The Power of Language

Equinox Textbooks and Surveys in Linguistics
Series Editor: Robin Fawcett, Cardiff University

Already published:

Multimodal Transcription and Text Analysis by Anthony Baldry and Paul J. Thibault
Meaning-Centered Grammar: an introductory text by Craig Hancock
Language in Psychiatry: a handbook of clinical practice by Jonathan Fine

Forthcoming titles in the series:

Genre Relations: mapping culture by J.R. Martin and David Rose
Intonation in the Grammar of English by M.A.K. Halliday and William S. Greaves
An Introduction to English Sentence Structure: clauses, markers, missing elements by Jon Jonz
The Rhetoric of Research: a guide to writing scientific literature by Beverly Lewin

The Power of Language

How discourse influences society

Lynne Young and Brigid Fitzgerald

LONDON   OAKVILLE

Published by

Equinox Publishing Ltd

UK: Unit 6, The Village, 101 Amies St, London, SW11 2JW
USA: DBBC, 28 Main Street, Oakville, CT 06779

www.equinoxpub.com

The Power of Language by Lynne Young and Brigid Fitzgerald
First published 2006
© Lynne Young and Brigid Fitzgerald 2006

British Library Cataloguing-in-Publication Data
A catalogue record for this book is available from the British Library.

ISBN 1–84553–014–4   (hardback)
ISBN 1–84553–015–2   (paperback)

Library of Congress Cataloging-in-Publication Data
Young, Lynne.
The power of language : how discourse influences society / Lynne Young
and Brigid Fitzgerald.
p. cm. – (Equinox textbooks and surveys in linguistics)
Includes bibliographical references and index.
ISBN 1–84553–014–4 (hb) – ISBN 1–84553–015–2 (pb)
1. Discourse analysis–Social aspects. 2. Functionalism (Linguistics)
I. Title. II. Series.
P302.84.Y68 2006
401'.41–dc22
2005021562

Typeset by Catchline, Milton Keynes (www.catchline.com)
Printed and bound in Great Britain and the USA

Contents

Acknowledgements

The authors and the publisher would like to thank the following copyright holders for permission to reprint material:

Chapter 2

Melanie Anne Phillips for permission to reproduce excerpts from *Melanie Speaks*. Penguin Group UK for permission to reproduce and adapt excerpts from Moir, A. and Jessel, D. Originally published by Dell Publishing, New York, 1989.

Chapter 3

Vernellia R. Randall, Professor of Law and Director, Academic Excellence Program, University of Dayton, U.S., for permission to reproduce the Race Relations Survey.

Gladys Hansen, Curator, Museum of the City of San Francisco, for permission to reproduce sections of the Pearl Harbor editorial.

Chapter 4

Cynthia Bouris, Subaru Canada, Inc., for permission to reproduce Subaru Forester and Subaru Legacy GT advertisements.

David McDonald, Wyeth, for permission to reproduce the text of a Centrum Performance advertisement.

Chapter 5

International Monetary Fund, for permission to reproduce excerpts from the following IMF Fact Sheets:
The IMF at a Glance
How the IMF Promotes Global Economic Stability
How the IMF Helps Poor Countries
The Poverty Reduction and Growth Facility (PRGF)

Hope Chu, 50 Years Is Enough Network, for permission to reproduce excerpts from *SAPs: The IMF, The World Bank, and Structural Adjustment*.

Andrea Buffa, Global Exchange, for permission to reproduce excerpts from *The Global Economy: World Bank & Int'l Monetary Fund, Introduction.*

Ministry of Labour and Citizens' Services, Government of British Columbia, for permission to reproduce *Message to Employees.*

Professor William Foster, Secretary-General, McGill University, for permission to reproduce the text 'Academic Integrity' from the McGill University website.

Chapter 6

Liisa Tuominen, *The Ottawa Citizen*, for permission to reproduce the photo by Rod McIver to accompany story: 'Students Protest Fee-Hike Proposal: Pilot project would let schools increase tuition to cover full cost of education'.

Leann Swalwell, CanWest Interactive, for permission to reproduce sections of the story 'Students Protest Fee-Hike Proposal: Pilot project would let schools increase tuition to cover full cost of education' by Sarah Schmidt.

Andrea Gordon, CP Images, for permission to reproduce the photo by John Moorehouse to accompany the story 'No nudity please, I'm British Columbian'.

Infoline Sun and Province, for permission to reproduce sections of the story 'No nudity please, I'm British Columbian' by David Wylie, *The Vancouver Sun.*

Web Service Group, McGill University and Marci Denesiuk for permission to reproduce McGill Library photo.

Mark Shainblum, Manager of Communications and Publications, McGill University, for permission to reproduce excerpts from the Prospective Students section of the McGill website.

Cheng Lay Tin, Singapore Kindness Movement, Government of Singapore, for permission to reproduce Courtesy Poster.

Josh Boetler, Columbia.edu Web Team, Columbia University, for permission to reproduce excerpts from the Prospective Students section of the Columbia website, and the accompanying photo by Arjun Mehra, Columbia University Digital Knowledge Ventures.

Chapter 7

Kevin Brooks, Associate Professor, Department of English, North Dakota State University for permission to reproduce excerpts from *Dinner Conversation Transcripts: MVE Project.*

Dr. Miriam Locher, for permission to reproduce and adapt excerpts from Locher, M. *Power and Politeness in Action,* Mouton de Gruyter, Berlin 2004.

Chapter 8

Lisa Munns, Cato Institute, for permission to reproduce excerpts from *Cato Handbook for Congress, Policy Recommendations for 107th Congress.*

Richard Odermatt, The Heritage Foundation, for permission to reproduce excerpts from Daniel J. Mitchell, Backgrounder #1109: *Creating a Better Social Security System for America.*

David Seitz, The New York Times Agency, for permission to reproduce excerpts from the editorials 'Little Black Lies' and 'Many Unhappy Returns' by Paul Krugman.

Palast Office, for permission to reproduce the column 'Bush Tort Reform Executive Clemency for Executive Killers' by Greg Palast.

The Controller of HMSO and the Queen's Printer for Scotland, for a licence to reproduce excerpts from Prime Minister Tony Blair's April 1999 speech 'Doctrine of the International Community'.

Abdia Mohamed, World Bank Publications, for permission to reproduce excerpts from a speech by James Wolfensohn, given at Cambridge University in June 2000.

Eleanor S. Abaye, Director of Communications, Lakehead University, for permission to reproduce text and graphics from the Lakehead University website.

Patricia Hort, Manager, Creative Services, Thompson Rivers University, for permission to reproduce text and graphics from the Thompson Rivers University website.

While every effort has been made to contact copyright holders of material used in this book, we would be happy to hear from any we have been unable to contact, and we will make the necessary amendment at the earliest opportunity.

Preface

The Power of Language: How Discourse Influences Society is the result of many years' teaching university students about language as a social practice, focusing on the role of discourse in the structuring of societal relations. Students who engage in this type of discursive analysis have shown their need for methodological tools to understand the key role that language plays in producing and maintaining unequal relations among different social groups and in different social situations. *The Power of Language* combines a functional theory of language with a critical approach to the analysis of discourse to provide a comprehensive methodological guide to critical analysis.

Throughout the writing of this book there were several people who made valuable contributions. Jaffer Sheyholislami, Instructor in the School of Linguistics and Language Studies, Carleton University, field-tested all chapters of the book in three different courses and gave us valuable feedback. We would like to thank Michael and Saira Fitzgerald for their editorial suggestions; we also thank Claire Harrison for her input into earlier stages of this book; finally we extend thanks to the undergraduate and graduate students who used earlier versions of the book and who provided us with many useful ideas.

Lynne Young and Brigid Fitzgerald
1 May 2006

Introduction

The Power of Language focuses on how power in society is realized through language, specifically on the role of language in producing and maintaining powerful relations. We do this by answering questions such as the following:

1. How do people get and hold on to power through language?

2. What kinds of communities of people take different positions on contentious current issues such as abortion and race relations? How could you clearly identify the positions taken in a particular article? How would you identify the ideologies they might reflect?

3. When you read newspapers, have you ever asked yourself whose voices you are reading about? Who is being quoted or referred to? What other voices could have been, but are not, heard?

4. In short, how do powerful people control public discourse? How do the less powerful discursively resist?

The Power of Language is designed to answer these questions by combining a theory of language called Systemic Functional Linguistics and an approach called Critical Discourse Analysis to examine different discursive events in daily life.

By 'discursive', we mean any event in which language plays a role and helps to shape that event. We use the term 'discourse' to refer to the general categories of language found in descriptive labels such as racist discourse or gendered discourse. We use 'text' to refer to a particular language sample we have selected for analysis. The terms 'discourse' and 'text' are also used interchangeably and in their broadest sense in the book.

The Power of Language provides a comprehensive methodology to help you to critically analyze a wide variety of types of verbal and visual texts. It presents a theory of language that provides the underpinning for critical analysis of public discourses such as newspapers, political speeches, and advertisements.

Using the methodological tools provided, by the end of the book you will be able to:

- Describe the content, structure and context of any article you encounter.

- Explore how social interactions among participants are expressed.

- Examine how these interactions may reproduce or challenge relations of power and dominance in society.

- Gain a fuller understanding of the role of language in producing and reproducing social inequalities in relation to issues such as gender, race and politics.

Organization of the book

The book has eight chapters. Each chapter consists of discursive samples on a particular issue, e.g., Language and Gender or Language and Advertising, accompanied by explanations, examples and activities that introduce you to different aspects of functional and critical analysis. There are five types of activity:

1. Practice

In these activities you will practice identifying the language features present in the discursive texts.

2. Discussion

Here, you engage with the discursive issue being presented through directed analytical questions.

3. Application

These activities give you opportunities to analyze discursive samples on the basis of the language features you have identified in previous analyses.

4. CDA questions

These questions use the methodological tools presented in each chapter for critical analysis. They focus on the issues of power or ideology that have motivated the language choices in the discursive samples.

5.   Critical Discourse Analysis (Chapters 6–8)

These activities extend those in CDA questions. Here, you can apply your critical analytical skills to more in-depth examination of new discursive samples on the issues raised in the chapter.

Each chapter contains four additional features. The first is a series of excerpts labeled 'Views from the theorists', which provide additional brief but in-depth explanations from those working in the fields of SFL and CDA to reinforce theoretical points raised in the chapter. The second contains examples of either a CDA or SFL analysis to demonstrate how different theorists carry out analyses and discuss their analytical findings. The third is a glossary at the end of each chapter, explaining the new terms introduced in that chapter. Finally, each chapter ends with 'Further Readings' in the fields of SFL and CDA, which provide specific references to the work of different linguists who discuss the points presented in each chapter.

Chapter overview

Chapter 1 explores politics in general, and war speeches of political leaders in particular. This chapter introduces students to the kinds of questions that can be asked about discourse from the perspective of SFL and CDA.

Chapter 2 focuses on the very complex issue of the relationship between language and gender to examine how discursive choices result from people's interactions in different social practices. The focus of the chapter is on an analysis of a discourse from one area of the SFL perspective introduced in Chapter 1 – the Ideational Metafunction.

Chapter 3 examines how, in subtle and more overt ways, discourses can play an important role in producing and reproducing racism. Analysis in this chapter focuses on another aspect of SFL methodology – the Interpersonal Metafunction – which concerns the attitudes, and stances of interactants on this issue.

Chapter 4 explores the discursive role of language in advertising through the study of the Textual Metafunction. By examining thematic and other cohesive patterns within advertisements, you will gain a better understanding of how producers of advertisements place readers in a consumer position so that they will purchase the advertised products.

Chapter 5 'pulls it all together' as you use what you have learned to 'unpack' the language involved in the development and maintenance of power and hierarchy in organizations such as government bureaucracies.

Chapter 6 introduces you to the visual mode of communication, and the interaction of the visual with the verbal mode. In this chapter, you will examine multimodal resources from educational settings and the print media through the lens of SFL in relation to issues of power and ideology.

Chapter 7 examines spoken discourse in a variety of settings. Here you will begin to examine how the context of a language event influences spoken discourse. We demonstrate how different discursive events (called 'registers') such as casual conversation, interviews and courtroom interactions stem from distinctive contexts of situation and show the influence of situational constructs on discursive choices.

Chapter 8 explores modern trends in language, trends that both result from and reflect major changes in modern Western societies. The trends are 'technicalization', which involves the use of scientific language for social and political policy; 'conversationalization', which exhibits and reflects the crossing of boundaries between public and private discursive domains; 'marketization', or 'commodification', which reflects the degree to which growing consumerism has affected discourse in areas such as education, health or social services not traditionally thought of as commodities; 'globalization', which is an economic ideology that incorporates a number of distinctive discursive features to promote itself.

Throughout *The Power of Language: how discourse influences society*, the pedagogical focus is on SFL and CDA in tandem, and fully illustrates how the two are connected and how SFL informs CDA questions. This dual focus grounds critical considerations in a sound methodological approach to the study of language, and provides you with a foundation for developing analytical skills.

Lynne Young and Brigid Fitzgerald
1 May 2006

Chapter 1 contents

Language in time of war

Reading texts and listening to other people are important parts of everyone's life. Through these actions, you learn about your family, your friends, your society, your culture, your country, and the larger world. You learn through all kinds of media such as television, film, newspapers, and magazines and through a variety of genres such as dramas, documentaries, articles, poetry, and so on. For the sake of simplicity, let us call all these, and anything else you read or hear, *discourses*. In fact, with technologies like the Internet and wireless communications, we are so bombarded with discourses from every direction that we live in what is often referred to as the 'Information Age.'

Norman Fairclough, one of the major researchers in discourse analysis, believes that discourse is more important today than at any other time in human history. Noting that modern society is 'knowledge-based' or 'knowledge-driven,' he suggests that 'language may have a more significant role in contemporary socioeconomic changes than it has had in the past' (2004: 104).

Views from the theorists:
Norman Fairclough

Living in the 'knowledge society'

However, you are not just a passive reader and listener, taking in every fact and opinion like a sponge. To every new discourse, you bring your own knowledge, experiences, and point of view. Perhaps you choose to accept what you read or are told as the truth, or perhaps you question it. You may even decide that you don't believe it. No matter what your reaction is, you approach most discourses in an analytical way. You try to 'dig' below the surface of a discourse to find out *what* is being said, *why* it is being said, and *how* it evokes feelings in you.

The purpose of this book is to help you find these answers by subjecting each discourse to a *critical* examination. But we don't use *critical* in a negative sense. Rather, we use the term to describe a way of looking at language *reflectively*, that is, asking why a speaker/writer has chosen certain words and structures, and not others; and *interpretatively*, that is, analyzing the connections between language use within a society and societal structures.

This manner of looking at language will provide you with tools to analyze different types of discourse used in a variety of situations – discourses in which issues of power may arise. By examining the relationship between language and power, you will gain a greater understanding of the role that language plays in producing and reproducing social inequalities as they relate to issues such as race and gender.

This approach to language, which analyzes discourse to highlight inequality that is expressed, produced, and reproduced through language, is called Critical Discourse Analysis (CDA). CDA focuses on linguistic analysis to expose misrepresentation, discrimination, or particular positions of power in all kinds of public discourse such as political speeches, newspapers, and advertisements.

To start, we will begin with an exploration of a specific type of discourse in which the position of power always plays a dominant role: a political speech involving war 'talk.' Analyzing this type of discourse allows you to explore how groups are identified and portrayed (positively or negatively), and how this exploration can lead to a better understanding of the conflict involved.

1.2   A sample discourse: a 'call to arms'

On 11 September 2001 (9/11), members of the Islamic organization Al-Qaeda hijacked two airliners and flew them deliberately into the twin towers of the World Trade Center (WTC) in New York City. This event had an extraordinary political impact. In the United States, for example, it turned a government that was primarily interested in domestic affairs to focus on foreign affairs, and eventually to undertake military actions in Afghanistan and the Middle East. Most observers agreed that 9/11 was an event that had a significant impact on the United States, particularly from a political point of view.

9/11 was the first time that the United States as a nation had been attacked within its borders by a foreign force, and Americans were, not surprisingly, upset, frightened and angry. However, U.S. political leaders took many different political approaches as to what should be done beyond taking national security measures. Some leaders urged caution, discussion, and reflection; others were more hawkish. Among the latter were many members of and advisors to the Bush administration. The result was that, on 15 September 2001, President George W. Bush made the following 'call to arms' in a speech to the American people.

> I've asked the highest levels of our government to come to discuss the current tragedy that has so deeply affected our nation. Our country mourns for the loss of life and for those whose lives have been so deeply affected by this despicable act of terror.
>
> I am going to describe to our leadership what I saw: the wreckage of New York City, the signs of the first battle of war.
>
> We're going to meet and deliberate and discuss – but there's no question about it, this act will not stand; we will find those who did it; we will smoke them out of their holes; we will get them running and we'll bring them to justice. We will not only deal with those who dare attack America, we will deal with those who harbor them and feed them and house them.
>
> Make no mistake about it: underneath our tears is the strong determination of America to win this war. And we will win it.

http://www.whitehouse.gov/news/releases/2001/09/print/20010915–4.html (Accessed September 2003)

This type of discourse, a 'call to arms', occurs when a national or military leader uses words in a way that he/she hopes will convince citizens or soldiers to mount an offensive against an enemy. A 'call to arms' is intended to inspire patriotic feelings that will overcome other types of reactions such as fear, caution, cynicism, and disbelief.

So it's clear what type of discourse this is. The first important question that a discourse analyst would ask is: 'How do I know this?' If your answer is: 'It's in the words', you're absolutely right. But what does 'in the words' really mean? How can investigating this response reveal more about this discourse than appears on the surface?

1.3   Asking analytical questions

In this section, we will examine the kinds of questions you could ask in an analysis in order to identify key features in this discourse. As we go through these questions, we suggest the following procedure:

1) look at the questions;
2) go back to the text to see what answers you can find;
3) discuss them with others; and
4) then see if your answers are similar to ours, which are shown below each set of questions.

1.3.1   Type I questions: Who is doing what to whom?

1.	Who is the discourse aimed at?
2.	Who is involved in this discourse?
3.	What is the intention or purpose of this discourse?

1. Who is the discourse aimed at? We suggest that the President's speech has three target audiences: American citizens, friends and allies of the United States, and the enemy – the unknown people who planned the attack against the World Trade Center.

2. Who is involved in this discourse? The President is talking about three different participants:

1) himself through the word *I*;
2) *we/us*, referring to the President and the American people/government; and
3) *them/those*, referring to the enemy.

3. What is the intention or purpose of this discourse? We suggest that the purpose of this discourse is threefold:

1) To reassure and rally citizens and make them feel that their country is still powerful despite their vulnerability to terrorist attacks.
2) To rally friends and allies to the American cause as well as to reassure them that the United States will not yield to such attacks.
3) To intimidate enemies by making sure that they know that the United States will fight back and that they will suffer for their

actions. As well, we suggest that the President is trying to discourage them from any further attacks.

1.3.2 Type II questions: Attitudes, beliefs, and opinions

1.	What is your overall impression of the speaker's feelings?
2.	Can you point to the words/phrases that indicate these feelings to you?
3.	What kind of phrases/sentences does he use that demonstrate his state of mind?
4.	Is there any phrase/sentence that stands out as an indicator of the speaker's feelings?

1. What is your overall impression of the speaker's feelings? We think that the President is sad, angry, and has a fierce desire to act on his feelings.

2. Can you point to the words and phrases that indicate these feelings to you? Circle the words/phrases and then check with our answers below.

> I've asked the highest levels of our government to come to discuss the current tragedy that has so deeply affected our nation. Our country mourns for the loss of life and for those whose lives have been so deeply affected by this despicable act of terror.
>
> I am going to describe to our leadership what I saw: the wreckage of New York City, the signs of the first battle of war.

The words and phrases that indicate the President's feelings to us are: *tragedy, mourns, loss of life, despicable act or terror*, and *wreckage*. These words and phrases are strong ones. No one would use such words about an event that was not catastrophic and didn't cause sadness and grief. Further, when someone describes an action as *despicable* or *an act of terror*, we believe he/she is making a judgment about what has occurred and, in this case, it is a judgment tinged with anger. Would you agree?

3. What kind of phrases/sentences does the President use that demonstrate his state of mind? In this case, at some points in the text, he seems to be threatening or warning. We found phrases that point to the President's desire to act upon his feelings of sadness and anger. The third paragraph provides strong clues regarding these emotions.

> We're **going to meet** and **deliberate** and **discuss** – but there's no question about it, this act **will not stand**; **we will find those** who did it; **we will smoke them** out of their holes; **we will get them running** and **we'll bring them to justice. We will not only deal with** those who dare attack America, **we will deal with those** who harbor them and feed them and house them.

These bolded phrases, we believe, demonstrate that the President is uttering threats and making promises of future action. They have features in common that make them different from the words and phrases he used before and afterwards.

1) Each includes the word *will* or *going to*.
2) They all have the same form; they are *statements* (as opposed to *questions* and *commands*).
3) They are all short and to the point, making the threat very easy to identify.

Why did these features lead us to believe that these statements are both threats and promises? Look at the bolded words and think about them for a moment. The most important indicator is the repetitive use of the future tense through *will* and *going to* – words that are almost always used in threats and promises, that is, statements about certain types of actions that will take place in the future. Whether an action is a threat or a promise depends on the identity of the speaker/writer, the identity of the listener/reader, and the consequences. In this case, the President and, by implication, the United States can threaten because they have the power to undertake these actions. Therefore, these statements are a threat – that is, a promise of adverse consequences. In fact, since the President is sure that he can carry these actions out successfully, he uses *will* or *going to*, rather than other words such as *might* or *could* that suggest possibility or probability, but not certainty.

The second feature that these features have in common is that they are all *statements*. Why are statements so often used to create threats and promises? First of all, it is much more effective to make a threat or promise by using a statement rather than a *question*. Try it and see. Secondly, if the President had used *commands* – for example: *fight them, find them, smoke them out* – they would no longer be threats or promises but direct orders to the American people. But this speech is aimed not only at American citizens but also at their enemies. Commands, then, would not have been appropriate. Nor would commands describe what the President intended to accomplish, or promise action. Only the statement can play these two roles – as a description and as a promise – in a 'call to arms.'

Finally, the parallelism of the statements also contributes to their quality of threat and promise. Say the speech aloud, and hear how rhythmical this paragraph sounds as each threat/promise builds on the one before it, the whole accumulating a much greater power than any one threat/promise would have if it stood alone.

In sum, the President's discursive choices serve to assure listeners that he is determined to take action, and is rallying his people and potential allies to align themselves with his position.

4. Is there any phrase/sentence that stands out particularly as an indicator of the speaker's feelings? We found one sentence in the speech that stands out because it is so different from the others.

> **Make no mistake about it**: underneath our tears is the strong determination of America to win this war. And we will win it.

Make no mistake about it is a command. The President is issuing an order to make sure that all his listeners understand what his previous statements have meant. What makes this an order? The President's use of a verb in the first position in the clause: *Make no mistake about it*. If he had said, *There is no mistake about it*, it is likely that this statement would not have a strong impact on listeners because it lacked the 'punch' of a command.

Also, the President placed this command at the end of his 'call to arms' to ensure it would be noticed. The placement of words, phrases, and sentences is also a significant aspect of a discourse. Beginnings and endings are often where the most important ideas are stated; rarely will a speaker/writer bury his/her best 'stuff' in the middle of a discourse.

1.3.3   Type III questions: Holding the discourse together

1.   What words and phrases does the speaker use to let us know that he is focusing on particular themes or topics?

2.   How can listeners/readers, in general, and listeners of this speech, in particular, recognize that a specific discourse is a unified whole as opposed to just a collection of individual sentences?

1. What words and phrases does the speaker use to let us know that he is focusing on particular topics? At a first go-through, we found five topics that emerge very clearly. Each is reflected in a group of words or *chains*. These chains include two major themes: *war* and *tragedy*, and three types of participants: the *President* representing personal leadership, *we/us* referring to the United States, and *them/those* – the enemy whose identity was unknown immediately after the September 11 attacks.

Practice

Read through the speech again, pick out the words in each chain, and then fill in the chart.

I've asked the highest levels of our government to come to discuss the current tragedy that has so deeply affected our nation. Our country mourns for the loss of life and for those whose lives have been so deeply affected by this despicable act of terror.

I am going to describe to our leadership what I saw: the wreckage of New York City, the signs of the first battle of war.

We're going to meet and deliberate and discuss – but there's no question about it, this act will not stand; we will find those who did it; we will smoke them out of their holes; we will get them running and we'll bring them to justice. We will not only deal with those who dare attack America, we will deal with those who harbor them and feed them and house them.

Make no mistake about it: underneath our tears is the strong determination of America to win this war. And we will win it.

Vocabulary chains				
War	Tragedy	President	We/Us	Them/Those

2. How can listeners/readers, in general, and listeners to this speech, in particular, recognize that a specific discourse is a unified whole as opposed to just a collection of individual sentences? A vocabulary chain throughout a discourse holds it together by creating links from one sentence to another, and one paragraph to another. This type of 'tying together' is one element of *cohesion*. This is one strategy that speakers/writers use to help readers/listeners make sense of a discourse. Several vocabulary chains, all acting simultaneously in this discourse both support one another – for example, the linked themes of war and tragedy – and reinforce the unity of the text. As well, the speech uses connecting words (conjunctions) such as *but* and *and* to help connect different ideas.

In sum, these features – vocabulary chains and conjunctions – work together to ensure that we see or hear the text as a unified whole, rather than as a collection of sentences with no relationship to one another and therefore, not a discourse at all.

Through these questions (Types I, II, and III), you have just started a simple, but meaningful, language analysis that you could apply to any discourse that you read or hear. However, your ideas (and ours) have been based primarily on personal feelings and intuition, which lead to a *subjective* analysis that is open to the challenge of being biased. In the next section, we will demonstrate methods to critically analyze a discourse using linguistic tools which allow for a more *objective* analytical viewpoint.

1.4   Starting systemic functional linguistics

Critical discourse analysts use several different methods to help them 'dig' beneath the surface of the discourse to answer their questions. One widely used theoretical framework is Systemic Functional Linguistics or SFL – a way of understanding the functions that language performs and the choices people make when they speak/write to exchange meaning with readers/listeners. We will discuss SFL throughout this book because it will provide you, as an analyst, with an excellent methodology that should help protect your analyses from bias.

In this next section, we will rephrase the Type I, II, and III questions within the framework of SFL and examine the President's speech with this analytical method. If you have been taught traditional grammar (and some of us have), you have looked at parts of speech that were classified as nouns and verbs, and studied them as the structures that help to build sentences. But in SFL, analysts examine nouns and verbs, not only as structural items, but also in terms of the meanings they represent or *realize*.

1.4.1   SFL question 1

a)   Who are the participants?

b)   What are the processes and circumstances?

Participants are nouns/pronouns that describe who and what is involved in different mental/physical actions and different states.

Processes are represented or 'realized' by verbs that describe what is happening.

Circumstances describe the when, where, and how of the process.

When studying a discourse, SFL researchers are interested in the meanings that participants, processes, and circumstances are creating. Using these labels helps analysts figure out '*who* is doing *what* to *whom*: *when*, *where*, and *how*' – an important consideration in CDA because, as we mentioned earlier, one of its goals is to determine who has power in a society and how that power is wielded linguistically.

Let's look at two examples from the speech to explain these labels and demonstrate how SFL tools can be applied to discourse to describe 'who is doing what to whom: when, where, and how.'

> Example 1:   *We will find them.*
> Participants: *we, them*
> Process: *find*

Note that, in the above example, the participants are different: *we* and *them*. Let's look at their different properties. The *we* is:

- doing the action;
- undertaking the action of finding;
- playing the role of Actor in the sentence.

On the other hand, the *them* is:

- being acted on, that is *being found*;
- playing the role of Goal in the sentence – the participants being sought and then found.

The Actor and the Goal in this sentence are connected by *find* – a type of process that SFL researchers call *Material* because a 'material' thing is happening or being done – that is, something identifiable as a physical action. When describing relationships in a sentence, SFL researchers often use diagrams such as the one below.

Actor	**Process: Material**	**Goal**
we	*find*	*them*

Let's look at another example that shows how SFL allows us to understand what is happening in a discourse.

> Example 2:   *We will smoke them out of their holes.*
> Participants: *we, them*
> Process: *smoke out*

In Example 2, the participants are the same as those in Example 1: *we* is doing the action and *them*, is being acted on. In other words, *we* is doing the *smoking out* while *them* will be *smoked out*. (Notice that the process includes both *smoke* and *out* even though the two words are split up by *them*.) In this example, *we* is the Actor in the sentence, *them* is the Goal, *smoke out* is a Material process, and *of their holes* is the circumstance of *where*. (We will discuss the use of *will* in the processes later.)

Actor	Process: Material	Goal	Circumstance: Where
We	*smoke out*	*them*	*of their holes*

Let's now look at the President's speech. By using SFL, we can see that the President used the *Actor + Process: Material + Goal* 12 times in paragraphs 3 and 4. We have numbered and bolded them for you.

> We're going to meet and deliberate and discuss – but there's no question about it, this act will not stand; 1) **we will find those** 2) **who did it**; 3) **we will smoke them out** of their holes; 4) **we will get them running** and 5) **we'll bring them** to justice. 6) **We will not only deal with those** 7) **who dare attack America**, 8) **we will deal with those** 9) **who harbor them** and 10) **feed them** and 11) **house them**.

> Make no mistake about it: underneath our tears is the strong determination of America to win this war. 12) And **we will win it**.

(Note that in 10 and 11 the Actor *who* is not identified, but is easily understood by listeners.)

Twelve repetitions of language usage in such a short speech are significant because they demonstrate a pattern in the President's speech.

- What does this pattern mean?
- Does it have a purpose?
- What does it show about his intent?

These are the kind of questions CDA researchers ask in order to *interpret* their SFL findings – questions that we will explore later in this chapter.

1.4.2   SFL question 2

> What are the speaker's or writer's attitudes and stances?
>
> Attitude refers to the combination of opinions and beliefs that a speaker or writer holds about a subject.
>
> Stance results from the attitude of the speaker/writer and is the position that he/she takes in relation to a subject, that is, to the proposition he/she is making.

In Type II questions discussed earlier in the chapter, we tried to determine how the President felt by analyzing his words and phrases. What we were trying to do was determine his attitude and stance. These two aspects of discourse are always significant because they have a strong effect on all interactions among people.

Attitude and stance are strongly connected. For example, there are two groups of people who hold opposing attitudes and stances on capital punishment: let's call them the *pros* and the *cons* and lay out their attitudes and positions/stances in a simple way.

Attitude	Stance
Pros: believe that taking a human life is an appropriate form of punishment for certain types of crimes.	Pros: are in favour of capital punishment.
Cons: believe that it is wrong to take human life as a form of punishment no matter what the type of crime.	Cons: are not in favour of capital punishment.

To find out how speakers/writers *represent* their attitudes and stances in a discourse, a CDA researcher first uses SFL methods to identify language choices that indicate these attitudes and stances. For example, in paragraphs 3 and 4 of the President's speech, there are nine instances of the use of *will* or *going to*. As we noted during the discussion of Type II questions, the use of *will* and *going to* makes listeners aware that the President is making threats and promises.

We're **going to** meet and deliberate and discuss – but there's no question about it, this act **will** not stand; we **will** find those who did it; we **will** smoke them out of their holes; we **will** get them running and **we'll** bring them to justice. We **will** not only deal with those who dare attack America, we **will** deal with those who harbor them and feed them and house them.

Make no mistake about it: underneath our tears is the strong determination of America to win this war. And we **will** win it.

This strategy of repeating *will* solidifies the President's attitude to the September 11 attacks firmly in the minds of his audience. He obviously believes this type of warfare is outrageous and he is taking a resolute stance against it. The repetition also serves to indicate how strongly the president wishes to make his position clear.

The President also reinforces his attitude and stance through another technique: switching from statements to the command: *Make no mistake about it* (in italics above). By making this switch, the President seems to be ensuring that his audience knows how strongly he feels about the issue.

1.4.3   SFL question 3

What holds the discourse together?

Cohesion refers to ways a discourse is held together so that readers and listeners can follow and understand it. It is accomplished by means such as:

- Chains – associated words/phrases that highlight certain topics that appear throughout the discourse.
- Themes – the word(s) that are the main 'starting point' for each 'message' in the discourse.

When we discussed Type III questions earlier, we were examining features of discourse that 'work' to create cohesion so that 1) different sentences relate, and are connected, to each other, and 2) listeners/readers can understand the discourse and follow it. One of the features of cohesion that we identified is the *vocabulary chains* of associated words/phrases that identify topics that appear throughout the discourse. Earlier, we identified five topics in the President's speech: *war, tragedy*, the *President, we/us*, and *them/those*.

Another form of *cohesion* involves how speakers/writers order their words for purposes of logical flow and emphasis. *Theme* is the word SFL researchers use to describe the word(s) and phrase(s) speakers/writers use to start their messages.

theme versus Theme

Theme is a word that can be used in two senses. The first is more popular and general; it refers to the main topic of a discourse such as a *theme* in an essay. In SFL research, the term *Theme*, when capitalized, has a more specific meaning; it refers to the initial word(s)/phrase(s) in a clause.

These messages occur in *clauses*, that is, sentences or the parts of sentences that contain a full thought. Clauses can start with different Themes, but each clause must have a *Topical Theme* – this may be a participant, a process, or a circumstance.

Below, we have separated the President's speech into its major clauses, bolded each Topical Theme, and indicated in brackets whether it is a participant, process or circumstance. As well, we have italicized another kind of Theme, called Textual, because words in this category, such as *and* and *but*, do important work in holding a discourse together.

1) **I've** asked the highest levels of our government to come to discuss the current tragedy that has so deeply affected our nation. (participant)
2) **Our country** mourns for the loss of life and for those whose lives have been so deeply affected by this despicable act of terror. (participant)
3) **I** am going to describe to our leadership what I saw: the wreckage of New York City, the signs of the first battle of war. (participant)
4) **We're** going to meet and deliberate and discuss (participant)
5) *but* **there's** no question about it, (participant)
6) **this act** will not stand; (participant)
7) **we** will find those who did it; (participant)
8) **we** will smoke them out of their holes; (participant)

9)   **we** will get them running (participant)
10) *and* **we'll** bring them to justice. (participant)
11) **We** will not only deal with those who dare attack America, (participant)
12) **we** will deal with those who harbor them and feed them and house them. (participant)
13) **Make** no mistake about it: (process)
14) **underneath our tears** is the strong determination of America to win this war. (circumstance)
15) *And* **we** will win it. (participant)

When we examine the Topical Themes, we see a very strong pattern. Of the 15 Topical Themes, 12 are about the United States. In other words, the Themes hold the speech together by repeating words that represent Americans: the *I* standing for the President in his role as leader, *our country*, *we*, and *underneath our tears*.

Topical Themes in President Bush's speech

United States	Other
I (2x)	there
our country	this act
we (8x)	make
underneath our tears	
Frequency: 12	Frequency: 3

In sum, then, we see that the three types of questions we asked at the beginning of the discussion can also be answered from an SFL perspective.

Views from the theorists: Michael Halliday

Understanding and evaluating texts

Michael Halliday, the foremost figure in SFL, believes that people who analyze discourse from a linguistic perspective have two goals for research. The first is to make 'a contribution to the **understanding** of the text: the linguistic analysis enables one to show how, and why, the text means what it does. In the process they are likely to reveal multiple meanings, alternatives… and so on.' The second is to contribute to 'the **evaluation** of the text: the linguistic analysis may enable one to say why the text is, or is not, an effective text for its own purposes – in what respect it succeeds and in what respect it fails, or is less successful' (Halliday, 1994: xv).

As you continue reading this book, you will begin to notice that we have extended the question of *why* to include the motivations of speakers/writers, that is, not only why a text is effective, but also why the speaker/writer made this word choice or used that expression. In other words, *why* also encompasses questions of motivation, particularly with regard to how the speaker's/writer's choices constitute, maintain, and/or challenge relationships of power in our society. You will be reading more about this type of *why* question in the next section: Adding critical discourse analysis.

Adding critical discourse analysis   1.5

So far in this chapter, we have explored different ways of analyzing a discourse, in this case, President Bush's speech made after the 9/11 attacks. We noted that, just by both asking certain kinds of questions and using personal intuition to answer them, you would be able to find out a great deal about the speech. We then demonstrated how the theoretical framework of SFL allows us to answer these questions in a more objective way. However, to carry out an analysis that is *critical* in the sense that we are using it, that is, examining the ways in which discourse is connected to, reflects, and in turn exerts power, we have to ask and be able to answer questions about

- **why** a speaker or writer made these types of choices; and
- **how** they reflect relationships between powerful and weaker groups.

One way to do this is by combining SFL and CDA – two approaches to language that are connected but have a different focus. SFL, as we have noted, provides you with the methodological tools to answer questions that provide a *description* of a discourse. You can then take the description supplied by SFL and answer CDA questions that provide an *explanation* and *interpretation* of a discourse in terms of the relationships between language, power and ideology. The two approaches are joined in a continuum relationship because their focus on issues such as power and ideology begins with SFL and is extended by CDA. SFL's concern with the roles that language plays in exerting, reflecting and reinforcing power has always been present. This focus has been taken up by critical discourse analysts in their concern with the interconnections among power, ideology and language. Of particular relevance is their examination of the discursive role in unequal relations of power.

Views from the theorists:
Ruth Wodak

Principles of CDA

Ruth Wodak, an important figure in current discourse research, sets out principles for CDA that will help you understand how analysts in this field approach the role of language in society.

1. CDA addresses social problems: Wodak says that 'The focus in CDA is not upon language or the use of language in and of themselves, but upon the linguistic character of social and cultural processes and structures.' In particular, CDA researchers concentrate on those processes and structures that produce and maintain inequality.

2. Power relations are discursive: Our social relationships are established and maintained by discourse. We talk, listen, read, and write and, therefore, create relations with others in and through language. As a result, 'power relations are exercised and negotiated in discourse.'

3. Discourse does ideological work: Wodak defines ideologies as 'particular ways of representing and constructing society, which reproduce unequal relations of power, relations of domination and exploitation,' and she notes that 'they are often false and ungrounded …'

4. Discourse is historical: No written or spoken discourse exists by itself. Rather, it is connected to discourses that came before it and is affected by the people and events around it. Therefore, Wodak notes that 'discourse… cannot be understood without taking [its] context into consideration.'

5. Discourse is a form of social action: Wodak describes CDA as 'a socially committed scientific paradigm' that aims to change discourse practices that create social inequality. She says that researchers 'have had some success in changing discourse and power patterns in organizations' (Wodak, 1996: 17–20).

Let's move on to an example of how SFL and CDA can work together. We noted earlier that a *we/us* versus *them/those* pattern existed in the President's speech. An important critical linguistic question we should ask is **What is the purpose of this pattern?** One way to find an answer is to examine how *we/us* and *them/those* are represented in the President's 'call to arms' by looking at the processes associated with each group.

Actor	Processes
we	*meet, deliberate, discuss, find, smoke out, get, bring, deal with*
them	(none)

As this shows, there are no clauses in which *them/those* exists in the Actor position. In other words, the unnamed enemy is not credited with any power to perform an action. President Bush never said: *They attacked our people* or *They created this tragedy* although, as listeners, we know that they did, in fact, carry out these actions and did create this tragedy.

Is this kind of choice deliberate? Did the President or his speechwriters sit down and make a decision never to give the enemy an Actor role in the speech? People who are very sensitive or aware of language may consciously do this, but most native speakers instinctively choose the words that will most effectively get their message across. Their language choices are based on their ideological beliefs and opinions which they share in common with other people in their own social group. President Bush's speech reflects commonly held attitudes among Americans – attitudes about their country's ability to face an enemy and win – and this is evident in the choice of participants in the Actor group. The *we/us* are performing all the actions: *meeting, finding, smoking out, getting* (them) *running, bringing* (them to justice) and *dealing with* (them).

Contrast this with the processes involving *them/those* as shown below.

Goal	Processes
we/us	*mourn for*
them/those	*be found, be smoked out, be caught running, be brought to justice, be dealt with*

Rather than Actors, members of this group are Goals, that is, people being acted on. They are being *smoked out of holes, are running*, and *are being brought to justice*. It is quite clear in this context that the President wants his listeners to understand that Americans are the ones '*who* have the power to do *what* to *whom*' in this speech. Choices such as these are one way a nation can be rallied, especially a nation that has been attacked in a new and frightening way.

The chart below provides you with questions from both SFL and CDA perspectives. These questions can be applied to any discourse. They will enable you to undertake a thoughtful and careful analysis that minimizes bias.

SFL questions	CDA questions
Who are the main participants?	Who in this discourse is acting on whom and, therefore, has the power?
Who are the other participants?	Do you think they are less important? Why?
What are the processes in which the two sets of participants are involved?	What do the actions carried out by the *we/us* participants tell you about the use of power?
What do the circumstances in the discourse focus on?	How do the circumstances differ according to participants?
What are the attitudes and stances of the speaker/writer?	Do you agree with or differ from these attitudes? Are you in agreement with the President's position/stance? Why?
What are the Topical Themes in the text?	What do these Theme choices tell us about the focus and organization of this discourse? And, thus, the President's preoccupation with a particular Theme? How do the Theme choices reinforce the power of the President in the speech?
What features make this discourse a cohesive one instead of a group of unrelated sentences?	Are these features selected to emphasize a particular position/stance?
In sum: • What are the main patterns in terms of participants, processes and circumstances? • What are main patterns of choices that expresses attitudes, opinions, and judgements? • What are the main features that make this discourse a unified whole?	In sum: • Can you identify who has the power in this text by identifying who is doing what to whom – when, where, and how? • How do the attitudes and opinions reinforce the impression of power of the main participant? • What more do the cohesive features of the discourse – chains and Themes – tell us about who is in power and who is not?

You now have some of the basic tools for undertaking your first critical discourse analysis. The discourse we provide below is another 'call to arms,' that is similar in many ways to President Bush's speech. This 'call to arms' is from a famous speech given by Winston Churchill, the Prime Minister of Great Britain more than 50 years ago, when he wished to rally his country during World War II. In fact, this type of speech could be referred to as a genre, a recognizable form of speech no matter when it occurs in history, although there will always be some features that change in order to be more suitable to one era than another.

> Even though large tracts of Europe and many old and famous States have fallen or may fall into the grip of the Gestapo and all the odious apparatus of Nazi rule, we shall not flag or fail. We shall go on to the end, we shall fight in France, we shall fight on the seas and oceans, we shall fight with growing confidence and growing strength in the air, we shall defend our Island… we shall fight on the beaches, we shall fight on the landing grounds, we shall fight in the fields and in the streets, we shall fight in the hills; we shall never surrender.

Adapted from http://www.winstonchurchill.org/index.html (Accessed September 2003)

To begin, it will be useful to do some basic SFL analyses. Then, using the information you have gathered through these analyses, you will be able to answer SFL and CDA questions.

Undertaking a basic SFL analysis   Practice

In order to help you carry out your SFL analysis, we have separated Churchill's 'call to arms' into its major clauses and analyzed several for you. Complete the charts. Go back to each clause and circle the Topical Themes. Discuss your answers with other students in your class. (Note: we have bolded the Topical Theme for you.)

1. Even though large tracts of Europe and many old and famous States have fallen or may fall into the grip of the Gestapo and all the odious apparatus of Nazi rule

Actor(s)	Process(es): Material	Goal(s)	Circumstance(s): Indicate if the circumstance is a *when, where* or *how*
Even though large tracts of Europe and many old and famous States	*fall into*	*the grip of the Gestapo and all the odious apparatus of Nazi rule*	

2. we shall not flag or fail.

Actor(s)	Process(es): Material	Goal(s)	Circumstance(s): Indicate if the circumstance is a *when, where* or *how*

3. We shall go on to the end,

Actor(s)	Process(es): Material	Goal(s)	Circumstance(s): Indicate if the circumstance is a *when, where* or *how*
we	*go on*		**When:** *to the end*

4. we shall fight in France,

Actor(s)	Process(es): Material	Goal(s)	Circumstance(s): Indicate if the circumstance is a *when, where* or *how*

5. we shall fight on the seas and oceans,

Actor(s)	Process(es): Material	Goal(s)	Circumstance(s): Indicate if the circumstance is a *when, where* or *how*

6. we shall fight with growing confidence and growing strength in the air,
(hint: this clause has two different types of circumstances)

Actor(s)	Process(es): Material	Goal(s)	Circumstance(s): Indicate if the circumstance is a *when*, *where* or *how*

7. we shall defend our Island…

Actor(s)	Process(es): Material	Goal(s)	Circumstance(s): Indicate if the circumstance is a *when*, *where* or *how*

8. we shall fight on the beaches,

Actor(s)	Process(es): Material	Goal(s)	Circumstance(s): Indicate if the circumstance is a *when*, *where* or *how*

9. we shall fight on the landing grounds,

Actor(s)	Process(es): Material	Goal(s)	Circumstance(s): Indicate if the circumstance is a *when*, *where* or *how*

10. we shall fight in the fields and in the streets,

Actor(s)	Process(es): Material	Goal(s)	Circumstance(s): Indicate if the circumstance is a *when*, *where* or *how*

11. we shall fight in the hills;

Actor(s)	Process(es): Material	Goal(s)	Circumstance(s): Indicate if the circumstance is a *when*, *where* or *how*

12. we shall never surrender.

Actor(s)	Process(es): Material	Goal(s)	Circumstance(s): Indicate if the circumstance is a *when*, *where* or *how*

Application

Answering SFL and CDA questions

You now have the material to help you answer the SFL questions in order to *describe* Churchill's 'call to arms' and to undertake a CDA *interpretation*.

Complete the following chart.

SFL questions	Your answers
Who are the participants?	
What is the type of processes in which the participants are involved?	
What are the circumstances surrounding the processes and what kind of pattern do they create?	
CDA questions	**Your answers**
Who is involved in the processes? How do you know who has the power?	
What do the processes tell us about Churchill's presentation of participants? Is it a positive or negative representation? How do the processes reveal the dominance and power of the participants?	

With your own analysis in mind, read the following example of a critical discourse analysis.

You have seen how both President Bush and Prime Minister Churchill used the *we/us* in their speeches to make their discourse more persuasive and compelling. This type of *we/us* is called 'inclusive' because it always includes the speaker/writer and all of his/her audience. The 'exclusive' *we*, on the other hand, excludes the audience – as in the sentence: '**We** don't want you sitting here.'

Norman Fairclough, CDA scholar, demonstrates how the 'inclusive' *we* in editorials can exert a different kind of power by implying that a whole nation has only one perspective.

Fairclough analyzed the following sentence that appeared in an editorial in the English newspaper, the *Daily Mail*, when Argentina invaded the British-governed Falkland Islands in 1982, creating a military conflict in which the U.K. was eventually victorious.

> We cannot let our troops lose their edge below decks while Argentine diplomats play blind man's bluff round the corridors of the United Nations.

By using the 'inclusive' *we*, Fairclough notes that 'the newspaper is speaking on behalf of itself, its readers, and indeed all British citizens. In so doing it is making an implicit authority claim… that it has the authority to speak for others. Notice, also, that *Britain* or *the government* could both happily replace… [the]… *we*; the newspaper's way of showing its identification with the government and the state is to treat them as equivalent to its composited *we*, i.e., all of the British people.'

Fairclough also states that, when an editorial conflates everyone and all institutional entities into the one *we*, 'One aspect of this reduction is that it serves corporate ideologies which stress the unity of a people at the expense of recognition of divisions of interest' (Fairclough, 1989: 127–128).

Example of a CDA analysis: the role of the inclusive *we*

Chapter 1 Glossary

Actor: the *who* in '*who* is doing *what* to *whom*'.

Attitude: the combination of opinions and beliefs that a speaker/writer holds about a subject.

Circumstance: the *when*, *where*, and *how* of a process.

Clause: a part of a sentence that is composed of at least two elements – a Subject and a Verb.

Cohesion: features that tie a text together.

Critical Discourse Analysis (CDA): an approach to language that examines how ideology and power are expressed, produced, and reproduced through discourse.

Discourse: any form of written or spoken text or visual depiction that is a unified whole.

Goal: the *whom* in '*who* is doing *what* to *whom*'; that is, the element that receives the action of the process.

Ideology: particular ways of representing and constructing society which can reproduce unequal relations of power.

Material process: a physical action.

Participant: the entity that is involved in different mental and physical actions and states.

Process: the *what* in '*who* is doing *what* to *whom*'; realized by verbs involving actions or states which take place in and over time.

Realize: a word used by SFL researchers to indicate that a grammatical choice expresses a certain meaning.

Stance: results from a speaker/writer's social attitudes which are, in turn, based on his/her sets of beliefs.

Systemic Functional Linguistics (SFL): a linguistic theory that examines the functions that language performs, that examines language in terms of the purposes it serves in a society.

Theme: the first word(s)/phrase(s) in a clause.

Topical Theme: the first participant, process or circumstance in a clause.

Textual Theme: conjunctions such as *and* and *but* that appear at the beginning of a clause.

Vocabulary chain: a series of words related in meaning in a discourse.

SFL readings

Butt, D., Fahey, R., Feez, R., Spinks, S. and Yallop, C. (2000) *Using Functional Grammar, An Explorer's Guide.* This is a very accessible introduction to SFL and Chapter 1 will help novice analysts with the concepts presented here.

Eggins, S. (1994) *Introduction to Systemic Functional Linguistics.* Eggins explains Halliday's theories and approaches in a clear manner. Students should read her Chapter 1 and take a look at Chapter 9 which, although a bit advanced, offers a clear explanation of some of the basic concepts introduced here.

Halliday, M. A. K. (1994) *Introduction to Functional Grammar.* This 'bible' is the major resource for researchers in SFL. A good section to read in relation to this chapter is the Introduction, pages xiii–xix.

CDA readings

Fairclough, N. (1989) *Language and Power.* To build your knowledge of critical analysis, start with Chapter 1, pages 1–6 and Chapter 5, pages 109–124. A new edition of this book appeared in 2001.

Fowler, R. (1996) 'On critical linguistics'. In *Texts and Practices* (Edited by Carmen Rosa Caldas-Coulthard and Malcolm Coulthard) pages 3–15. Roger Fowler's essay discusses CDA and its connections to SFL.

Wodak, R. (1996) *Disorders of Discourse.* For more discussion of the main principles of CDA, see pages 17–20.

Chapter 2 contents

Language and gender

Before beginning to analyze different gender discourses, we should first discuss what is meant by gender and why it is worth exploring from a Critical Discourse Analysis (CDA) perspective. As you can see from the two definitions below, gender can be defined in different ways: in a biological way that includes all organisms (definition 1), or as an identity issue involved in being part of a human society/culture (definition 2).

Definitions of gender

1   The male or female sex, or the state of being either male or female.

    Cambridge Dictionary of American English

2   Sexual identity, especially in relation to society or culture.

    The American Heritage® Dictionary of the English Language (2000) Fourth Edition

Which of these definitions of *gender* is most appropriate for critical discourse analysis? We suggest the second, because when researchers consider the issues of power between men and women, they are approaching gender, not as a biological issue, but as a *social construction*. Gender issues involve complex sets of social practices between and among people, media, and government. These practices affect personal feelings, social identity, and power relations in both overt and subtle ways. In other words, gender is *constructed* by the attitudes, beliefs, and opinions of a particular society at a given time. This means that gender as a social construction can vary within one society over time. It also means that gender is viewed differently from one culture to another.

When thinking about gender issues as a social construction, it is very important to remember that gender cannot be reduced simply to generalizations about all men or all women. Gender also includes social identity and social practices. For example, recent research in gender and language shows that men and women speak the way they do because of who they are and what they are doing, not simply because they are male and female. Therefore, we cannot say that men and women talk in this way or that way; rather, they talk in certain ways depending on the social situations in which they find themselves.

For example, a female judge and a male judge speak in very similar ways because they are both judges (their social identities) and involved in the activity of judging (their social practice.) On the other hand, a male student and a female professor will speak differently because their social identities and their social practices are different. This points to gender and language as being dependent, not on gender, but on social constructions.

Views from the theorists:
J. Holmes and M. Meyerhoff;
Eckert and McConnell-Ginet

Approaches to the study of language and gender

J. Holmes and M. Meyerhoff suggest that 'recent research on the relationship between language and gender has been dominated by approaches that examine the ways in which gender is socially constructed in interaction, rather than existing as a fixed social category to which individuals have been assigned at birth…' (1999: 180). Other researchers, Eckert and McConnell-Ginet, to whom Holmes and Meyerhoff refer, add another construct to the study of language and gender, that of 'Communities of Practice' (CofP) which they define as:

> An aggregate of people who come together around mutual engagement in an endeavour. Ways of doing things, ways of talking, beliefs, values, power, power relations – in short, practices – emerge in the course of mutual endeavor. As a social construct, a CofP is different from the traditional community, primarily because it is defined simultaneously by the membership and by the practice in which that membership engages (1992: 464)

Eckert and Mcdonnell – Ginet further indicate what this construct has to offer, saying that instead of emphasizing gender differences that result from differing patterns of early socialization, gender researchers can now examine 'people's active engagement in the reproduction of or resistance to gender arrangements in their communities' (1992: 466).

In this chapter we will look at a discourse about male and female differences. This topic is very popular. It has been studied and discussed from a wide range of perspectives, ranging from scientific investigations to discussions on popular talk shows. Sometimes the beliefs expressed in these studies and discussions are grounded in fact and based on research findings. In other cases, there is very little factual basis for belief. Yet somehow, people have arrived at what linguist Norman Fairclough calls 'common sense' assumptions, which he says are 'implicit conventions according to which people interact, linguistically, and of which people are generally not consciously aware' (1989: 2). Such assumptions are usually ideologically 'loaded' and can be very hard to challenge and change if we decide that they are wrong. CDA is particularly helpful in identifying ideologically driven perspectives, as you will find when you have analyzed the following discourse.

The Brain Sex discourse   2.2

In the following excerpt, which we call the Brain Sex discourse, the authors make a very general, broad, and strong claim about the origin of the differences between men and women. Take a few minutes to read it and see what you think and how you feel about it.

> Men are different from women. They are equal only in their common membership of the same species, humankind. The sexes are different because their brains are different.
>
> The brain, the chief administrative and emotional organ of life, is differently constructed in men and in women; it processes information in a different way, which results in different perceptions, priorities and behaviour.
>
> In the past ten years there has been an explosion of scientific research into what makes the sexes different. The findings of some researchers have been, if not suppressed, at least quietly shelved because of their potential social impact.

The truth is that virtually every professional scientist and researcher into the subject has concluded that the brains of men and women are different. There has seldom been a greater divide between what intelligent, enlightened opinion presumes – that men and women have the same brain – and what science knows – that they do not.

Adapted from Moir (1989) *Brain Sex: the real difference between men and women.*

2.2.1 Nature versus Nurture: background to the Brain Sex discourse

Until the twentieth century, some Western cultures treated men and women differently. Women were, in general, considered second-class citizens. In many countries, they did not have the right to vote, own property, or have their own bank accounts. Men were considered to be superior not only in strength, but also in intelligence, temperament, skills, and capabilities. In other words, people believed that nature had designed women to be less than equal to men. However, feminism – a mid-1960s movement based on earlier women's movements such as suffragism (the right to vote) – radically changed the way Western cultures thought about the abilities, roles and rights of women. People who argued for greater equality for women believed that women and men were not different from one another except in physical terms of height and strength. Feminists maintained that women and men were equal in intelligence, temperament, and capabilities, and that any differences observed in these areas were the result only of nurture – social conditioning and expectations. Beliefs and assumptions built up around this idea created a strong ideology about women that affected every aspect of Western societies, from education to health to the workplace.

However, bio-medical and technological advances that began in the 1980s enabled researchers to study the human brain in ways never before possible. The Brain Sex discourse was written in 1989 when some of this research was starting to reveal that, in fact, women and men were not born equal, because their brains developed differently, beginning almost at conception. In other words, the nature argument was 'raising its head' once again. People with a strong belief and investment in the nurture argument possibly felt threatened. They might have feared that talk of natural differences between the sexes might reverse years of advancement in women's equality. Therefore, the authors of the Brain Sex discourse knew that their book would provoke controversy.

2.2.2 Analyzing the Brain Sex Discourse

In Chapter 1, we looked at a number of ways of analyzing discourse – through 1) participants and processes, 2) attitudes and positions/stances, and 3) cohesion, achieved by chains and Themes. As you will also recall from Chapter 1, these three ways of analyzing a discourse stem from the linguistic theory called Systemic Functional Linguistics (SFL). This theory states that, when people interact through language, they are simultaneously exchanging three kinds of meanings:

1. They are talking/writing about their ideas and experiences.
2. They are talking/writing about their attitudes and positions/stances towards what they are saying and who they are interacting with.
3. They are making sure that what they are communicating is cohesive and coherent – in other words, has meaning for listeners/readers.

In this chapter, you will be exploring in greater depth the first way of making meaning – when speakers/writers communicate their ideas and experiences. In SFL, this is a general function of language called the Ideational Metafunction and it involves the participants, processes, and circumstances in a discourse. When you analyze this metafunction, you are finding *who* does *what* to *whom, when, where*, and *how*.

The Ideational Metafunction

• Expresses speakers/writers' ideas and experiences.		
• Answers the question: Who is doing what to whom, when, where, and how?		
Who and whom	= Participants	(nouns/pronouns)
Is doing what	= Processes	(verbs that realize actions/states)
When, where, and how	= Circumstances	(adverbs, prepositional and adverbial phrases)

Views from the theorists:
Michael Halliday

View of processes

Michael Halliday, in his discussion of the Ideational Metafunction, says that reality as we experience it is made up of processes. 'Our most powerful impression of experience is that it consists of 'goings-on' – happening, doing, sensing, meaning and being and becoming. All these goings-on are sorted out in the grammar of the clause.'

The grammar '…distinguishes rather clearly between our outer experience, the processes of the external world, and inner experience, the processes of consciousness. The grammatical categories are those of MATERIAL process and MENTAL process.'

There are processes of a third type: 'those of classifying and identifying; we call these RELATIONAL processes'.

'A process consists, in principle, of three components:
    (i) the process itself;
    (ii) participants in the process;
    (iii) circumstances associated with the process'. (1994: 106–107)

In this chapter, you will explore the Ideational Metafunction in the Brain Sex discourse. Your analysis will help you understand more about the way our society/culture thinks about gender issues.

As you learn about participants, processes, and circumstances, it is important to remember that you are **not** studying the grammar to find out the correct word order. Rather, you are discovering the ways in which the grammar *realizes* meanings, that is, the meanings that are expressed in a particular discourse, and how these relate to meanings in similar and different discourses. As you learn to use the CDA tools, you will develop the skills to help you study how people exchange meanings, and how these meanings are sometimes used to exert power and influence over others.

Practice

Identifying participants, processes, and circumstances

In this section, we have divided the Brain Sex discourse into clauses so that you can do some basic SFL analysis.

1. Underline the participants. Remember that participants can be Actors or Goals.

2. Circle the processes. Each clause contains one or more Finite processes, that is, verbs that indicate past, present or future. It may also contain other words that indicate time. We will only identify the processes that are realized by Finite verbs because these express time.

Finite vs. non-finite verbs	
Finite verb	**Non-finite verb**
Definition: a verb or the auxiliary that precedes it which indicates the past, present or future.	Definition: a verb form that has no indication of past, present or future.
Examples: I *am* happy. He *went* to the restaurant. She *has* eaten in the cafeteria for the whole year.	Examples: *To be* happy is important. *Going* to restaurants is a way to relax. *Eating* in the cafeteria all year is terrible.

3. Highlight the circumstances. Remember that circumstances describe when, where, and how and occur in two constructions: prepositional phrases and adverbs/adverbial phrases.

- Prepositional phrases begin with prepositions such as *in, around, of, through,* and *above.*
- Adverbs/adverbial phrases contain words such as *differently, in a different way.*

1. Men are different from women.
2. They are equal only in their common membership of the same species, humankind.
3. The sexes are different
4. because their brains are different.
5. The brain, the chief administrative and emotional organ of life, is differently constructed in men and in women;
6. it processes information in a different way,
7. which results in different perceptions, priorities and behaviour.
8. In the past ten years there has been an explosion of scientific research

9.   into what makes the sexes different.
10.   The findings of some researchers have been, (a) if not suppressed, (b) at least quietly shelved because of their potential social impact.
11.   The truth is
12.   a) that virtually every professional scientist and researcher into the subject has concluded b) that the brains of men and women are different.
13.   There has seldom been a greater divide
14.   between what intelligent, enlightened opinion presumes
15.   that men and women have the same brain
16.   and what science knows
17.   that they do not (have the same brain)

2.3   The Brain Sex discourse: processes and participants

You've likely noticed that the Brain Sex discourse has many differences from President Bush's speech in Chapter 1, particularly in vocabulary, tone, and style. In the President's 'call to arms,' the processes were Material, such as *we will find them*. SFL researchers call such processes *Material* because a 'material' thing is happening or being done by one participant (sometimes to another), that is, something we can identify as a physical action. It isn't surprising that so many of the processes in President Bush's speech were Material, because the speech was about action. On the other hand, the Brain Sex discourse has very few Material processes. Rather, we find two other kinds of processes: Mental and Relational. In this section of the chapter, we examine each type of process along with its participants. We begin with an SFL analysis, and follow it with a CDA discussion.

2.3.1   Material processes and participants

You will recall from Chapter 1 that the participants played one of two roles in a Material process. The participant doing the action was the Actor, and the participant receiving the action was the Goal. When speakers/writers put the Actor in the Subject position in a clause, this indicates that the clause is in the **active voice.** The following demonstrates the active voice in the clause: *we find them.*

Actor(s)	Process: Material	Goal(s)
we	*find*	*them*

Now, compare this with the two Material processes and their participants in the Brain Sex discourse. You may immediately notice that the construction is quite different from that in *We find them*. Look at what has happened to the Actor and the Goal:

10a: *Their findings have been suppressed*
10b: *Their findings have been shelved*

In each of these cases, the participants realized by nouns in front of the processes are still Subjects, but they are no longer Actors. Why? Because they are not doing the action of shelving or suppressing. In fact, these participants are playing a similar role to *them* in *we find them*, that is, they are Goals which are being acted on. Here is how these clauses look.

Goal	Process: Material
Their findings	*have been suppressed*
Their findings	*have been shelved*

When English speakers/writers use this kind of construction, in which the Goal comes first, the clause is in the **passive voice.**

Active vs. passive voice

Important note: When the active voice changes to the passive, only the form changes. The meaning is the same, but the emphasis is different.

Active	Passive
Actor is in the Subject position before the process.	Goal is in the Subject position before the process.
Goal is after the process.	Actor, if one exists, is after the process.
Example: *They* (Actor) have suppressed *the findings*. (Goal)	Examples: *The findings* (Goal) have been suppressed by *them* (Actor). *The findings* (Goal) have been suppressed (no Actor).

Two important things happen when speakers/writer use the passive voice.

- First, the Goal receives the reader's primary focus because it occurs first in the sentence. In other words, the authors want listeners and readers to focus on the Goal and not the Actor.

- The Actor can be eliminated, as it has been in these two clauses. This means that, as readers, you cannot find out who has suppressed and shelved the findings because the text does not give you this information.

In the section below, we have included the types of questions a CDA researcher could ask about the Material processes in this discourse. Try to answer them and then check your answers with ours in the discussion which follows.

CDA questions

Material processes and participants

1. What voice predominates in the Material processes? Active or passive?
2. Why do you think the authors might have chosen to use that voice?
3. Since the authors have not identified the Actors, can you guess who they are?
4. Is this important to know? Why?

Our responses

What we find interesting in the Brain Sex discourse is that all its Material processes are in the passive voice. This tells us that when the authors do describe actions, they do not seem to want readers to know *who* is doing *what* to *whom*. When the authors wrote: *The findings have been, if not suppressed, at least quietly shelved*, they were suggesting that many scientists who have found certain things to be true have not been able to publish or publicize their results. For social and/or political reasons, some people, not identified, have not accepted or liked their results.

When Actors are eliminated as they have been in this case, it is difficult for you to evaluate the truth of this statement. Who are the 'suppressors?' What are their credentials? Are they qualified to make the decision to suppress information? You will have trouble trying to determine whether this judgment is right or wrong without knowing the Actors involved.

Is it important to know who has suppressed these scientific findings? We think so. We also think that the authors are deliberately not identifying the many people who support the social and political aspirations of women. For this reason, we suggest that the lack of Actors in the instances of the passive voice here is significant.

Mental processes and participants

All of us have experiences that are not action-oriented, but instead involve mental activities. SFL researchers describe these activities – sensing, thinking, feeling, reacting – as Mental processes. In the Brain Sex discourse we see four Mental processes.

6. it **processes** information
12. a) *every professional scientist and researcher* **has concluded**
    b) *that the brains of men and women are different.*
14. *what intelligent, enlightened opinion* **presumes**
16. *what science* **knows**

Who feels, thinks, and senses?

Not surprisingly, Mental processes can **only** be experienced by a conscious being. However, it is very common for speakers/writers to *anthropomorphize* inanimate objects or entities by attributing human feelings to them. For example, if you were to say: *My computer hates this software*, you are anthropomorphizing your computer, that is, giving the computer human-like qualities.

When SFL researchers discuss the Participants involved in Mental processes, they do not talk about Actors or Goals, because mental activities such as feeling, thinking, sensing, and reacting are different from the physical actions that constitute Material processes. Researchers use the term *Senser* for the one involved in the mental activity, and the *Phenomenon* for what is being 'sensed.' The Phenomenon is what a Senser thinks of or about, feels, senses, likes or dislikes. An interesting fact about the Phenomenon is that it can be realized by a single word, a phrase or a whole clause, as the following chart of the Mental processes in the Brain Sex discourse demonstrates.

Senser	Process: Mental	Phenomenon
it	processes	information
scientist and researcher	has concluded	that the brains of men and women are different
opinion	presumes	what (that men and women have the same brain)
science	knows	what (that they do not have the same brain)

We find it rather strange, given that Sensers are defined as conscious beings, that in the Brain Sex discourse, two out of four Sensers are not animate. To highlight this oddity, before reading the discussion which follows, study the questions in the box below and try to answer them.

CDA questions

Mental processes and participants

1. Who or what are the Sensers?
2. Is the Senser always a conscious being?
3. If not, what is 'standing in' for the conscious Senser?
4. Why?

Our responses

There are three different kinds of Sensers in the Brain Sex discourse:

1. Part of the human body – *it* referring to the brain;
2. Conscious beings – *scientists and researchers*; and
3. Non-animate entities – *opinion* and *science*.

How can *opinion presume* and *science know*? The answer is that they can't. Neither *opinion* nor *science* are conscious beings, although both are human activities. *Science*, of course, is done by scientists, while *opinion* refers to views and concepts held by others.

We suggest that the authors are doing two things by choosing *science* and *opinion*. First, they are obscuring agency (*who* is doing what), as you have seen in passive constructions with Material processes. They seem to be doing this because they do not want readers to know exactly who opposes the information they provide in this discourse.

Secondly, they are in a sense setting up two opposing 'camps' for readers – those who agree that men are different from women, and those who don't. The first camp is *science*, which includes the researchers and scientists already mentioned in the text. The authors may be hoping that by saying *science* instead of *scientists*, their statement will be stronger since 1) it implies that everyone in the scientific field knows that men and women are different; and 2) *science*, in general, is a discipline that is presumably based on fact, not opinions.

The second camp consists of people who don't agree that men are different from women. Although their views are described as *intelligent, enlightened opinion*, these people only *presume*; they do not *know*. In other words, this group only expresses views, not facts; they are not in nearly as strong a position as those in the science camp. The authors can present this group in this manner because they do not identify the members.

This leaves the reader with two choices. We can decide that the members of the second camp are truly intelligent and enlightened individuals, and therefore their opinions and presumptions are correct. Or we can decide the reverse – that no matter how intelligent and enlightened the members of the second camp may be, they are wrong. However, we will never know whether or not we are correct, because we do not know who these people are.

2.3.2 Relational processes and participants

The majority of processes in the Brain Sex discourse are Relational processes. Their predominance in this discourse reinforces the authors' main points. Relational processes allow speakers and writers to show a *relationship* between and among Participants. Another way to describe Relational processes is to say that they allow speakers/writers to tell us about 'how things are' in the past, present, and future, that is, about 'states of being.' For this reason, many Relational processes use the verb *to be*. However, many different verbs can 'stand in' for *to be* – for example, *has, owns, appears, equals, seems, means, represents*, and *signifies*. The Brain Sex discourse has 12 clauses that contain Relational processes.

1) Men **are** different
2) They **are** equal
3) The sexes **are** different
4) Their brains **are** different
5) The brain, the chief administrative and emotional organ of life, **is** differently **constructed** in men and in women
7) Which **results in** different perceptions, priorities and behaviour
8) There **has been** an explosion of scientific research
9) Into what **makes** the sexes different
11) The truth **is**
12b) The brains of men and women **are** different
13) There **has** seldom **been** a greater divide
15) Men and women **have** the same brain
17) They **do not** [**have** the same brain].

You will find it easy to identify those processes that use the verb *to be* or *to have* as Relational. However, the processes in clauses 5, 7, 9 may be more difficult to identify as Relational processes. Let's examine them more closely to see why they are Relational.

- *The brain* **is** *differently* **constructed** (5): The verb *to construct* is usually considered a Material process when it is used in clauses such as *he constructed a house* and *the building was constructed*. However, in these two examples, there are Actors, either identified or not identified, who undertake a physical action in order to create a building. Is there an Actor who constructs a brain?

  We could possibly argue for biology or a deity, depending on our beliefs. However, innate human characteristics such as eye colour, height, and size are generally considered as a 'state of being,' that is, attributes in Relational processes. Therefore, in this text, *the brain is constructed* is similar to a statement such as *the human brain is large*. Both *constructed* and *large* are attributes of the brain.

- *which **results in** different perceptions, priorities and behaviour* (7): The verb *to result in* may also seem at first glance to be Material because it implies a physical action of change. However, the idea here is that in processing information, the brain creates a new situation, that is, a new 'state of being'. Therefore, this process is also Relational.

- *what **makes** the sexes different* (9): Again, the verb *make* is very often a Material process as in *cooks make cakes*. However, here the authors want to convey the idea that 1) there has been a vast amount of scientific research that has led to the understanding that the sexes are different; and 2) this research accounts for and explains that difference. A synonym for *makes* in this context would be *leads to* which realizes a new 'state of being'.

It is not uncommon for a discourse to have one predominant process. When this occurs, it reveals a pattern. As we mentioned in Chapter 1, patterns are often significant because they tell us something about the attitudes, beliefs, and choices writers/speakers make to convey experience. In this discourse Relational processes predominate. As critical discourse analysts, we ask why this is so, and what it means. In the box below, we have listed the kinds of questions a CDA researcher might ask when looking at this pattern of Relational processes. First, read the questions and try to answer them. Then compare your answers with our responses below.

Relational processes and participants   CDA questions

1. What do the Relational processes in this discourse focus on?
2. What basic stance/position towards gender difference is revealed by this choice?
3. What groups might agree with the position taken here?
4. What groups might oppose it?

Our responses

The Relational processes in the Brain Sex discourse all involve gender differences. In general, they reflect the authors' version of the state of things or the relation between things, ideas, and states as they may have occurred in the past, are occurring in the present, and might occur in the future. In this text, 10 of the 12 Relational processes are in the present tense. The authors, in other words, are telling you the 'facts' as they see them today. They inform you of this in the first four clauses. Notice how strong these statements are because of the use of *are* and the lack of any qualifying words such as *perhaps*, *maybe*, or *probably*.

1.   Men **are** different from women.
2.   They **are** equal only in their common membership of the same species, humankind.
3.   The sexes **are** different
4.   because their brains **are** different.

There is no question here about the authors' position on differences between the brains of the two genders. Even the two Relational processes that occur in the present perfect tense (the tense that uses the auxiliary *has/have*) indicate that there was an activity that began in the past and continues today. In other words, the use of this tense does not subtract from the authors' position – it reinforces it.

8.   there **has been** an explosion of scientific research
14.   there **has** seldom **been** a greater divide

These statements, realizing Relational processes, seem to present facts that cannot be argued with. The large number of such statements make it difficult to disagree or offer opposition. The more such 'facts' pile up, the harder it may be to dispute the overall argument.

2.4   Summary: the Brain Sex discourse

In this section of the chapter, we will pull together what you have learned so far about the **Ideational Metafunction** in the Brain Sex discourse, and expand on that information. The table format helps us to organize our SFL and CDA findings.

2.4.1 Classifying participants

In Section 2.2, as part of the SFL analysis, we identified the participants in the discourse. The next step for the CDA discussion is to classify the participants to better understand who the authors are focusing on. In the chart below we list the different participants and note how frequently they are mentioned in the text. (Remember that nouns/pronouns in circumstances are *not* participants.)

Men/Women/Brain	Science/Scientists	Others (unidentified)
men	some researchers	intelligent, enlightened
women	every professional scientist	opinion
the sexes	and researcher	divide
they *(2x)*	an explosion of scientific	
their brains	research	
the brains	findings	
brain	science	
it		
different perceptions		
priorities and behaviour		
they		
Frequency: 10x	Frequency: 5x	Frequency: 2x

2.4.2 Creating a summary of the processes

In Section 2.2 we identified the processes, and in Section 2.3 we analyzed them in more depth, using SFL tools. The chart below presents this analysis in a tabular form to make the processes easier for you to identify.

	Clause	Process
1	Men **are** different from women	Relational
2	They **are** equal only in their common membership of the same species, humankind.	Relational
3	The sexes **are** different	Relational
4	because their brains **are** different	Relational
5	The brain, the chief administrative and emotional organ of life, **is** differently constructed in men and in women;	Relational
6	it **processes** information in a different way	Mental

7	which **results in** different perceptions, priorities and behaviour	Relational
8	In the past ten years there **has been** an explosion of scientific research	Relational
9	into what **makes** the sexes different	Relational
10	The findings of some researchers **have been**, (a) if not **suppressed**, (b) at least quietly **shelved** because of their potential social impact	Material (passive) and Material (passive)
11	The truth **is**	Relational
12	that virtually every professional scientist and researcher into the subject **has concluded** that the brains of men and women **are** different	Mental and Relational
13	There **has** seldom **been** a greater divide	Relational
14	between what intelligent, enlightened opinion **presumes**	Mental
15	that men and women **have** the same brain	Relational
16	and what science **knows**	Mental
17	that they **do not** [**have** the same brain]	Relational

2.4.3 Classifying the circumstances

In Section 2.2, we noted that circumstances describe *when*, *where*, and *how*. It is useful to ask what the circumstances in this text tell us about the speaker's/writer's representation of ideas and experiences. As you'll note from the classification in the chart below, the frequency of types of circumstances is similar to the frequency of types of participants. In other words, there are more circumstances in the category of *men/women/brain* than any other category.

Men/Women/Brain	Science/Scientists
from women	in the past ten years
in their membership of the same species, humankind	of scientific research
differently	quietly
in men	into the subject
in women	
in a different way	
of men and women	
Frequency: 7x	Frequency: 4x

2.4.4 Putting SFL and CDA together

The chart below summarizes what we have found out about the ideational function, which forms the basis for our CDA questions and answers.

SFL questions	Our answers
Who are the main participants?	The vast majority of participants are human beings or the brain, men and women, the brain, the sexes, scientists, researchers, findings, explosion of scientific research, science.
What are the processes?	The majority of processes are Relational and in the present tense. There are a few Mental processes and a few Material processes, with the latter all in the passive voice.

CDA questions	Our answers
According to the authors, who seems to have all of the power in terms of knowledge? How do we know?	The most powerful entity here is science and the people, research and findings related to science. We know this because of the seven occurrences of these participants, second only to the men and women and their brains – the topic of this discourse.
Are the science participants represented positively or negatively in the processes in which they are involved? How are other participants presented and why?	The processes present a strong case for the scientists' being right about brain differences in the two sexes. These people are portrayed very sympathetically. People who disagree with the point of view presented in this discourse are described as intelligent and enlightened; however, they only hold opinions and can only presume to know anything. This slightly negative portrayal suggests that anyone who disagrees with the authors is probably wrong.

As we discussed in the Introduction, one can view the two perspectives on language, SFL and CDA, as being on a continuum, where SFL's concern with issues of ideology and power are extended by those working in the critical discourse framework. J. R. Martin's work has been situated in SFL but he also has concerns and interests that bring him into CDA. In an analysis he carries out on a child's book in which he focuses on the different and unequal roles of the men and women in the household, he examines ideational meaning:

Views from the theorists:
J. R. Martin

Connections between SFL and CDA

From the perspective of ideational meaning we are interested in how a text of this kind constructs power. In the experience of CDA analysts one relevant part of language is TRANSITIVITY; its purpose is to construct processes, the participants involved in them and the circumstances in which they take place. … Clearly this dimension of meaning is central to the analysis of the inequality and power in discourse. It allows us to ask questions about who is acting, what kinds of actions they undertake, and who or what if anything they act upon. (2000: 276)

2.5   Sample gender discourse: 'Melanie Speaks'

The following discourse has been adapted from an audio guide called 'Melanie Speaks'. The guide provides advice to transsexual men who wish to speak more like women. Read the text and focus on the language and gender aspects of this discourse.

One of the dead giveaways of masculinity is the wrong vocabulary. For example, men use the word 'want' much more than women use it. Women don't 'want' things, they 'like' things. A guy will go up to the little speaker box at a fast food restaurant and say, 'I want a Big Mac,' whereas a woman will say, 'I'd like a small salad please.'

Men have power in our society. They are in control. Women believe that they have less power and less control over their own lives.

When a man says that he 'needs' to do something, he is really saying, 'I have a goal, a purpose.' On the other hand, a woman has a tendency to feel that she's not in control of achieving goals so she feels that she 'should' do something. It has more of a sense of obligation than a sense of instigation, and that is a very big difference in the mental attitudes of men and women.

Now, I know this is anathema to feminism, but this is not about how to break stereotypes, it's about how to become one. For feminizing your voice, stay away from those assertive words and go with the 'kinda-sorta' words, and words that don't have command value to them, and you will find that your voice will be considered a lot more feminine.

Melanie Anne Phillips (2003) http://heartcorps.com/journeys/ (Accessed March 2006)

We find this discourse worth exploring because it examines the issue of language and gender. In the past, popular magazines often advised women how to speak in order to succeed in life. For example, in the 1990s, *Glamour* had an article, 'Girl Talk, Boy Talk,' which advised women to speak in a straightforward way to male subordinates and not to shy away from blatant orders.

The assumption that women and men had two different ways of talking was based on early research that suggested that men's speech was the norm and that women spoke differently. There were two theories about this difference. The first was that it was just a difference, nothing more. The second, called the deficit theory, said that women's speech was deficient or deviant; one implication was that, for women to be successful, they had to take on male speech characteristics. This theory makes very strong assumptions about the differences between male and female language and has implications for a wide variety of social contexts such as education, business, and personal relationships.

Earlier, when discussing the background for the Brain Sex discourse, we talked about the controversies involved in the 'nature versus nurture' approaches to understanding differences between the brains of men and women. The issue of language and gender also generates the same controversies. The deficit theory assumes that male and female differences in speech habits are innate (nature), instead of questioning what social functions these differences serve and where they come from (nurture). When women are given advice on how to talk, the nature approach is reinforced: women have to change, but men do not. (This is also a variation on the theme of deviance, in which male speech is set up as normal and anything that differs is deviant.)

It is also important to keep in mind that the media interpret very selectively research findings made by linguists – often emphasizing what they think the public will find interesting, rather than providing a complete picture. The result is that popular opinion does not adequately reflect all the complexities involved in the issue of language and gender.

Another issue to remember as we discuss the 'Melanie Speaks' discourse further is the one raised at the beginning of this Chapter, namely that *personal identity* and *social practices* have to do with conversational styles as well as gender. In different situations, men and women speak the way they do in relation to who they are, the particular activities in which they are involved, and their specific communities of social practice. In fact, a man and woman engaged in the same activity, in the same role, and with the same status may speak the same. A number of linguists are now studying how males and females interact as judges and plaintiffs, doctors/nurses and patients, and teachers and students. As you analyze this text, consider what 'common sense' assumptions it reveals, as opposed to findings from recent research on language and gender.

Practice

Identifying participants

As we indicated earlier, one of the first steps in analyzing a text is often to identify the participants. We have started the analysis in the chart below by listing the participants in the first paragraph of the 'Melanie Speaks' discourse. Fill in the participants from the next two paragraphs.

People	Others
men women women they (women) men a guy I Woman	one of the dead giveaways of masculinity wrong vocabulary word 'want' it things things Big Mac small salad
Frequency:	Frequency:

Now compare your answers with those of other students in the class.

Identifying processes

The next step is to identify the processes in the discourse. You already have learned about most of the processes in 'Melanie Speaks.' However, you will need more information about Mental processes and a new process – Verbal – in order to analyze this discourse.

More about Mental processes

In the Brain Sex discourse, the Mental processes involved thinking activities such as *knowing* and *presuming*. In the 'Melanie Speaks' discourse, the Mental processes involve feelings. Some examples of Mental processes in this discourse are:

4. women **don't** 'want' things
5. they '**like**' things
12. when a man says that he '**needs**' to do something,
15. so she **feels** that she 'should' do something

Like the Mental processes in the Brain Sex discourse, these processes also have a Senser and a Phenomenon.

Senser	Process: Mental	Phenomenon
they	*'like'*	*things*
she	*feels*	*that she 'should' do something*

Verbal processes

Verbal processes include *say* and its many synonyms, such as *talk, ask, state, announce, report*, and *indicate*. Verbal processes have:

- **Sayer** – someone who does the saying or talking;.
- **Receiver** – someone to whom the talk is directed; and
- **Verbiage** – what is being said.

The first paragraph in 'Melanie Speaks' ends with the sentence *A guy will go up to the little speaker box at a fast food restaurant and say, 'I want a Big Mac.'* This sentence has three clauses:

- Clause 1: A guy will go up to the little speaker box at a fast food restaurant
- Clause 2: and say,
- Clause 3: 'I want a Big Mac.'

The first clause contains a Material process, the second a Verbal process, and the third a Mental process. It is very typical of the Verbiage to be realized by a separate clause. It is easier to demonstrate this by diagramming the clauses separately.

Actor	Process(es): Material	Circumstance: Where	Circumstance: Where
A guy	*will go up*	*to the little speaker box*	*at a fast food restaurant*

Sayer	Process: Verbal
(A guy)	*(will) say*

Sayer	Process: Verbal	Verbiage
(A guy)	*(will) say*	*a big Mac.*

Many Verbal processes include direct or indirect quotes, as we saw above and see again in clauses 8 and 12. This type of clause construction actually contains two clauses – one with the Verbal process which projects another clause which has its own process. Here are two examples from the 'Melanie Speaks' text.

8. whereas a woman will say, 'I'd like a small salad please' (Verbal and Mental)
12. When a man says that he 'needs' to do something (Verbal and Mental)

There are no cases of Verbal processes with a Receiver in the 'Melanie Speaks' text, but there is an example in the first sentence of President Bush's 'call to arms' in Chapter 1: *I've asked the highest levels of our government to come to discuss the current tragedy that has so deeply affected our nation.*

Sayer	Process: Verbal	Receiver	Verbiage
I	*'ve asked*	*the highest levels of our government*	*to come to discuss the current tragedy that has so deeply affected our nation*

Identifying processes by clause and type

With this added information on Mental and Verbal processes, you should now be able to identify all the processes in the text by clause and by type in this discourse. Fill in the following chart and then compare your answers with those of other students. We have put in some of the answers to assist you.

	Clause	Process
1	One of the dead giveaways of masculinity **is** the wrong vocabulary	
2	For example, men **use** the word 'want' much more	Verbal
3	than women **use** it	
4	Women **don't** '**want**' things	Mental
5	they '**like**' things	Mental
6	A guy **will go up** to the little speaker box at a fast food restaurant	Material
7	and **say**, 'I **want** a Big Mac'	Verbal and
8	whereas a woman **will say**, '**I'd like** a small salad please'	Verbal and
9	Men **have** power in our society	
10	They **are** in control	
11	Women **believe** that they **have** less power and less control over their own lives	
12	When a man **says** that he '**needs**' to do something,	and Mental
13	he **is** really **saying**, 'I **have** a goal, a purpose'	Verbal and Relational
14	On the other hand, a woman **has** a tendency to feel	
15	that she'**s not** in control of achieving goals	
16	so she **feels** that she '**should**' **do** something	Mental and
17	It **has** more of a sense of obligation than a sense of instigation	
18	and that **is** a very big difference in the mental attitudes of men and women.	
19	Now, I **know** that this **is** anathema to feminism	

20	but this **is** not about how to break stereotypes	
21	it's about how to become one	
22	For feminizing your voice, **stay away from** those assertive words	Verbal
23	and **go with** the 'kinda-sorta' words	
24	and words that **don't have** command value to them	
25	and you **will find** that your voice **will be considered** a lot more feminine	

Identifying processes associated with each gender

Now that you have identified the participants and processes, you should be able to 'tease out' the processes that are associated with men and women. Complete the charts below. Discuss your answers with members of your class.

Men			
Material	Mental	Relational	Verbal
Frequency:	Frequency:	Frequency:	Frequency:
Women			
Material	Mental	Relational	Verbal
Frequency:	Frequency:	Frequency:	Frequency:

Now that you have carried out these basic SFL analyses, examine the CDA questions below and try to complete them in paragraph form. This will be your first attempt at a mini-essay that discusses your findings.

1. Once you have isolated the processes associated with each gender, describe the differences in the process types that, according to the 'Melanie Speaks' discourse, characterize men and women's speech.
2. Summarize your findings and then add a paragraph based on your experiences, in which you agree or disagree with these findings.
3. Exchange paragraphs with other students and compare your findings and opinions. What are the differences? What are the similarities?
4. Read the discourse again. This time, think about how you could revise it based on your experience as a student. Write a paragraph directed towards a male or a female friend who is about to enter university.

With your own analysis in mind, read the following example of a critical discourse analysis.

Kate Clark looks at a British tabloid to examine the ways in which *The Sun* reports on crimes of violence and lays blame on victims as well as attackers. She does so to point out the underlying ideology of the newspaper in relation especially to issues dealing with sexual violence. She says that often the view of the paper is very blatant as in the following headline: 'VICTIM MUST TAKE THE BLAME'. Often, however, she says 'language is used to convey blame subtly...' (1992: 212).

> Blame or lack of responsibility, absence, emphasis or prominence of a participant can all be encoded into a report of *The Sun* through its choice of transitivity... Transitivity is concerned with language at the level of clauses. The elements in this theory most relevant to the reports studied are material processes and participants. Material processes

involve 'doing'. There are two possible roles for participants: the Agent who 'does' the process and the Goal who is affected by the process. (Clark, 1992)

Clark outlines the ways in which *The Sun* avoids mentioning the Agent so that the victim seems to receive the blame. She says that '… blame for the attack can be withheld from the attacker and transferred to the victim or to someone else' (ibid: 212–213). She then carries out an analysis to show how this is accomplished in the newspaper.

She examines one of the headlines dealing with a murder: 'GIRL 7 MURDERED WHILE MUM DRANK AT PUB'. The sentence has two clauses:

> …one details the murder, the other describes what the victim's mother… was doing at the time of the murder. The 'murder' clauses are passive and the murderer is made invisible by deletion. This minimizes the reader's awareness of his guilt: compare 'Girl 7 murdered' with 'Man murdered Girl, 7'. This structure – a 'drinking mother' clause linked to a 'murder-less-murder clause' is used in four out of the five sentences. This insistent repetition joins the child's death and the mother's absence so directly and so forcibly that a causal relationship is formed… The naming of Nicola (the young girl) and her mother underscores the mother's supposed responsibility. (ibid: 213)

Chapter 2 Glossary

Active voice: when the one undertaking a physical, mental or verbal action is in the Subject position in a clause.

Commonsense assumption: a belief based, not on fact, but on certain conventional ways of thinking within society.

Direct speech: enclosed by quotation marks, for example, 'She left'.

Finite: a Verb or the auxiliary that precedes it that indicates the past, present or future tense.

Ideational Metafunction: a general function of language that expresses speakers/writers' ideas and experiences.

Indirect speech: speech that is referred to indirectly without quotation marks; for example, I said that she left. (I said *that she was gone.*)

Mental process: realized by verbs that express the following: feeling, thinking, sensing.

Mood: whether a clause is a statement, question or command.

Non-Finite: a verb form with no tense.

Passive voice: form of a clause in which the Subject follows the Verb, allowing the Goal to receive the focus while the Actor can be mentioned or left out.

Phenomenon: what the Senser in a Mental process feels, thinks or senses.

Receiver: the one who is being spoken or written to in a Verbal process.

Relational process: describes a relation between participants or a state of being.

Sayer: the one who speaks in a Verbal process.

Senser: the one who feels, thinks or senses in a Mental process.

Verbal process: the act of saying realized by verbs such as *say, tell, order,* and *exclaim.*

Verbiage: what the Sayer says in a Verbal process.

SFL readings

Eggins, S. (1994) *Introduction to Systemic Functional Linguistics.* Her Chapter 9 provides a very thorough treatment of the Ideational Metafunction in which she clearly outlines processes and participants involved in transitivity.

Halliday, M. A. K. (1994) *Introduction to Functional Grammar.* Halliday's Chapter 5 is a very closely related treatment of processes and participants. It would be helpful to read both of these

Chapter 2
Further readings

works to get a thorough idea of Transitivity. See especially 106–161.

CDA readings

Clark, K. (1992) 'The linguistics of blame, representations of women in *The Sun*'s reporting of crimes of sexual violence'. In M. Toolan (ed.) *Language, Text and Context, Essays in Stylistics* 208–224. Her essay, as we have seen in 'Views from the theorists', offers further insights into transitivity analysis in which she indicates the relationship between language and blame as reported in *The Sun*.

Talbot, M. (1997) Randy fish boss branded a stinker: coherence and the construction of masculinities in a British tabloid newspaper. In S. Johnson, H. Meinhof and H. Ulrike (eds) *Language and Masculinity* 173–187. Talbot takes a similar linguistic approach to the study of language and gender in her examination of the construction of masculinity in relation to sexual harassment cases treated in *The Sun*.

Chapter 3 contents

Language and racism

In this chapter, we will be looking at the complex issue of racism, which can be examined from many perspectives. It has been the subject of literally thousands of articles and studies. We cannot, of course, consider all the ways that researchers have approached this issue. But we will examine the issue from a linguistic point of view, and more specifically from the point of view of SFL and CDA.

In order to understand what racism involves and who it affects, we will start by briefly examining four definitions of racism. Definitions are a genre, a specific type of discourse. Read through them and, as you do so, try to find some common elements, particularly at the start of each definition, that relate to the Ideational Metafunction which you learned about in Chapter 2 – the participants and processes.

Racism is the prejudice that members of one race are intrinsically superior to members of other races; racism is discriminatory or abusive behaviour towards members of another race. (Dictionary.com)

Racism refers to the belief that human races have distinctive characteristics which determine their respective cultures, usually involving the idea that one's own race is superior and has the right to rule or dominate others; offensive or aggressive behaviour to members of another race stemming from such a belief. (Macquarie University, Australia, 1998: Human Rights and Equal Opportunity Commission)

Racism is more than personal prejudice; it involves carrying into effect one's prejudices, resulting in discrimination, inequity and/or exclusion. Racism is understood as the negative valuing and discriminatory treatment of individuals and groups on the basis of their race. Racism can be manifested in both personal attacks and insults and in the structure of social institutions. (Carleton University, Canada: Human Rights Policies and Procedures)

Racism is a set of beliefs (often complex) which asserts the natural superiority of one racial group over another, at the individual but also the institutional level. In one sense, racism refers to the belief that biology rather than culture is the primary determinant of group attitudes and actions. This belief can then be used to extol the inherent superiority of certain 'races' and justify deferential treatment and social positions. Racism goes beyond ideology, however, involving discriminatory practices that protect and maintain the position of certain groups and sustain the inferior position of others. (Freeservers.com)

You likely noticed that each definition begins, not surprisingly, with the Topical Theme *racism*. As well, defining is a way of explaining a 'state of being' so each definition also begins with a Relational process: *is* or *refers to*. We only talked about Relational processes in general in Chapter 2, but there are in fact several different types. In this discourse, there are Relational processes of *Identification*, which has two participants – the object being identified, which is called the *Token*, and the *Value* attached to it. For example, we could chart the first clause of the first definition as follows:

Token	Process: Relational/ Identification	Value
Racism	*is*	*the prejudice that members of one race are intrinsically superior to members of other races*

To explore commonalities and differences between these definitions, we list below all the Values associated with the Token *racism*.

- discriminatory or abusive behaviour …
- belief that human races have distinctive characteristics…
- offensive or aggressive behaviour…
- more than personal prejudice…
- negative valuing and discriminatory treatment…
- set of beliefs which asserts the natural superiority of one racial group over another
- the belief that biology rather than culture…
- discriminatory practices…

What this list of Values tells us is that racism is about beliefs and behaviours, or, more specifically, that racism goes beyond a belief – the way one views people of another race – to have a significant impact on behaviour – how one acts towards them.

We have examined definitions of what is thought of as traditional racism. Peter Teo writes of a new type of racism that is, according to him, more subtle and thus 'insidious'. He looks at:

Views from the theorists:
Peter Teo

View of racism

> … the changing nature of racism and ethnic domination in modern and increasingly cosmopolitan societies such as the United States of America, Western Europe and Australia. The people who practice this 'new racism' believe in and uphold the basic values of democratic egalitarianism, and would thus emphatically deny that they are 'racist' (as defined by van Dijk, 1993). Nevertheless they would speak or act in such a way that distances themselves from the ethnic minority, engaging in discursive strategies that *blame* the victims for their circumstances on their own social, economic and even cultural disadvantages. For instance, the vicious circle of low educational achievement, limited employment opportunities, poverty and consequent assimilation into a culture of drugs and crime among African Americans would be rationalized by these 'new racists' as stemming from the minority's alleged lack of drive and desire for achievement and over-reliance on social welfare. (Teo, 2000: 2)

The Ideational Metafunction has allowed us to identify the main features of these definitions in terms of the first set of participants and processes. However, there is another general function of language called the Interpersonal Metafunction that also contributes to how a discourse creates meaning for readers and listeners. This function has to do with two related aspects of a discourse: how people exchange information, and the speech roles that people play when they interact with one another. The writers of definitions, for example, are givers of information and they provide this information in the form of statements. As the readers of definitions, our role is as receivers – in this case, silent receivers because we have no way of responding.

Definitions are characterized by statements. In fact, we would find it very odd if a definition included a question or a command – the two other ways that people exchange information. When SFL researchers talk about these three different ways of communicating – statements, questions, and commands – they are talking about one aspect of the Interpersonal Metafunction called *Mood*.

mood versus Mood

'Mood' is a word that can be used in two ways. The first is more popular and general; it refers to how people feel. In SFL research, the term Mood has a more specific meaning; it refers to whether a clause is a statement, question or command. To distinguish between these two meanings, we will use 'Mood' with a capital 'M' for our SFL and CDA analyses.

In this chapter, we are going to start with an overview of Mood. Then you will have a chance to explore one particular Mood – question – in a CDA analysis of a racism discourse called the Race Relations Survey. As you do this, you will be looking at how people interact with each other in terms of speech roles, attitudes and positions towards each other and the information they are exchanging. We will then move on to another aspect of the Interpersonal Metafunction called *modality* – a term used to describe one way that people express their positions through language. Later in this chapter, you will use what you learn about modality to analyze how attitudes are realized in an editorial on racism.

3.2   Mood: an overview

Mood is a term that SFL researchers use in general terms to describe what happens to the arrangement of the Subject and Verb in a clause.

However, we want to emphasize that, in our discussions, we are only dealing with clauses with Finite Verbs.

3.2.1 Reviewing the Finite

You may recall that we discussed the Finite versus the non-Finite in Chapter 2. As a reminder, we have included the chart from Chapter 2 dealing with this topic.

Finite vs. non-finite verbs	
Finite verb	**Non-finite verb**
Definition: a verb or the auxiliary that precedes it which indicates the past, present or future.	Definition: a verb form that has no indication of past, present or future.
Examples: I *am* happy. He *went* to the restaurant. She *has* eaten in the cafeteria for the whole year.	Examples: *To be* happy is important. *Going* to restaurants is a way to relax. *Eating* in the cafeteria all year is terrible.

What you see in the box is that we can achieve Finiteness, that is, rooting the discourse in a particular time – past, present or future – either through the main Verb or through the Auxiliary that precedes it. Why is the Finite element important? It 'anchors' the clause so that its meaning can be discussed, argued about, and contested. For example, let us look at a clause from one of the racism definitions: *Racism goes beyond ideology.* In this clause, we know that the Verb is *goes beyond*. Here is how this clause could be argued about in a sample discourse.

Joe: *According to the book, racism goes beyond ideology.*
Mary: *I don't think it does.*
Joe: *Why not?*
Mary: *Racism doesn't have to go beyond because it automatically includes it.*

The reason this argument can take place is because the Finite is rooted in the 'here-and-now' and is debatable. What happens if we use a non-Finite to talk about racism and ideology? Can we argue about it?

Joe: *Going beyond ideology is included in racism.*
Mary: *It isn't.*
Joe: *It is.*
Mary: *It's not included.*
Joe: *Oh, yes it is.*

As you may have noticed, Joe and Mary are not arguing about whether or not racism *goes beyond* ideology in the second example. Rather, they are arguing about whether ideology *is included* in racism because *going beyond* is non-Finite and cannot be argued about. On the other hand, *is included* is Finite and, therefore, can be contested.

Views from the theorists:
Jim Martin

Finite versus non-Finite

Martin (2000: 281) succinctly discusses the non-Finite and the Finite and the roles each can or cannot play in discourse. He explains that the non-Finite Verb is not negotiable:

> Non-finite clauses, in other words, are clauses which might have been part of an argument, but have been backgrounded, to take them out of the repartee. Non-finite clauses simply remove the dialogic potential by eliminating the meaning which makes a clause negotiable – its finiteness.

3.2.2 Arrangement of Subject and Verb

As we noted above, Mood involves the arrangement of the Subject and Verb in a clause. The arrangement is important because it generally creates the three different ways of communicating that we mentioned above – stating, asking, and commanding. Look at how the Subject and Verb rearrange themselves in the following three examples to create meaning.

- **Statement**: *The teacher defined racism.* (Subject + Verb)
- **Question**: *Did the teacher define racism?* (In English we often have to add an additional auxiliary to the Verb such as *do, does, did, has, have* and *had*, or *is* and *are* in order to create a question. So the arrangement here is Auxiliary + Subject + Verb.)
- **Command**: *Define racism.* (Verb only; Subject understood)

Of course, native speakers of English do not have to think about these arrangements when they decide to switch from one Mood to another. It is something they learned as they acquired the language. Let us look at each of these Moods more closely to determine their significance.

3.2.3   The three types of Mood

Declarative: the speaker/writer gives information in the form of a statement.

Interrogative: the speaker/writer asks for information in the form of a question.

Imperative: the speaker/writer gives or asks for information or action in the form of an order/command.

The Declarative Mood: making statements

Statements are a way that speakers/writers provide information. Look at this example from one of the definitions: *Racism is discriminatory or abusive behaviour towards members of another race.* As we discussed above, the Ideational meaning is realized by the participants *racism* and *discriminatory or abusive behaviour*, as well as by the Relational process of Identification: *is.* As you have also seen, the writer of this definition is taking on the speech role of the giver of information. The Mood choice of Declarative is an important way to tell people what you think about things. When you make this choice, you do two things:

1) take on the speech role of being a provider of your viewpoint about a subject/issue; and
2) put your listener/reader in the speech role position of being a receiver of that viewpoint.

From a CDA perspective, the Declarative Mood, which indicates the ability to give information, can place the speaker in a position of power; in many situations, the exchange of information may not be between equals. So CDA researchers typically analyze discourses in different situations to determine whether the two interactants in the discourse/situation are equal. For example, the doctor-patient relationship is one of inequality. Although the patients provide information to the doctor about their history or symptoms, doctors then define the patients' problems and tell the patients what they should do. Another obvious case of unequal power occurs in the classroom where a teacher is the power figure, and is generally the giver of information. Students may also be able to give information, but the teacher has the power to affirm or reject the student's information. If you think about your culture, you will realize that there are many other people who have the power to give information or tell you what to do, such as politicians, judges, and policemen.

Declaratives: summary

- Structure: Subject + Verb
- Speech role of speaker/writer: Giver of information
- Example: *Racism is a social issue.*
- CDA perspective: Who has the power to be the giver of information, and why? How does the giver of information use this power?

Interrogatives: asking questions

But what happens if you do not know something about a subject or issue and you want to learn more? Then you must choose another Mood – the Interrogative. If you decide to play the speech role of questioner, then you are not giving information, but requesting it. There are two ways of asking questions.

1) The first type is in the form of the question we discussed earlier: *Did the teacher define racism?* This type of Interrogative generally requires only a *yes/no* answer.

2) The second type is called a *wh-interrogative*, and can be identified by any question that begins with *who, what, which, when, why* and *how*. An example of this question would be: *Why did the teacher define racism?* This kind of Interrogative has several characteristics:
    - The question word: *who, what, which, when, why* or *how* comes before the Verb.
    - The question is open-ended with the answer probably beginning with: *because...*

Again, let us look at questions from the point of view of CDA. The power issue is who has the right to ask questions, and why?

Interrogatives: summary

- Structure: Auxiliary + Subject + Verb (except for wh-interrogatives)
- Speech role of speaker/writer: Requester of information

- Example 1: *Did the teacher define racism?*
- Example 2 (who-interrogative): *How did the teacher define racism?*
- CDA perspective: In the above examples, who has the power to ask questions? Why? What does the 'right to question' tell us about the relationship between the asker and the responder?

Imperative Mood: issuing commands

You may recall that, in Chapter 1, President Bush spoke mostly in statements except for one important instance. Near the end of the speech, he switched from the Declarative Mood to the Imperative Mood when he said: *Make no mistake about it.* People who can issue orders are generally those who are in a more powerful position in a relationship – as the President was as regards other Americans and (he believed) his unknown enemy. Let's take another example. In a classroom, who could use the Imperative Mood and say: *Tell me what you know about racism* – the teacher or a student? Clearly, in a classroom situation, the teacher has the power to be in the speech role of demander.

The Imperative Mood has several characteristics:

- As we noted above, it is the only Mood in which the Verb comes first in the clause.
- The Subject *you* is understood. We would never say: *Define racism* unless there was someone to whom we were addressing the order. This someone could be either present or imagined in the case of written instructions.
- The Imperative can be softened by the use of the word *please* as in: *Please define racism.*

Although most recognizable when in the form of commands, orders can be realized not only by commands, but also by questions and statements:

- Use of a question: *Would you define racism?* Note here that this is asked by a teacher; the command is being realized by a question. But it is nonetheless a command. How often have you been commanded through questions?
- Use of a statement: *It would be a good idea for you to learn the definition of racism.* What the teacher is really saying is: *Learn the definition of racism. It will be on the next test.*

CDA researchers are interested in studying situations in which some people issue orders and others follow these commands because of precedent or assumptions that both parties may hold. Commanding and obeying are often indications of inequality in relations; CDA researchers want to make people aware of the linguistic features of situations in which the interactants are not equal.

Imperatives: Summary

- Structure: Verb; no Subject (understood)
- Speech role of speaker/writer: Demander of information
- Example 1: *Define racism.*
- CDA perspective: Who has the power to command? Why? What does this power tell us about the relationship between the commander and the person who obeys?

To sum up: Mood is realized by Declaratives, Interrogatives, and Imperatives. In each case, CDA researchers focus on the speech roles that speakers/writers and listeners/readers assume in their interactions with each other, as demonstrated by Mood. This focus is very different from the one we discussed in Ideational considerations, where we were interested in who was doing what to whom in a variety of discourse events. With Mood, we explore how people position themselves interpersonally, that is, towards each other, while exchanging information in these different situations.

Views from the theorists:
Suzanne Eggins

Mood

Eggins points out that a clause has two components:

> There is one component (*you can't...*) that gets bandied about, tossed back and forth to keep the argument going, while the second part of the clause (*do that these days...*) disappears once the argument is underway.

> The component that gets bandied back and forth is what we call the MOOD element of the clause... The rest of the sentence is called the RESIDUE. To discover which part(s) of the clause constitute the MOOD element, we ask which part of the clause cannot disappear when the responding speaker takes up his/her position... (1994: 154–155)

Eggins also points out how we can identify the part of the clause that is the MOOD element by adding a Tag at the end of a declarative sentence to turn it into a question. We may do this to soften or to 'temper' our words, as Eggins puts it. So, in the sentence 'He is smart, isn't he?' we have added a tag to pose a question. The parts of the clause that get picked up in the tag 'are the MOOD constituents of the clause' (ibid: 155).

To sum up, clauses have two elements: the MOOD and the RESIDUE. The first carries forward the argument while the latter can be left out.

The Race Relations Survey   3.3

The Race Relations Survey below is a discourse characterized by questions and answers. First, study and then respond to the Survey. As you do so, consider the five questions below. We have purposely left them open-ended. We thought it would be interesting for you to answer them based on your initial responses and then to compare them with the answers provided by the SFL and CDA analyses that follow the Survey. Jot down your reactions and discuss them with the class. Then compare them with the analyses.

Questions to consider   Discussion

1. What is the speech role of the questioner?
2. What speech role do I play in answering the questions?
3. How do different forms of questions change the position of the responder?
4. Are some of the questions 'stacked,' leading to specific kinds of answers?
5. How do the different questions reflect the writer's attitudes and positions?

The Race Relations Survey

1. What is your opinion about race relations in the United States/Canada? For the purpose of this survey minorities always refers to:
    *   African or African Descendants
    *   Asians or Asian Descendants including (Pacific Islander i.e., Native Hawaiians)
    *   Indigenous Peoples (such as American Indians/Native Americans, Eskimo)

2. In your view, are racial minorities routinely discriminated against or not?
    *   Yes
    *   No
    *   No opinion

3. How serious a problem do you think racial discrimination is where you live?
    *   Very serious
    *   Somewhat serious
    *   Not too serious
    *   Not serious
    *   No opinion

4. How serious a problem do you think racial discrimination is at your place of employment or school?
    *   Very serious
    *   Somewhat serious
    *   Not too serious
    *   Not serious
    *   No opinion

5. How serious a problem do you think racial discrimination is in health care?
    *   Very serious
    *   Somewhat serious
    *   Not too serious
    *   Not serious
    *   No opinion

6. How serious a problem do you think racial discrimination is in the practice of law?
    *   Very serious

- Somewhat serious
- Not too serious
- Not serious
- No opinion

7. How serious a problem do you think racial discrimination is in the administration of justice?
   - Very serious
   - Somewhat serious
   - Not too serious
   - Not serious
   - No opinion

8. Do you think that relations between racial minorities and whites will always be a problem or that a solution will eventually be worked out?
   - Will always be a problem
   - Will eventually be worked out
   - No opinion

9. How do you think white people feel about racial minorities?
   - Only a few white people dislike minorities
   - Many white people dislike minorities
   - Almost all white people dislike minorities
   - No opinion

10. How do you think racial minorities feel about white people?
    - Only a few minorities dislike whites
    - Many minorities dislike whites
    - Almost all minorities dislike white
    - No opinion

11. Who do you think is more responsible for poor status of race relations?
    - Whites mostly responsible
    - Minorities mostly responsible
    - Neither
    - Both
    - No opinion

12. On the whole, do you think most white people want to see minorities get a better break, or do they want to keep minorities down or don't you think they care either way?
    - Minorities to get a better break
    - To keep minorities down

- Don't care either way
- No opinion

13. Over the last 10 years, how has the quality of life changed for racial minorities?
    - Has gotten better
    - Has stayed about the same
    - Has gotten worst
    - No opinion

14. What do you think about racial minorities chances for good employment?
    - As good a chance as whites
    - A better chance than whites
    - Not as good a chance as whites
    - No opinion

15. What do you think of racial minorities chances of getting a good education?
    - As good a chance as whites
    - A better chance than whites
    - Not as good a chance as whites
    - No opinion

16. What do you think of racial minorities chances of getting quality health care?
    - As good a chance as whites
    - A better chance than whites
    - Not as good a chance as whites
    - No opinion

17. What do you think of minorities chances of being stopped by a police officer?
    - As good a chance as whites
    - A better chance than whites
    - Not as good a chance as whites
    - No opinion

18. What do you think of racial minorities chances of being imprisoned?
    - As good a chance as whites
    - A better chance than whites
    - Not as good a chance as whites
    - No opinion

http://academic.udayton.edu/race/ (Accessed February 2003)

Analyzing the Race Relations Survey: Questions 1–10

You probably noticed that the Survey has a range of question types. Some are simple, only asking for *yes/no/no opinion* answers. Others are more complex and the form of the question leads to different kinds of answers. As you will see in our analysis below, questions are not neutral, although at first glance they seem to be so, and the speech role assigned to you as the responder can vary in subtle ways. A survey such as this one also provides answers from which readers can make choices. As analysis will also show, the answers can be as value-laden as the questions.

Questions, like statements and commands, originate in the writer's/speaker's view of the world. One of the goals of CDA is to make these views more transparent so that we can better understand both the intentions of the interactants and the Mood choices that people have made.

Changing the reader's speech role

Questions 1 and 2 provide examples of the way the survey writer puts readers into different speech roles.

1.   What is your opinion about race relations in the United States/Canada? For the purpose of this survey minorities always refers to:

2.   In your view, are racial minorities routinely discriminated against or not?

Question 1 is an example of a wh-interrogative. This question is open-ended; you could answer it any way you like – with a sentence, a paragraph, even an essay. It does not compel you to make any choices except to stay on the topic. Question 2, on the other hand, essentially forces you to answer *yes* or *no*. (You may also answer *no opinion*; however, since the survey is designed to find out people's views, we will focus on the more meaningful answers.) The *yes/no* alternative puts you, as the responder, into a much more restricted speech role than you were in Question 1. You are forced into making a one-word answer, either *yes* or *no*, and you have no way of explaining this response. As we analyze the survey, you will see that the writer's choice of question types places the reader into different positions.

Assuming a problem

Questions 3–7 are a series of questions that start with *How* followed by the words *serious a problem*. Look closely at the questions and consider the ways they are different from Questions 1 and 2.

3. How serious a problem do you think racial discrimination is where you live?

4. How serious a problem do you think racial discrimination is at your place of employment or school?

5. How serious a problem do you think racial discrimination is in health care?

6. How serious a problem do you think racial discrimination is in the practice of law?

7. How serious a problem do you think racial discrimination is in the administration of justice?

The *how* questions are not open-ended as Question 1 was; nor do they restrict you in the same way as Question 2. These five questions control the reader in a different way. Take a look at them again and see if you can pick out the feature that makes them distinctive.

The significant difference is that the questions all begin with: *how serious a problem*, thereby assuming that a problem about racial discrimination does indeed exist, affecting many aspects of our society: health care, neighborhood relations, school, employment, law, and justice. As the responder, you must agree with this assumption in order to choose an answer. One way to see this clearly is to pose a question about racial discrimination that assumes the reverse – that the problem does not exist.

Let's take a few minutes and try to reword Question 3 in a way that makes the reverse assumption.

- How does it differ from the original Question 3?
- Does it sound like Questions 1 or 2?
- And how does it change the speech role of your reader – does it narrow or broaden it?

The important point is to understand that questions can be posed in a variety of ways and the speech roles of listeners/readers change accordingly.

Question 8 is not a wh-interrogative like Questions 3–7, but it is similar because it also makes an assumption – that relations between racial minorities and whites pose a problem.

8. Do you think that relations between racial minorities and whites will always be a problem or that a solution will eventually be worked out?

In Question 8, there are only two possible answers: *Will always be a problem* and *Will eventually be worked out*. In a way, this is like Question 2 with its *yes/no* choice – you have only two alternatives. However, unlike Question 2, your answers are predetermined by the question; you can only answer within the parameter that race relations are a problem, much like Questions 3–7. This obviously narrows your speech role. You cannot say that there is no problem (as you could in Question 2). You can only say the problem will always be bad or it will go away.

One way to rephrase this question in such a way that it does not make this assumption and thus narrow the readers' speech role would be to say: How do you think relations between racial minorities and whites will eventually be worked out?

Questions 9 and 10 are interesting because without the answers, these questions could be very open-ended.

9. How do you think white people feel about racial minorities?
    - Only a few white people dislike minorities
    - Many white people dislike minorities
    - Almost all white people dislike minorities
    - No opinion

10. How do you think racial minorities feel about white people?
    - Only a few minorities dislike whites
    - Many minorities dislike whites
    - Almost all minorities dislike white
    - No opinion

Notice, however, that the answers assume that 'dislike' exists between whites and racial minorities. In fact, the real question here is: *How much do you think x dislikes y?* except that the writer chose not to pose it in that fashion. We are not sure why this is so – perhaps because it would have been too strong an assumption. At any rate, the answers limit your speech role as provider of information because there is no choice that provides a more positive response. Imagine how different these questions would be if the answers had 'like' instead of 'dislike' in the possible responses.

Also consider what would happen if we rephrased 9 and 10 to read: *Do you think white people like or dislike racial minorities? Do you think racial minorities like or dislike white people?* and changed the possible answers to *like* or *dislike*. What kind of assumption underlies this new choice of answers? How do they broaden the readers' speech role or narrow it? From our perspective, this re-phrasing assumes strong feelings between whites and racial minorities and does not allow for any emotion between *liking* or *disliking*. According to this question, whites and racial minorities can have no neutral feelings about each other. This obviously narrows the speech role of the reader to an answer that is similar to *yes/no* with no opportunity to indicate any range in feeling.

Analyzing the Race Relations Survey: Questions 11–18

We have now provided you with different ways of looking at questions and their answers. In this section, you will have a chance to undertake your own critical discourse analysis of the remaining questions and answers.

CDA questions

Take some time to carefully read Survey questions 11–18. You will notice that after each Survey question, we pose one or more CDA questions. Answer each CDA question in writing.

Question 11

11. Who do you think is more responsible for the poor status of race relations?
    - Whites mostly responsible
    - Minorities mostly responsible
    - Neither
    - Both
    - No opinion

1. What are the assumptions on which this question is based? Check both the question and answers.
2. What would happen to the speech role of readers if the question was: *Do you think minorities or whites or neither are responsible for current race relations?*

Question 12

    12. On the whole, do you think most white people want to see minorities get a better break, or do they want to keep minorities down or don't you think they care either way?
- Minorities to get a better break
- To keep minorities down
- Don't care either way
- No opinion

1. How does Question 12 constrain readers?
2. Is there a way of asking this question that would broaden the speech role of readers?

Question 13

    13. Over the last 10 years, how has the quality of life changed for racial minorities?

1. Why do you think the writer posed this question?
2. Is the speech role of readers who are members of racial minorities different from those who are not? If so, why? If not, why not?
3. What assumptions are contained in the question?

Questions 14 to 18

    14. What do you think about racial minorities chances for good employment?
- As good a chance as whites
- A better chance than whites
- Not as good a chance as whites
- No opinion

    15. What do you think of racial minorities chances of getting a good education?
        (same answers as 14)

    16. What do you think of racial minorities chances of getting quality health care?
        (same answers as 14)

    17. What do you think of minorities chances of being stopped by a police officer?
        (same answers as 14)

18. What do you think of racial minorities chances of being imprisoned? (same answers as 14)

1. What are the assumptions underlying questions 11–18?
2. Have you seen this kind of assumption elsewhere in the Survey? Where?
3. How narrow or broad is your speech role as a responder? Why?

Summing up Interrogatives

CDA researchers closely examine Interrogatives in a variety of discourses such as the Survey. It is important to recognize the assumptions on which the questions are based, and how these assumptions place listeners/readers into speech roles with only a narrow choice of answers. Without being aware of it, listeners/readers can be strongly influenced by the way questions are posed. This Survey, for example, limits a responder's perspective on the issue of racism in ways that ensure that the responder expresses the same beliefs as the writer. The CDA researcher could then ask: What are the interests of the people who created the Survey? How do they want to influence readers? Why? In doing this, the researchers can begin to make transparent the underlying assumptions. Such demonstrations allow you to become more sensitive to, and aware of, how language choices influence the ways in which you can respond. If you are ever the developer of a survey or questionnaire, you will be able to take a CDA approach by posing questions that do not constrain your readers, thus allowing for a broader discussion. In other words, you may be in a position to bring about change.

3.4   Modality: an overview

When President Bush said in his speech: *Our country mourns for the loss of* life, he was not expressing his opinion. Rather, he was stating what he considered to be a truth – as in *yes, this is happening*. Similarly, *this is not about how to break stereotypes* in the 'Melanie Speaks' text is true according to the writer. When you studied the Ideational Metafunction, you found out how participants, processes, and circumstances allowed speakers/writers to tell others how they viewed the world through their presentation of information. But what happens when a speaker/writer wishes to modify his/her discourse to express a position that is not *yes* but not *no* either? This in-between area is what SFL analysts call *modality* and it expresses four different stances:

1) **Probability**: how likely the speaker/writer feels that something may occur. For example: *Racial discrimination* **might** *come to an end.*

2) **Frequency**: how often the speaker/writer feels that something may happen. For example: *Racial discrimination* **usually** *takes place in the legal system.*

3) **Obligation**: when the speaker/writer feels that something has to be done. For example: *Racial discrimination* **must** *come to an end.*

4) **Inclination**: how the speaker/writer assesses the tendency of something to occur. For example: *I'll help you move tomorrow.*

3.4.1 What happens to the Ideational Metafunction when modality occurs?

One of the most important things to remember about the metafunctions of language is that they *work together* to realize meanings. The Ideational Metafunction realizes the content of our information. The Interpersonal Metafunction realizes the ways in which we modify the *yes/no* aspect of our information in order to express our attitudes and positions.

Modality can be added to simple statements by adding modal auxiliaries to the main Verb. Look at the bolded words in the clauses below and consider how they alter the propositions. Are the statements/questions still propositions? Or have they been changed in some way? How?

- President Bush's speech: *we* **will** *win it*
- Prime Minister Winston Churchill's speech: *Even though large tracts of Europe and many old and famous States have fallen or* **may** *fall into the grip of the Gestapo*
- Race Relations Survey. *Do you think that relations between racial minorities and whites* **will** *always be a problem*
- 'Melanie Speaks': *she* '**should**' *do something*

As you may have noted, these modal auxiliaries mean that the propositions are no longer exactly *yes* or *no*. Rather, they are somewhere in between. The modals allow us, as speakers/writers, to express a wide range of attitudes and stances. When we analyzed President's Bush's speech in Chapter 1, we noted that phrases such as *we will win it* allowed the President to make a combined threat and promises.

How does *will* do this? It does it with the choice of a modal indicating a high degree of probability so that it almost is a definite event (but not quite – because it has not happened yet). Churchill makes many strong *shall* statements in his speech, which have the same high degree of probability as *will*. However, when it comes to discussing whether or not more land will fall into the hands of the Germans, he uses *may* – a modal auxiliary which has a lower degree of probability – in order to show how unlikely he thinks it is that Germany will win the war despite this possibility.

When analyzing the Race Relations Survey, we noted how the questions were based on strong assumptions. Notice that Question 8: *Do you think that relations between racial minorities and whites will always be a problem?* uses *will* instead of *could* or *might* – two modals that indicate a lower level of probability than *will*. The use of *will* ensures that the assumption remains strong even though the writer is asking readers to look into the future.

The clause *she 'should' do something* in 'Melanie Speaks' does something quite different. Instead of demonstrating probability, the *should* demonstrates obligation or necessity. Without the *should*, the clause would be: *she does something* – a simple fact. What the clause does say is that she feels the obligation to do something, because of her socialization as a female, a point that Melanie makes forcefully with the sense of explicit obligation evident in the choice of 'should.'

In sum, modal auxiliaries alter simple propositions. As they do so, they indicate a speaker/writer's attitude towards the discourse, that is, his/her position or stance on whether, to varying degrees, something will or must happen.

Another way to take a stance towards propositions is through adverbs, because adverbs also express modality. Speakers/writers can use adverbs to modify a statement, as in *Racial discrimination* **usually** *takes place in the legal system*. They can also use adverbs to modify a modal auxiliary and its main verb: *Racial discrimination will* **certainly** *come to an end*. We have numerous adverbs in English that help us express modality in this way – for example, *usually, often, sometimes, possibly, probably, definitely*.

3.4.2   The Interpersonal Metafunction: summary

In Chapter 2, you learned that the Ideational Metafunction was a general function of language that allowed speakers/writers to express their ideas and experiences. One of the founders of SFL, Michael Halliday, calls this 'the clause as representation.' The Interpersonal Metafunction is a second general function of language that Halliday calls 'the clause as exchange.' When people exchange information, they introduce attitudes and stances into their discourse. This includes both attitudes and stances (1) toward their topic and (2) toward their listeners/readers.

As you have seen, speakers/writers can demonstrate attitudes and positions/stances is through modality. Through the use of modal auxiliaries and adverbs, speakers/writers can add elements that modify the propositions in their discourses, changing these propositions to statements marked by their opinions, beliefs, and perspectives.

As the exchange occurs, the interactants are also placed into different speech roles through Mood – whether they are giving information, asking for information or demanding it.

Interpersonal Metafunction

Demonstrates how people exchange information and the speech roles that people play when they interact with one another.

Answers the question: What are the speaker's writer's attitudes and positions/stances? through:

1) *Mood*: whether the speaker/writer is giving information, asking for information or giving orders.
2) *Modality*: how the speaker modifies factual statements through use of modal auxiliaries and adverbs.

As we have noted throughout this chapter, CDA researchers find the Interpersonal Metafunction, particularly Mood, a rich source of information about equality and inequality among people. They have used this aspect of SFL to research a wide variety of discourse events that involve people with differing levels of status, including doctors/patients, teachers/students, managers/workers, politicians/the electorate, media/readers, police officers/criminals, social workers/people who need assistance, and judges/accused persons. The focus of their research is to expose how inequalities are produced and maintained through discourse.

In the next section of this chapter, you will have an opportunity to analyze the Interpersonal Metafunction in a discourse in which writer(s) in the media contributed to a situation involving racial discrimination that impacted the lives of thousands of people.

3.5   The Pearl Harbor editorial

Editorials in newspapers are written to influence readers – to get them to share or, at least, be swayed by, the opinions of the editorial writers, which are most often a reflection of the position of a particular newspaper. For this reason, editorials can be a very rich source of research for CDA analysts. They want to find out how people in positions of power, such as newspaper publishers and editorial writers, view current issues that arise most of the time through specific agencies in society – government and business. The purpose of the editorials, then, is not to provide facts about current events but rather to serve, as CDA linguist Teun van Dijk says, persuasive, political, social, and cultural functions. These purposes are particularly evident in the editorial discourse we will discuss below.

3.5.1   Background to the Pearl Harbor editorial

The Pearl Harbor editorial is an example of a newspaper supporting government-sanctioned racism. Although this editorial and its events occurred more than 50 years ago, it demonstrates a clear case of *racial profiling* – an issue as important today as it was then. Racial profiling occurs when a person identifies someone as a member of a racial minority and makes an assumption about that person's background, psychology, temperament, and intentions based on what he/she believes about that minority. Racial profiling is dangerous. If it occurs in law enforcement, for example, police may use race, religion, ethnicity or national origin to decide who should be stopped and investigated for suspicion of breaking the law in situations such as selling illegal arms, using drugs or any other activity. In other words, racial profiling is the singling out of groups on the basis of race or ethnicity for some negative reason.

This editorial that we are about to examine was written in 1942 just after the Japanese made an unexpected and therefore highly successful bombing attack on American troops and ships in Pearl Harbour, Hawaii. One result was that Japanese-American citizens and immigrants became objects of suspicion in the United States. Some people thought they were loyal to Japan and they were thus suspected of spying. The U.S. government encouraged this belief when the Secretary of the Navy released a statement saying that the Pearl Harbor attack was the result of sabotage on the part of Japanese-Americans, even though there was no evidence to support it. In fact, no American citizen of Japanese descent was ever found to have committed an act of espionage or sabotage against the United States. Military influence and inflammatory editorials such as the one you will analyze, however, provided a rationale for the U.S. actions taken against its own citizens in 1942.

Many Japanese – approximately 120,000 – were interned in prison camps for the duration of the war. They lost their homes and businesses; they often lived in very difficult conditions in the internment camps and frequently experienced great hardship. It wasn't until 1988 that the U.S. government passed the Civil Liberties Act, offering a $20,000 reparation and letter of apology to each of those imprisoned in the camps still alive at that time.

3.5.2   Analyzing the Pearl Harbor editorial

Read through the editorial once. Then read it again, noticing, specifically, the modal verbs (bolded) and adverbs (bolded and italicized).

> Japanese leaders in California who are counseling their people, both aliens and native-born, to co-operate with the Army in carrying out the evacuation plans are, in effect, offering the best possible way for all Japanese to demonstrate their loyalty to the United States.
>
> Many aliens and practically all the native-born have been protesting their allegiance to this Government. Although their removal to inland districts outside the military zones **may** inconvenience them some-what, even work serious hardships upon some, they **must** *certainly* recognize the necessity of clearing the coastal combat areas of all possible fifth columnists and saboteurs. Inasmuch as the presence of enemy agents **cannot** be detected *readily* when these areas are

thronged by Japanese the only course left is to remove all persons of that race for the duration of the war.

Real danger **would** exist for all Japanese if they remained in the combat area. The least act of sabotage **might** provoke angry reprisals that *easily* **could** balloon into bloody race riots.

We **must** avoid any chance of that sort of thing. The most sensible, the most humane way to insure against it is to move the Japanese out of harm's way and make it as easy as possible for them to go and to remain away until the war is over.

Their Best Way to Show Loyalty, *The San Francisco News*, 6 March 1942.

3.5.3   Examining modality

When we discussed modality at the beginning of this section, we noted that there are four types: probability, frequency, obligation, and inclination. As we discussed different uses of modal auxiliaries, we noted that that some showed greater certainty than others – described as high, medium or low.

Practice

In the chart below, analyze each modal auxiliary in the discourse by type and certainty. If there is a modal adverb, write down how you think the adverb affects the modality. We have done the second one as an example.

	Modal Auxiliary	Type	Certainty	Adverb
1	Although their removal to inland districts outside the military zones **may** inconvenience them somewhat,			

2	they **must *certainly*** recognize the necessity of clearing the coastal combat areas of all possible fifth columnists and saboteurs	obligation	high	emphasizes the certainty
3	Inasmuch as the presence of enemy agents **cannot** be detected ***readily***			
4	Real danger **would** exist for all Japanese			
5	The least act of sabotage **might** provoke angry reprisals			
6	that ***easily* could** balloon into bloody race riots.			
7	We **must** avoid any chance of that sort of thing.			

Application

A discourse make-over

The *Japanese-American Journal* is a (hypothetical) weekly newspaper that served Japanese Americans in the United States in the 1940s.

Re-write the Pearl Harbor editorial as if you were an editorial writer for the *Journal* at that time. Cover the topics included in the original, but write from the perspective of being in a racial minority that is under threat of internment in prison camps for political reasons.

- After you have written the editorial, note the Moods and Modality that you chose to get your point across.
- Describe your discourse in terms of the stances evident in your choices. Compare them with the original and, while doing so, identify the ways in which the stances in each discourse reflect power.
- Compare your editorial with that of your classmates and discuss differences and similarities.

Example of a CDA analysis: the role of Mood

Read the following example of a critical discourse analysis of Mood.

Jim Martin, whose Ideational analysis we have seen in Chapter 2, looks here at the role of the interpersonal in analysis focusing specifically on Mood. As part of a larger project in which he was involved in the 1990s, he examines '...the ways in which popular music could be deployed to challenge power' (2000: 280). He looks at a text by the musical group U2 called *Sunday Bloody Sunday*, a song about the troubles in Ireland. As Martin explains, the song was performed many times but because it was so controversial it was eventually banned in Northern Ireland by the then Prime Minister of England, Mrs. Thatcher. Bono, the lead singer, phased the following rap into the song:

> I'm going to tell you something. I've had enough of Irish Americans
> who haven't been back to their country in 20 or 30 years, come up to me
> and talk about the resistance, the revolution back home, and the glory

of the revolution and the glory of dying for the revolution. Fuck the revolution! They don't talk about the glory of killing for the revolution. What's the glory in taking a man from his bed and gunning him down in front of his wife and children. Where's the glory in that? Where's the glory in bombing a Remembrance Day parade of old age pensioners, their medals taken out and polished up for the day. Where's the glory in that? To leave them dying or crippled for life or dead under the rubble of the revolution that the majority of people in my country don't want. No more. Say 'No more.' No more-No more. No more.

Martin examines, through the system of Mood, how this kind of text exerts power, especially over American fans. He says it does so because of the ways in which it positions its speakers into different roles – stating, questioning, commanding and explaining. As he says, if one examines the different choruses one will note how Mood '…positions its listeners to receive information, to provide information, to perform a service or to empathize with the feeling' (ibid: 281).

Martin then gives some illustrations from the text of how the song thus positions its listeners:

The song begins with the declarative mood giving information: 'I'm going to tell you something,' 'I've had enough of Americans who…'

He (Bono) then switches to the imperative, to dismiss the way in which he feels some Irish Americans glorify the revolution. 'Fuck the revolution!' (imperative) This is followed by the declarative clause, giving information about the acts of killing the revolutions has involved: 'They don't talk about the glory of killing for the revolution'.

Then there are more interrogatives and the song ends with what is called a minor clause, one without a verb: 'No more', which is repeated several times.

Martin's final analysis of this song clearly illustrates the thrust, the power of the use of the Mood system:

What seems crucial to the interpersonal enactment of Bono's power is not just the number or type of mood selections he makes, but the manner in which he moves from one selection to the next… His goal is to align the audience with his position, a significant objective given the amount of funding for the IRA donated by Irish expatriates in America. He pursues this by first tabling a proposition about the glory of the revolution, then dismissing it (Fuck the revolution), then subverting it (Where's the glory…), then undermining it (the revolution that the majority of the people in my country don't want), then pleading for an end to the violence (No more), and closes by aligning the audience to plead with him, chanting in response to the cue.

This then is how Martin illustrates the 'ways in which interpersonal meaning (through the Mood system) is used to enact power,' and shows how important it is to look at how 'meanings unfold in a text' (ibid: 284).

Chapter 3 Glossary

Declarative Mood: giving information.

Frequency: when modality indicates 'likelihood'.

Imperative Mood: demanding information or action.

Inclination: when modality indicates 'tendency'.

Interrogative Mood: requesting information.

Interpersonal Metafunction: how people express their attitudes and positions/stances in discourse.

Modal auxiliary: a word that modifies the main verb to express attitudes.

Modality: how speakers/writers demonstrate their attitudes and positions/stances.

Mood: whether a clause is a statement, question or command.

Obligation: when modality indicates 'must-ness'.

Probability: when modality indicates 'possibility'.

Relational process of Identification: a Relational process in which a Token – an object or a person – is identified by its Value.

Speech role: the identity taken on by speakers/writers and listeners/readers during a discourse.

Token: the object being identified in a Relational process of Identification.

Value: the information about the Token in a Relational process of Identification.

wh-interrogative: any question that begins with *who, what, where, which, when, why* and *how*.

SFL readings

Eggins, S. (1994) *Introduction to Systemic Functional Linguistics*. We have encountered Eggins before; her chapter on Interpersonal components is very thorough. The most relevant sections of her Chapter 6 are pages 146–164 in which she covers different aspects of Mood. Later in the same chapter she also discusses modality and modulation. It might be interesting for you to compare her treatment with Halliday's, which we describe below. Pages 178–183 are particularly relevant.

Halliday, M. A. K. (1994) *Introduction to Functional Grammar*. In Chapter 10 Halliday talks about modality and contrasts it with modulation. In very succinct and clear charts, he illustrates the range of each area of the grammar. See in particular pages 354–362.

Thompson, G. (1996) *Introducing Functional Grammar*. For yet another very clear discussion of modality see Thompson's Chapter 4, in particular pages 56–64.

CDA readings

Teo, P. (2000) 'Racism in the news: a critical discourse analysis of news reporting in two Australian newspapers'. In this article Teo uses many SFL tools that we have studied for his analysis of racism in the Australian press.

Chapter 3
Further readings

van Dijk, T. (1993) *Elite Discourse and Racism.* This is a book in which van Dijk summarizes much of his work and study of racism in Europe and the United States. In it he focuses on the role of the media in racism and in particular on what he calls elite racism. His Chapter 7, Media and Racism, is particularly relevant to our work in this chapter because he looks at racism as conveyed through the print media.

Chapter 4 contents

Language and advertising

In the past three chapters, you have looked at different social issues and the role of language in these issues. You have considered political language, language and gender, and language and racism, and have seen how speakers/writers use language to produce, reproduce, and maintain power and social inequalities. In this chapter, we are going to explore the nature of advertising discourse. We will use SFL methodology to describe what the language is doing in advertisements. At the same time, we will also examine the role of advertisements in our society and see how, from a CDA perspective, they express ideology and how the influence exerted through them on listeners/readers is another expression of power.

Advertising is, generally, a multimodal form of discourse. In print, it usually involves the use of text and graphics such as colour, typography, illustrations, and photographs. Later in this book, we will discuss multimodal discourses, but for the purposes of this chapter, we will focus just on the written text in advertising.

The first example is a discourse from an advertisement for a Sports Utility Vehicle (SUV). We will call this the Forester ad.

Look at the ad and read the reprinted copy below.

FITS TIGHT SPACES
BUT PREFERS
WIDE-OPEN ONES
FORESTER

What's this? A sport-utility that's easy to park, yet can climb like a mountain goat? It's the 2002 Subaru Forester. Instead of being big and bulky, it's handsomely svelte. Incredibly easy to load. And equipped with the rugged traction of full-time All-Wheel Drive. So your options are wide-open. To take a closer look at the Forester, call 1–800– 876–4AWD or visit www.subaru.ca

The ABCs of Safety: Air Bags, Buckle Up, Children in back.
Forester S-limited shown in Platinum Silver Metallic.
SUBARU The beauty of All-Wheel Drive

Discussion

Having seen the advertisement, can you express in your own words how it differs from the ones you have analyzed in previous chapters? Discuss this with your classmates.

Consider the following questions and use the information you have learned about the Ideational and Interpersonal Metafunctions to answer them.

- Who are the main participants in this discourse and who is this discourse addressed to?
- How does the target audience affect the style of the discourse?
- Are there different Moods in the discourse and how do they affect its style?
- Why have the producers of the ad chosen this style?

Compare your responses with ours below.

Our responses

We find that the Forester ad differs considerably from the other discourses because it attempts to engage the audience as if the advertisers and readers were friends. At first glance, this may appear to be similar to the chatty style of the 'Melanie Speaks' discourse. One reason is that both discourses are addressed to *you*. However, there is an important difference between the two. 'Melanie Speaks' was an excerpt from a larger discourse, written by an individual about certain sexual issues and concerns to a very specific audience with similar experiences and problems. The Forester ad, on the other hand, may appear in magazines and perhaps newspapers with a large circulation and with many different kinds of readers. When such discourses are addressed to *you* in this way, linguist Norman Fairclough calls this *synthetic personalization* – synthetic because the intimacy that writers are trying to establish is a bit artificial. The advertisers do not know you or your issues and concerns. But they talk in a conversational way as if *you* were an acquaintance with whom they can exchange information and to whom they can give advice.

The second major difference in the Forester ad is that it is the only discourse we have discussed that includes all three types of Mood – Interrogative, Declarative, and Imperative. The first clause is Declarative, and the last is an Imperative, with the clauses in between in both Interrogative and Declarative Moods. Why would the advertisers choose three different Moods in such a short text? Advertising is one of the most researched types of discourse in the world. Companies spend a great deal of money developing advertising campaigns and focus-testing the results. When we look at an ad, we can expect to find discourse that has been very carefully chosen for maximum impact on readers. Discourse analysis research on advertising has revealed that Interrogatives and Imperatives play important roles in persuading you – the reader – to take time to read the ad and buy the product advertised.

Let's examine the questions, responses and one command in the Forester ad to see how this is accomplished.

> What's this? A sport-utility that's easy to park, yet can climb like a mountain goat?

The purpose of these kinds of questions is different from those you saw in the Race Relations Survey in Chapter 3. Here, they are rhetorical questions – ones that the speaker/writer poses without expecting an answer. The ad's producers ask the questions to engage your attention and to get you thinking about the qualities of SUVs.

They then answer the question themselves by providing the most common features of SUVs that an audience would value in terms of capability, parking, appearance and performance:

> It's the 2002 Subaru Forester. Instead of being big and bulky, it's handsomely svelte. Incredibly easy to load. And equipped with the rugged traction of full-time All-Wheel Drive.

In a sense, they are asking you to compare your criteria for SUVs with theirs. But, more importantly, they are setting up a standard of quality which tries to make their values yours.

Advertisers often use commands in their text:

> To take a closer look at the Forester, call 1–800–876–4AWD or visit www.subaru.ca

How do they do this without offending readers? Research has suggested that orders of this kind are accepted for two reasons. The first is because the producers introduce the word *you* in the text. Once they have created a synthetic relationship with their audience, they can give commands that are more likely to be accepted. The second reason is that commands in advertising are never negative or onerous, but are designed to appear like advice and suggestions given between friends – a relationship established through synthetic personalization. For example, in this ad, it is suggested that you 'take a closer look' at the Forester by calling Subaru or visiting their website. This combines two things the ad creators want you to do: notice the difference between their product and others and then contact the manufacturers (to buy it).

Now we can move on to other features of ads. We will focus in this chapter on the third metafunction of language. We will start by giving you an overview of two aspects of the Textual Metafunction: cohesion and coherence, and then apply them to the Forester ad.

The Textual Metafunction: cohesion and coherence   4.3

You learned a bit about the Textual Metafunction in Chapter 1 when we examined the SFL question: *What holds the discourse together?* and then discussed how cohesion results from vocabulary chains and Topical Themes. The Textual Metafunction involves the ways in which writers/speakers connect parts of their discourse so that listeners/readers can understand what is being said or written. And, like the other metafunctions, it does not act alone, but works together with the Ideational and Interpersonal Metafunctions to allow speakers/writers to make meaning for listeners/readers.

Let's start by examining the paragraph in the box below. Take a moment to read it and then answer the questions below.

Is this a discourse?

> Our country mourns for the loss of life. The brain, the chief administra-
> tive and emotional organ of life, is differently constructed in men and
> in women. In your view, are racial minorities routinely discriminated
> against or not? Now, I know this is anathema to feminism. Many
> aliens and practically all the native-born have been protesting their
> allegiance to this Government. We shall not flag or fail.

1. Does each clause make sense by itself?
2. Do you know the context in which each clause occurred?
3. Does the paragraph make any sense to you?

It's likely that you had no problem understanding the individual clauses
and recognized them from the different discourses you have analyzed
in Chapters 1–3. But they clearly do not make a meaningful discourse
when merged together. SFL researchers would say that this paragraph
is not a discourse because 1) the clauses are not related to each other in
any way you can identify; and 2) they are not related to any one situation
that you can easily identify.

Now look at the following piece of discourse. Read it through and think
about why it is a unified discourse.

Is this a discourse?

> 'That toy is mine.'
> 'It isn't.'
> 'Is so.'
> 'Is not.'
> 'Is!'
> 'Not!'

This piece of writing – a hypothetical argument between two children
– contains only fragments of clauses – most of which are missing Subjects
and parts of their Verbs. Yet, unlike the example above, this dialogue
is a discourse. Why? What makes this piece of writing different from
the one above? What features hold it together? Your answer might go
something like this:

- I know that this is about two children fighting over a toy but they don't have to repeat the word *toy* in every clause to make sense.
- Also, their opposing positions are very clear even though they don't have to say the whole verb or clause for me to figure out what's going on.

The Textual Metafunction

This answer is correct, but let us put it in SFL terms. Any discourse, no matter how short or long, makes meaning for others when it contains two essential elements: cohesion and coherence.

- Cohesion: refers to internal connection among its clauses.
- Coherence: refers to the external connection between the discourse and the situation in which it occurs.

The Forester ad: cohesion   4.4

Let's look again at the Forester ad. However, this time, we will separate the discourse into its clauses to examine how it achieves cohesion and coherence. As we discussed in Chapter 3, we can only analyze clauses with Finite elements.

1) Fits tight spaces
2) But prefers wide-open ones
3) What's this?
4) A sport-utility that's easy to park,
5) yet can climb like a mountain goat?
6) It's the 2002 Subaru Forester.
7) Instead of being big and bulky, it's handsomely svelte.
8) Incredibly easy to load.
9) And equipped with the rugged traction of full-time All-Wheel Drive.
10) So your options are wide-open.
11) To take a closer look at the Forester,
12) call 1–800–876–4AWD
13) or visit www.subaru.ca

4.4.1 Achieving cohesion

Cohesion, the way words and phrases are connected within the discourse, is achieved through a number of elements. In Chapter 1, you learned about the use of vocabulary chains as a means of holding a discourse together. That is one form of cohesion. In this section, we will discuss three other forms – ellipsis, anaphoric reference, and repetition.

Features of cohesion

1) *Vocabulary chains* enable speakers or writers to connect a discourse by using words or phrases that are related to one another by meaning. (See Chapter 1.)
2) *Ellipsis* enables speakers or writers to omit words or phrases that can be 'retrieved' by listeners or readers from the surrounding clauses.
3) *Anaphoric reference* enables speakers or writers to connect words or phrases that come first in a discourse with ones that come later.
4) *Repetition* enables speakers or writers to hold a discourse together by repeating words or related forms of the words.

Ellipsis

One form of cohesion especially evident in the Forester ad is *ellipsis* (the omission of certain words or phrases.) To understand ellipsis, first take a look at clauses 8 and 9 and see if you can figure out what is missing.

8.   Incredibly easy to load
9.   And equipped with the rugged traction of All-Wheel Drive.

Here are the clauses with the elided words – that is, the omitted words – bolded and put back into the discourse.

8.   **The Forester is** Incredibly easy to load
9.   And **it is** equipped with the rugged traction of All-Wheel Drive.

Speakers and writers often leave out words or phrases when they are not necessary for comprehensibility, especially in face-to-face conversations. In the Forester ad, which imitates casual conversation, words or phrases are left out because readers can 'retrieve' them from the surrounding clauses. We are all accustomed to full statements being reduced to shorter forms when we talk with other people, and we have no problem filling in the omitted words.

We can even fill in omitted words using non-verbal clues like the image of the SUV in the ad. The first two clauses each contain an instance of ellipsis:

1. Fits tight spaces
2. But prefers wide-open ones.

Even before we read the rest of the ad, we can complete the statement by supplying the bolded words:

1. **The SUV in the picture** Fits tight spaces
2. But **it** prefers wide-open ones.

If the ad writers have done their jobs properly, once we have read the ad, we will probably change our first replacement (*The SUV in the picture*) to *The Subaru Forester*.

Anaphoric reference

A common way to connect meanings in discourse is through *anaphoric reference*, a language feature by which speakers and writers connect words and phrases throughout a discourse. The connection is between words and phrases that come first with ones that come later. Let's begin by looking at the connections in clauses 1 and 2:

1. Fits tight spaces
2. But prefers wide-open ones

As a reader, you have no trouble identifying that the pronoun *ones* – which is called a *referent* – in clause 2 connects back to the noun *spaces* in clause 1. One of the reasons speakers/writers choose to use a pronoun such as *ones* instead of repeating the noun *spaces* is to avoid too much repetition. If the ad writers had written *Fits tight spaces but prefers wide-open spaces* the connection would be clear, but it simply doesn't sound as good. Using pronouns as referents establishes the connections among the clauses even more effectively.

We can see further use of anaphoric reference in clauses 4, 5, 6, and 7:

4.   A sport-utility that's easy to park,
5.   yet can climb like a mountain goat?
6.   It's the 2002 Subaru Forester.
7.   Instead of being big and bulky, it's handsomely svelte.

As we discussed earlier, the readers of the Forester ad are being asked a question in clauses 4 and 5 concerning the qualities that they should look for in SUVs. Clauses 6 and 7 both begin with the Topical Theme *it*. This pronoun connects back in the first case to *sport-utility* in clause 4, and in the second case, to *the 2002 Subaru Forester* in clause 6.

Other examples of anaphoric reference are found in clauses 8 and 9. Here, however, the pronoun has been left out, because the ad writers have used ellipsis. Can you identify the omitted pronouns and the earlier word or phrase to which they refer?

8.   Incredibly easy to load.
9.   And equipped with the rugged traction of full-time All-Wheel Drive.

If you supplied the omitted pronoun *it* in each clause as the referent for *the 2002 Subaru Forester*, your answer is correct. In this very short ad, there are five instances of anaphoric reference and, in each case, the pronoun referent – *ones* or *it* – points back to an item in a previous clause. However, it is important to remember that anaphoric reference only works when listeners/readers can connect the referent to the item to which it refers. For example, *it* has no meaning on its own; it only takes on meaning when tied to *sport-utility* or *the 2002 Subaru Forester*.

Repetition

A third cohesive feature appears in the Forester ad – *repetition*. The repetition is subtle, but if you look closely, you will find three instances of the word Forester, and three instances of the word Subaru, in this ad. They occur in clauses 6 and 11, in the two logos, and in the Web site URL. It is not, of course, surprising that the advertisers repeated the brand and model names whenever possible so that readers would remember the product being advertised.

Repetition is a common way for speakers/writers to make internal ties to achieve cohesion. One word gets repeated in the same or related forms. For example, we have bolded all the ways that Subaru and the Forester are mentioned in the discourse (with ellipses in parentheses) – ten times in 70 words, a total of more than 14% of this discourse.

1. **(The Subaru Forester)** Fits tight spaces
2. But **(it)** prefers wide-open ones
3. What's **this**?
4. A **sport-utility** that's easy to park,
5. yet can climb like a mountain goat?
6. It's the 2002 **Subaru Forester**. Instead of being big and bulky,
7. **it** 's handsomely svelte.
8. **(It**'s) Incredibly easy to load.
9. And **(it**'s) equipped with the rugged traction of full-time All Wheel Drive.
10. So your options are wide-open.
11. To take a closer look at the **Forester**, call 1–800–876–4AWD
12. or visit www.**subaru**.ca

The Forester ad: Theme/Rheme   4.5

In Chapter 1, we discussed an aspect of the Textual Metafunction known as Theme, which refers to the first element in the clause – the word or phrase that is its starting point. In English, speakers/writers use this starting point in a clause to let listeners/readers know what their message is about. For example, in the Forester ad, clause 6 is *It's the Subaru Forester*. The bolded and italicized word *it* is the Theme and it refers to the Subaru Forester.

4.5.1 Theme versus theme

To review, *theme* is a word that can be used in two senses. The first is more popular and general; it refers to the main topic of a discourse such as a theme in an essay. In SFL research, the term *Theme* has a more specific meaning; it refers to the initial word(s)/phrase(s) in a clause.

If the Theme, then, 'sets the stage' for the message, the function of the rest of the clause is to provide the message itself. This part of the clause is known as the *Rheme* – for example *is the Subaru Forester*. As this clause demonstrates, when speakers and writers give us new information, they generally do so in the Rheme portion of the clause.

Theme/Rheme

- Theme: starting point for the message of the clause
- Rheme: completes the message of the clause

The important thing to understand about Theme and Rheme is that it helps listeners and readers identify how speakers and writers organize their discourse and develop their topics. By doing this, we and SFL and CDA researchers can explain how speakers and writers focus their discourse.

Here are some more examples of clauses from the Forester ad broken into Theme and Rheme.

Theme	Rheme
What	*is this*

Theme	Rheme
And (it)	*is equipped with the rugged traction …*

Theme	Rheme
So your options	*are wide-open*

Types of Themes

In Chapter 1, you learned about two types of Themes: Topical and Textual. However, there is also a third type of Theme that is interpersonal in nature and allows writers/speakers to mark their stance at the very beginning of a clause. Here is a summary, then, of the three types of Themes:

1) *Topical Themes* are those that realize elements from the Ideational Metafunction: participants, processes or circumstances. Every clause **must** have a Topical Theme.
2) *Interpersonal Themes* are those that demonstrate the speaker's/ writer's position towards the information in the clause; they are often realized by adverbs such as *unfortunately* or *frankly*. A clause may or may not have an interpersonal Theme. It so happens that there are no interpersonal Themes in the advertising discourses in the chapter. However, you should be aware that they can exist and may occur in later chapters.

3) *Textual Themes* are those that contain connecting words such as *but* or *therefore*; they work to tie clauses to one another. A clause may or may not have a Textual Theme.

As you have seen in the last two examples above, there are two Themes: **And (it)** and **So, your options**. In both cases the first of the Themes is Textual and the second is Topical. We provided in parentheses the elliptted item that is understood as the actual Theme of the sentence. We will examine Textual Themes further after identifying the Themes in the clauses in the Forester ad in the following chart. Note that the words in parenthesis are the ones that have been elliptted but are assumed to be understood by the readers.

	Theme		Rheme
	Textual	**Topical**	
1		(The Subaru Forester)	Fits tight spaces
2	But	(it)	Prefers wide-open ones
3		What	Is this
4		(This)	(is) a sport utility
5		that	is easy to park
6	yet	it	can climb like a mountain goat
7		it	is the Subaru Forester
8	*Instead (of being big and bulky)	It	is handsomely svelte
9		(It)	Is incredibly easy to load
10	And	(It)	Is equipped with the rugged traction…
11	So	your options	Are wide-open
12		(To take a closer look at the Forester…)	1–800–876–4AWD
13	or	call	
14		visit	www.subaru.ca

*This clause is not analyzed separately because, as you will remember, it has non-finite verbal groups and we analyze only those clauses with finite verb forms.

Textual Themes

Textual Themes allow speakers and writers to combine clauses and to signal particular relationships between clauses to listeners/readers. In this ad there are in fact six Textual Themes; almost half of the clauses are joined by them. Let's examine some of the purposes Textual Themes achieve.

- *But* as a link between clauses typically introduces a contrast in the clause following it. In fact, that is exactly what is done in this discourse – indicating that although the Forester is small enough to be driven and parked in the city where there is little room, it prefers to go out into the open – to be in the wilderness. The explicitly-indicated contrast helps the reader to understand the varied capabilities of this car, and that it can be used in very different situations.
- *Yet* again indicates a kind of contrast, once more illustrating the versatility of the Forester: once again, it is easy to park in the city but can climb like a mountain goat in the wilderness. The contrast serves to show that the car is adaptable: it is capable of operating in different situations such as the city and the countryside, no matter how rugged the latter.
- *Instead (of being big and bulky)*: once more, there is a contrast created by the Textual Theme to counter a common expectation of SUVs. Most people consider them to be bulky but that image is being explicitly countered by the sentence that follows the contrasting statement.

It is interesting that each of the contrasts is designed to counter a popular belief about SUVs and to set the stage for additional positive information in the next Textual Theme:

- *And* indicates other features of this car; having dispelled the possible negative impressions of SUVs, the ad can now go on to add more positive information through additive themes such as *and*.
- *So* follows as the next to last Textual Theme, signaling the natural conclusion to be drawn from the positive picture created by previous Textual Themes. Here the readers are told that their options are open, but are in fact presented with options through the following choices: to call or visit the website.
- *To* really stands for 'in order to', indicating how to exercise the options presented by the **or** between the clauses.

There is, then, a logical progression of Textual Themes leading the reader to consider features of the Forester that they might not have thought possible in an SUV; having done so, more positive features are added, indicated by the use of 'and'. Readers are then told what actual options are available to them with the ultimate one, of course, being to buy the Forester. The use of these Textual Themes plays an important part in conveying the message of the discourse.

For an extended view of themes and in particular Textual Themes, we have included views from Butt et al. who discuss this further.

Views from the theorists:
Butt et al.

Theme

Their explanation of the different themes supplements our discussion very helpfully. They describe the Textual Theme's role as the connection between different parts of a message:

> When we do this, we create a cohesive text with well-signposted connections between messages. Conjunctions are most likely to occur at the beginning of clauses and when they do they must be considered thematic. Even so, they do not fulfill the primary requirement of Theme which is to signal the point of departure for the experiences in the clause. We refer to these text-creating meanings as TEXTUAL THEMES in order to distinguish them from the experiential meanings in the Topical Theme… There are also times when we begin clauses with interpersonal meanings indicating the kind of interaction between speakers or the positions they are taking. At these times, we are using interpersonal Themes. (2000: 137–138)

Now that you have been introduced to the basic elements of cohesion and different sorts of themes, it would be a good idea to practice these new skills.

Application

1. Look over several magazines and select one or more car ads. Analyze each first in terms of ellipsis, anaphoric reference, vocabulary chains and repetition.
2. Next, identify the themes in the discourse.
3. Identify each type of theme and decide whether each is marked or unmarked.
4. Discuss the use of these features in conveying central meanings in the ad.

4.6   Text 2: The Legacy GT advertisement

The next ad that we will analyze is for another type of Subaru, the Legacy GT. Look at the ad and read the reprinted copy below.

HUGS THE ROAD.
KISSES THE CORNERS.
HOW EUROPEAN.
LEGACY GT

The way the 2002 Subaru Legacy GT embraces a set of curves is enough to rival the most amorous European sedans. With the traction and control of full-time All-Wheel Drive, the GT clings to the road's every contour. While its racy boxer engine makes the heart pound, the pulse quicken. Sounds like love. To find out more about this sleek, Euro-style sedan, call 1–800–876–4AWD or visit us at www.sabaru.ca.

The ABC's of safety. Air bags. Buckle up. Children in back.

Discussion

1. After you have gone through the ad once, try to identify the
    features that create mental images that might appeal to readers.
2. With your classmates, discuss these mental images. Decide how
    attractive they are to you as individuals and as a group.

The Legacy GT ad: cohesion   4.7

4.7.1 Analyzing cohesion

When discussing the Forester ad, you learned about features of the
Textual Metafunction that help achieve cohesion. In addition to vocabulary chains, you examined ellipsis, anaphoric reference and repetition.

Read the Legacy ad below. We have numbered the clauses for ease of
reference.

Practice

1)   Hugs the road.
2)   Kisses the corners.
3)   How European
4)   The way the 2002 Subaru Legacy GT embraces a set of curves
     is enough to rival the most amorous European sedans.
5)   With the traction and control of full-time All-Wheel Drive,
     the GT clings to the road's every contour.
6)   While its racy boxer engine makes the heart pound,
7)   the pulse quicken
8)   Sounds like love
9)   To find out more about this sleek Euro-style sedan,
10) call 1–800–876–4AWD
11) or visit us at www.subaru.ca

Identify the features of cohesion in the Legacy GT ad by answering the
following questions.

1. Clauses 1, 2, 3, and 8 contain ellipsis. Identify the omitted words.
2. Identify words/phrases that demonstrate the major form of repetition in this discourse.
3. Underline the words/phrases in the vocabulary chain about the car's drivability.
4. In the list that follows, circle the words/phrases that present the car in terms of love, and especially love of a European sort. We have separated the clauses to assist you.

In analyzing ads, CDA researchers might ask, 'What do these choices accomplish?'

Ellipsis

As we discussed in the Forester ad, ellipsis enables speakers/writers to leave out words that listeners/readers can 'retrieve' from the surrounding text. What does ellipsis achieve in the Legacy GT ad? As with the Forester ad, the Legacy GT ad's writers are reproducing an informal conversation between two equals. By so doing, they reduce the distance between themselves and the readers, which allows them to offer advice as one friend to another. This paves the way for the commands in clauses 10 and 11.

Repetition

It is obvious that, when a product is being advertised, it is desirable to keep the name and category of product clearly in view. This is achieved through the kind of repetition we see above. It is a common feature of any ad to ensure that you, the potential consumer, are always aware of the product being advertised.

Vocabulary chains

As we noted earlier, the Legacy GT has two vocabulary chains – also known in SFL as *lexical chains*, which are made up of vocabulary choices that relate to each other – one chain involving the Legacy's drivability and the other relating its performance to love of a European kind. Although we have separated these two chains, they do, in fact, overlap and reinforce each other. The second lexical chain, which includes *hugs*, *kisses*, and *amorous*, suggests certain values of our western society in which we often seem to treat desirable consumer goods as love objects.

Given what you have learned about this ad, you are now in a position to answer some CDA questions.

---

1. What values are reflected in the first lexical chain of drivability?
2. How are the first and second sets of values related?
3. Do these values apply only to Western cultures?
4. Can you imagine another culture in which other values might be more important? Which cultures? What values?

CDA questions

The Legacy GT ad: Theme/Rheme   4.8

As we discussed earlier, the text in advertising is some of the most carefully crafted discourse you will read. The writers want to persuade readers to buy their product or service at a time when the market competition is global and fierce. Every word is weighed and measured for its 'strategic' power. Studying the Textual Metafunction in advertising will provide you with insights into how this type of discourse is constructed to have maximum impact on readers and influence their behaviour. In this section of the chapter, we will take a close look at the Themes and Rhemes in the Legacy GT ad to see how the discourse is organized and the themes developed. We repeat the clauses below; we have bolded Topical Themes which were cut through ellipsis just to show you what the producers of this ad could have written but didn't. We will explore why they might not have done so in our discussion of marked and unmarked themes which follows the Practice on identifying themes.

1) **(It)** Hugs the road.

2)   **(It)** Kisses the corners.
3)   How European (it is).
4)   The way the 2002 Subaru Legacy GT embraces a set of curves is enough to rival the most amorous European sedans.
5)   With the traction and control of full-time All-Wheel Drive, the GT clings to the road's every contour.
6)   While its racy boxer engine makes the heart pound,
7)   the pulse quicken
8)   **(It)**Sounds like love
9)   To find out more about this sleek Euro-style sedan,
10)   call 1–800–876–4AWD
11)   or visit us at www.subaru.ca

Practice

1. Make a list of the Themes in each clause above. Do not include the ellipted Themes which are understood.
2. Try to identify the different types of Themes that you have listed.
3. Discuss the types and possible reasons for these choices with other students.

Marked and unmarked themes

When undertaking a CDA analysis, it is always useful to look at the Themes to help you understand what speakers and writers want to emphasize and why. Emphasis often occurs when speakers and writers select unusual Topical Themes. The best way to understand how this happens is to understand the reverse: *What is the most ordinary way of speaking/writing?* In SFL terms the most ordinary case is the unmarked Themes, the most common way of speaking or writing. While it is the case that, as we have seen in discussion of the Forester ad, the Topical Theme can be realized by the participant, the process or the circumstance, a typical focus is on the participants, in the Subject position.

However, speakers and writers often vary from these common structures in order to create emphasis. When they do this, they create *marked* Themes; there are many ways this can occur in English. In order to see which of the clauses have marked Themes, go back to your Practice responses and identify those Themes that are not realized by subject and therefore are marked. List the marked Themes below.

You will see that there is a pattern in the marking; in 4 out of the 6 marked Themes in the Legacy GT ad, the focus is either on processes or circumstances to reinforce the lexical chain related to the Legacy GT, and love in the European Style: *Hugs the road, kisses the corners, How European, embraces a set of curves, amorous European sedans, makes the heart pound, pulse quicken, sounds like love, Euro-style sedan.*

It would seem to be the case that marking of Themes thus has a specific purpose in this ad: to draw particular attention to the association between the Legacy GT and love. In our Western society, car owners often speak of 'loving' their cars; the advertisers have therefore crafted their ad to focus on this specific set of values.

Having looked at the Themes and Rhemes, along with different kinds of Themes, we are now in a better position to begin to answer CDA questions about the Legacy GT ad.

After you read the following questions, write your answers in complete sentences. Compare your responses with at least one other person in the class.

CDA questions

1. Identify the Themes that are realized by processes. What purpose do they serve?
2. What other features in the ad serve to place you, the reader, in a consumer role? For example, the commands suggest that you as consumer should go out to find out more information about the car. What other features encourage you to act as a consumer?
3. The ad has been framed as a casual conversation between friends who share the same values. What do you think these values are?

Now that we have looked at the cohesive features of the two Subaru ads and also at the Themes in both, we are in a position to look further at another aspect of the Textual Metafunction: coherence.

Coherence: exophoric reference

Coherence in a discourse can be achieved in a variety of ways, all of which involve connecting the discourse to the immediate situation or the more general cultural context. Coherence is an aspect of the Textual Metafunction that refers to the connection between the discourse and the immediate and broader situation outside the discourse. The situation of any ad consists of two types of context: of situation and of culture. The context of situation is the actual situation surrounding the text in a particular ad. In both of the Subaru ads, there are visual elements which accompany the actual text. The context is created in part by these visuals. There is also the context of culture, which refers to the broader culture in which advertisements themselves take on meaning.

This is what is meant by coherence being created by exophoric reference, outside the text itself. So, in the Forester ad, the words 'Fits tight spaces but prefers wide-open ones' create at least in part a context for the ad that follows, by echoing the picture of the car in the countryside – the natural place for an SUV to operate. It is assumed that readers of this ad are aware of the value of the SUV being able to go anywhere you would like to go – and that this is a good thing with which you want to be associated. The picture itself creates an image of driving freely away from the city and into beautiful nature. In other words, the values that are assumed here and to which the ad is responding are (1) that it is good to be able to get away from congested cities out into nature, and (2) by buying the Forester, you too will be able to escape and to share the beauty of nature.

In the Legacy GT ad, the *hugs* and *kisses* in clauses 2 and 3 do not refer to an item within the discourse, but to one *outside* the discourse; in this case, the picture of the car that accompanies the text. This exophoric reference serves to tie the discourse to its immediate context in which there is a beautiful car and perhaps a beautiful person to share the car with, certainly in a beautiful setting. The exophoric reference thus refers not only to the immediate context but to the context of culture in terms of the values of such a luxury car in the Western world. While the words *hugs* and *kisses* do in fact refer to the car in the picture, the idea also has another association – to love itself.

The advertisers have thus created coherence through two kinds of connections, both achieved through exophoric reference. The first is to the immediate situation of the discourse – the picture of the car. The second is to the broader cultural context in which cars are desirable.

Norman Fairclough suggests that listeners/readers do not simply decode something they read or hear. Rather, they interpret these discourses by associating them 1) with representations they hold in their memories, and 2) with their positive or negative evaluations of these representations. Therefore, advertisers create images in readers about products or services considered to be desirable and/or valuable by their target audience. In this way, a product or service acquires the same desirable and/or valuable features as the created imagery. It seems in this ad that the target audience is men of a certain financial status, who are urbane and worldly enough to understand the 'European' references throughout the ad; the association between love, the car and Europe is designed to provide them with additional incentives to become buyers of a Subaru Legacy GT.

Views from the theorists:
Norman Fairclough

Advertising and consumerism

Norman Fairclough expresses this very clearly below. To Fairclough, advertisements work ideologically and they do so in three ways: first by 'building relations':

> Advertising discourse embodies an ideological representation of the relationship between the producer/advertiser of the product being advertised and the audience, which facilitates the main ideological work.

Second, by 'building images':

> Advertisements get their audiences to draw upon ideological elements in their MR (Member's resources) in order to establish an 'image' for their product being advertised.

Third by 'building the consumer':

> Advertisements, using the 'images' which audiences 'help' them to generate for products as vehicles, construct subject positions for 'consumers' as members of consumption communities… this is the major ideological work of advertising. (1989: 202–203)

CDA questions

After examining the Textual Metafunction in terms of cohesion, themes and coherence, you are now in a position to apply some of your knowledge to answer the following questions.

1. In both ads mental images have been created and directed at certain segments of society. Describe these images in both Subaru ads. What values do they hold and how do they draw on particular desires related to these values?
2. Are these images congruent with your values as students in a Western culture? Are there images that are incongruent, that is, against your values?
3. Do you think both ads are actually aimed at you, a student? Why or why not?
4. How do the two Subaru ads establish relations between the advertiser and you the audience?

In this section of the chapter, you will have an opportunity to analyze the Textual Metafunction in an ad promoting a health product. Consider what you have learned about this metafunction to explore the role it plays in influencing people as potential consumers. As you read through the Centrum ad below, jot down the answers to the questions which follow the ad.

4.9   Text 3: The Centrum ad

You're working out instead of eating out. Because there aren't enough hours in the day.

You're doing more, being smarter, and constantly performing at your best. It's a demanding life that uses up essential nutrients.

And you don't always eat the way you know you should to replenish them. That's why there's Centrum Performance. It starts as a complete Centrum multi, then we add higher levels of essential nutrients, including key B vitamins and antioxidants, plus ginko and ginseng to help energize your mind and body.

Here's a new kind of multi, specially designed for today's demanding life.

CENTRUM PERFORMANCE
LIFE DEMANDS IT

1. Who are the members of the target audience?
2. What are the values of the target audience? How do you know?
3. What kind of knowledge do the ad producers assume of their target audience? How do you know this?
4. What, overall, does this ad say about our cultural values related to health and images of health?

Finding the lexical chains   Practice

As you will recall, chains of related words contribute to the unity in a discourse. Certainly, two of the main chains in this discourse are about personal and product performance and medical products. Fill in the chart below to identify the vocabulary in these two lexical chains. Do you see any other chains in this discourse?

Personal/Product performance	Medical products

Practice

Identifying repetition, ellipsis, and reference

Below we have identified the 14 clauses in the Centrum ad. To analyze the use of reference, ellipsis and repetition in the ad, do the following:

1. Repetition: Circle words that are repeated in order to create cohesion.
2. Ellipsis: Identify the missing words where we have left blanks. Did you find these easy to complete because of the surrounding text?
3. Anaphoric reference: We have bolded the referents in the discourse. Identify the items that they refer back to.

1) You're working out instead of eating out.
2) Because there aren't enough hours in the day.
3) You're doing more, being smarter, and constantly performing at your best.
4) It's a demanding life
5) that uses up essential nutrients.
6) And you don't always eat the way you know you should _____ to replenish **them**.
7) That's why
8) there's Centrum Performance.
9) **It** starts as a complete Centrum multi,
10) then we add higher levels of essential nutrients, including key B vitamins and antioxidants, plus ginko and ginseng to help energize your mind and body.
11) Here's a new kind of multi, specially designed for today's demanding life.
12) LIFE DEMANDS **IT**
13) Use as part of a healthy lifestyle.
14) _____ Contains all nutrients with an RDL.
15) These statements (referring to above) have not been evaluated by the Food and Drug Administration.
16) This product is not intended to diagnose, treat cure or prevent any disease.

Analyzing Themes in the Centrum ad

Now that we have identified the clauses, you should also be able to separate out the Themes and Rhemes. Identify the types of Themes and determine whether they are unmarked or marked. Use the chart below for your analysis.

	Theme			Rheme
	Textual	Topical	Unmarked/ marked	
1				
2				
3				
4				
5				
6				
7				
8				
9				
10				
11				
12				
13				
14				
15				
16				

Application

Construct your own ad

The following activity will give you an opportunity to demonstrate your understanding of the techniques used by advertisers to get people to buy their products.

1. Select a product – this can be an actual product or an imaginary one – perhaps something that doesn't exist yet, but that you think people would buy.
2. Prepare plans for an advertising campaign that will persuade people to buy your product. Identify your target audience and their values in terms of the ideas suggested by Fairclough: building relations, building images, and building the consumer. This should include the knowledge you assume they have of your product, any other characteristics you think will be important, and the medium you will use (print, radio, TV, the Internet…).
3. Draft the text of an advertisement or series of advertisements to publicize your product. Use as many as possible of the techniques discussed in the chapter to create mental images that will persuade people that your product is desirable and valuable.
4. Make an annotated copy of your advertisement(s) with references to the strategic discourse features you have used to persuade your target audience to buy the product. Keep this for your own reference.
5. Exchange a non-annotated copy of the advertisement with another student.
6. Analyze the advertisement you have received, from both an SFL and a CDA perspective. Will it achieve its purpose? Could it be made more persuasive? Return your analysis to the ad creator, in exchange for the analysis of your own advertisement.
7. Compare the analysis you were given with your own analysis. Were all the features you intended to include actually present? Was there anything in your discourse that you were unaware of?

Anaphoric reference: enables speakers/writers to connect a word/phrase with an earlier word or phrase in a discourse.

Coherence: refers to the connection between the discourse and the situation in which it occurs or the broader context of culture.

Cohesion: the internal connection between the clauses in the discourse.

Ellipsis: enables speakers/writers to omit words/phrases that can be 'retrieved' by listeners/readers from the surrounding clauses.

Exophoric reference: when a word or phrase refers to something or someone outside of the discourse, thereby, enabling speakers/writers to make connections to the immediate situation and to the broader cultural context.

Interpersonal Theme: demonstrates the speaker's/writer's position towards the information in the clause.

Marked Theme: an unusual realization of Topical Theme.

Repetition: enables speakers/writers to hold a discourse together by repeating words or related forms of the words.

Rheme: the part of the clause that does not include any of the three types of Themes or the MOOD element.

Synthetic personalization: use of *you* in discourse where the speaker/writer is not acquainted with the audience.

Textual Metafunction: a general function of language that allows speakers/writers to create unified discourses.

Unmarked Theme: the most common word(s) or phrase(s) that realize the Theme.

Chapter 4 Glossary

Chapter 4
Further readings

SFL readings

Butt et al. (2000) *Using Functional Grammar, An Explorer's Guide*. The book by Butt et al. offers a very clear explanation of themes in Chapter 6 of their book. The authors make the distinctions between Topical and Textual Themes and also introduce Interpersonal Theme which we have not yet covered. Of particular relevance to our discussion are pages 136–141.

Halliday, M. A. K. (1994) *An Introduction to Functional Grammar*. In Chapter 9 Halliday sets out the basic concepts on cohesion and extends our discussion considerably. In particular, pages 308–316 are especially relevant to our treatment in this chapter.

CDA readings

Fairclough, N. (1989) *Language and Power*. Fairclough sets out his views on consumerism and advertising, which he sees as very important in our current society. In his Chapter 8 he discusses this influence in some detail on pages 197–211.

Chapter 5 contents

Language and organizations

This chapter, like previous chapters, has a dual focus. The first is on a new current issue: organizations and discourse. Second, by examining the role of language in organizations, we will also review the major components of SFL metafunctional analysis presented so far.

When considering the relationship between organizations and discourse, we are not interested in discourse that just happens to exist in different organizational settings. Rather, we are concerned with how such discourses are shaped, and in turn shape different organizations. We are also interested, as in previous chapters, in the relationships among discourse, power and ideology.

Specifically, our study concerns the language choices that both reflect and create the hierarchical power seen in different levels of organizations in international, national, state/provincial, and institutional settings. These varied settings will provide a wide base for discussion of the discursive role of language in organizational structures, and will allow us to review the major aspects of SFL presented in Chapters 1–4.

But first, we will consider some key definitions of organizations. Munby and Clair (1997) define an organization as '… a social collective, produced, reproduced and transformed through the ongoing, interdependent and goal-oriented communication practices of its members' (p.181).

The term 'organizational discourse' as we are using it is defined by Grant and Hardy (2004: 5) as '… the structured collections of texts embodied in the practices of talking and writing... that bring organizationally related objects into being as those texts are produced, disseminated, and consumed...' The focus, then, is on the discursive role of language in organizations. Munby and Clair also emphasize that 'Organizations exist only in so far as their members create themselves through discourse' (1997: 118). Given this view, the need to examine the role of language in the enactment of organizations takes on particular importance.

And given our focus on the critical discourse perspective, like many of those working in this area of organizational discourse, we are looking at questions of power and control in these organizational settings (Munby and Clair, ibid: 182). Munby and Clair also '... see organizations not as social collectives where shared meaning is produced, but rather as sites of struggle where different groups compete to share the social reality of organizations in ways that serve their own interests' (ibid: 183).

As they outline later on page 183 of their article, these scholars use CDA to show the relationship between talk, power and resistance to it in different organizations. They do so because they think of discourse as the '... principle means by which organizational members create a coherent social reality that frames their sense of who they are' (ibid: 181).

5.2   Overview of Chapter 5: Organizational discourse resources

We will focus on different examples of organizations in this chapter: international, national, provincial and institutional organizations. We will begin with a set of texts dealing with an international organization: the IMF (the International Monetary Fund), established in 1945 in response to WWII. We will examine three different views of the mandate and organizational purpose of the IMF. The three views interpret the mandate differently, considering the goals and intentions from positive and negative perspectives. The positive or negative evaluations of the IMF are prompted by the effects of its restructuring of economies in poorer countries in Eastern Europe and Latin America.

We will then move on to another type of discourse, drawn from a national setting. The text we will examine is a flyer put out by the United States Department of Health and Human Resources, more specifically from a section known as the Food and Drug Administration (FDA). The intention of the flyer is to discourage people from buying prescription drugs outside the U.S.

The third text is drawn from a provincial setting. It is a communiqué from the Deputy Minister to the Premier of the province of British Columbia in Canada, directed at provincial public service employees. The Deputy Minister to the Premier focuses on what has become known as 'workforce adjustment' plans in store for the Public Service of BC. We will examine the ways in which power emanating from the Premier's office is expressed through discursive choices related to these plans.

In the last text, drawn from the academic institutional level, we examine a communique from the administration of a large Canadian university, McGill, in Montreal. The purpose of the directive is to inform students about the policy of academic integrity.

In working with each of the texts, our focus is on linguistic choices that reflect power, and how this power is used to inform, coerce and influence people in different ways. Our examination will be rooted again in SFL, which grounds the CDA questions that arise in relation to each of the texts and organizational settings.

Review of SFL analytical tools   5.3

In Chapter 1 we provided an overview of the main areas in SFL, simply discussing each in non-technical terms. We considered the following questions: Who is doing what, to whom, and in what circumstances? We now know that these questions concern the Ideational Metafunction, which we examined in more detail in Chapter 2. There we looked at different process types – Material, Mental and Relational – and the different participants and circumstances involved in each. We also introduced general questions focusing on speakers' and listeners' interactions with each other, and the attitudes and stances expressed in the discourse.

In Chapter 3, we answered these questions in a more formal way. We examined how the Interpersonal Metafunction is realized through choices of Modality and Mood, to reveal the judgements and stances of writers and speakers. We looked at the three main Moods: Declarative, Imperative and Interrogative (with the last breaking down into two sub-categories: wh and polar interrogatives):

1) Declarative: *I love fish.*
2) Imperative: *Love all fish!*
3a) Polar Interrogative: *Do you love fish?*
3b) Wh Interrogative: *What do you love about fish?*

In these examples, the speakers take different positions. In 1, the speaker is informing his or her listeners; in 2a and 2b the speaker takes on the role of questioner, while in 3 the speaker takes on a more authoritative role, commanding listeners and readers to do something.

We also saw in Chapter 3 that only finite clauses carry Mood choices, and that each finite choice indicates tense and person. Non-finite clauses, on the other hand, in Martin's words, '… simply remove the dialogic potential by eliminating the meaning which makes a clause negotiable – its finiteness' (2000: 282). In other words, it is the MOOD element that we argue about and negotiate. For example, we can say to a friend, 'We will go'. She, in turn can say, 'No, you won't'. And we could continue arguing because of the finite element here: 'will go'. If we said instead 'going is wonderful', you could say 'no it isn't'. But notice here that you are arguing about the 'is', not the 'going'. So, finite clauses have a MOOD element which allows a speaker or writer to negotiate.

Another way in which speakers/writers inject themselves and their attitudes into a text is through modality, realized by modals such as 'can' and 'might', which indicate a speaker or writer's stance toward the possibility of something happening.

Chapter 4 focused on the Textual Metafunction, in terms of cohesion and coherence. In the first category, cohesion, we looked at the ways in which writers and speakers choose to connect their ideas through vocabulary or lexical chains as well as through ellipsis, anaphoric reference and repetition.

Let's consider an example of each. In the following exchange, notice the ellipsis:

Do you like ice cream?
Yes.

The ellipsis is in the answer, which the respondent simplifies with a simple 'Yes'. That is all that is needed to make the sentences cohesive; it is not necessary to say 'Yes. I do like ice cream.' Because of its informality, ellipsis usually occurs in conversations rather than in writing.

In the following example, we see anaphoric reference used to connect different utterances in the discourse.

Tom always came late to class. He went to bed too late every night.

The referent 'he' only makes sense because we as listeners or readers understand that it refers to Tom, who was mentioned in the first sentence. This relationship has meaning only if we can connect the referent to what it refers to, in this case, 'Tom.'

In the third example, repetition (of words, phrases or complete sentence) is another cohesive device. The repetition may be seen in the reiteration of the same word, or in the use of a different form of the word, as in the following sentences:

There is a lot of competition among cars. There are many ways in which they can compete.

The last cohesive choice that we looked at in Chapter 4 involved two types of Themes: Topical and Textual. In the first sentence below there is the more typical Topical element which begins the sentence. The second sentence beginning with the Textual Theme 'But' connects the two sentences through the idea of contrast.

1) *Mary doesn't like fish.*
2) *But she loves meat.*

As we discussed in the previous chapter, the thematic element occurs first in a sentence; in the example above the first element is the Topical Theme 'Mary'. In the second sentence, beginning with the Textual Theme 'But' tells the reader that something must have come first, because it introduces a contrast to it.

The Topical Theme of the sentence is, as we have seen, 'Mary' – and every sentence must have at least one such theme, although it may occur together with Textual and Interpersonal Themes. In other words, there must be a Topical Theme present in each sentence, regardless of how many other types of Themes exist. Topical Themes realize a process, participant or a circumstance, because they convey Ideational meanings.

In the last Chapter one type of coherence, exophoric reference, was also presented. We discovered this type of reference in the car ad, where the text referred outward to the picture accompanying the text, not to other sentences within the text.

5.4   Review of CDA questions

In each of the preceding chapters we also examined issues from a CDA perspective, based on our SFL analysis, and considered questions such as the following:

1. Who seems to have the power in a particular situation? How do you know?
2. How are the participants represented in relation to the activities they carry out in a discourse?
3. Are there examples of strategic discourse in which readers are being directed to do something?
4. How does the structure of the discourse help to persuade readers to act?
5. How does the advertising industry exert power over readers?
6. How does CDA make this power more transparent?

We will be examining questions like these throughout this chapter as we review our SFL analytical tools and revisit CDA questions and concerns. By doing this, we will examine how language reflects and creates hierarchical power in different organizational settings.

5.4.1   Example 1: International organizations

In the following texts, 1, 2, 3, you will read about the International Monetary Fund (IMF); three views are presented as you will immediately notice. Text 1 (a series of excerpts from fact sheets on the IMF website) presents a neutral view. Texts 2 and 3 reflect negative views of this organization. We have numbered each sentence of each text for reference.

Text 1: IMF

1. The International Monetary Fund was created in 1945 to help promote the health of the world economy.

2. Headquartered in Washington DC, it is governed by and accountable to the governments of the 184 countries that make up its near-global membership.

   http://www.imf.org/external/np/exr/facts/glance.htm
   (Accessed January 2005)

3. The IMF advises and assists member countries in implementing economic and financial policies that promote stability, reduce vulnerability to crisis, and encourage sustained growth and high living standards.

   http://www.imf.org/external/np/exr/facts/globstab.htm
   (Accessed January 2005)

4. The IMF provides low-income countries with policy advice, technical assistance, and financial support.

5. Low-income countries receive nearly half of the technical assistance provided by the Fund, and financial support is extended at low interest rates and over relatively long time horizons.

6. Low-income countries with high external debt burdens are also eligible for debt relief.

   http://www.imf.org/external/np/exr/facts/poor.htm
   (Accessed January 2005)

7. The Poverty Reduction and Growth Facility (PRGF) is the IMF's low-interest lending facility for low-income countries. PRGF-supported programs are underpinned by comprehensive country-owned poverty reduction strategies.

http://www.imf.org/external/np/exr/facts/prgf.htm (Accessed January 2005)

Text 2: 50 Years is enough, on the IMF

1. The IMF and World Bank are controlled by the wealthy governments of the world, led by the U.S., the U.K., Japan, Germany, France, Canada, and Italy – the 'Group of 7', which holds over 40% of the votes on their boards.

2. Their function is to impose economic austerity policies in the countries of the so-called 'Third World' or 'global South' and the 'transition economies' of the former Soviet bloc.

3. Once countries build up large external debts, as most of those in Africa, Asia, Latin America, and the Caribbean have, they cannot get credit or cash anywhere else and are forced to go to these international institutions and accept whatever conditions are demanded of them.

4. None of the countries has emerged from their debt problems; indeed most countries now have much higher levels of debt than when they first accepted IMF/World Bank 'assistance.'

5. IMF/World Bank conditions, known as 'structural adjustment programs' (though the institutions are trying to escape that term's negative reputation by changing the name to 'poverty reduction and growth programs'!) force countries to promote sweatshops, exports to rich countries, and high-return cash investment.

http://www.50years.org/factsheets/SAPs-FactSheet_3.9.04.pdf (Accessed January 2005)

Text 3: Global exchange on the IMF

1. Created after World War II to help avoid Great Depression-like economic disasters, the World Bank and the IMF are the world's largest public lenders, with the Bank managing a total portfolio of $200 billion and the Fund supplying member governments with money to overcome short-term credit crunches.

2. But the Bank and the Fund are also the world's biggest loan sharks.

3. When the Bank and the Fund lend money to debtor countries, the money comes with strings attached.

4. These strings come in the form of policy prescriptions called 'structural adjustment policies.'

5. These policies – or SAPs, as they are sometimes called – require debtor governments to open their economies to penetration by foreign corporations, allowing access to the country's workers and environment at bargain basement prices.

6. Structural adjustment policies mean across-the-board privatization of public utilities and publicly owned industries.

7. They mean the slashing of government budgets, leading to cutbacks in spending on health care and education.

8. They mean focusing resources on growing export crops for industrial countries rather than supporting family farms and growing food for local communities.

9. And, as their imposition in country after country in Latin America, Africa, and Asia has shown, they lead to deeper inequality and environmental destruction…

http://www.globalexchange.org/campaigns/wbimf/ (Accessed January 2005)

On first reading, it is obvious that there are significant differences in position among the three writers regarding the purpose and origin of the IMF. To get a better idea of the similarities and differences, begin by becoming familiar with the topic.

Look at the questions below, which focus on the different characterizations of the IMF. Jot down your responses to each of the questions. Your notes will form the basis of your discussion with other students in the class.

Discussion

1. In general, how would you characterize Text 1 in terms of the writer's view about the IMF? Similarly, How would you characterize Texts 2 and 3?
2. What is there in the texts that tells you this?
3. Which text(s) provide you with the most neutral information about this organization? Which one(s) are negative or positive? How do you know?
4. What traits or characteristics are attributed to the IMF in each of the versions?

After discussing your ideas with others in your group, did you agree or disagree with other students' responses? What did you disagree about? Why?

5.5.1   SFL analysis: Text 1

Looking at the texts in SFL terms will help you to substantiate your answers more completely and more impartially. After analyzing the texts according to the guidelines we provide below, you should be in a very good position to argue or persuade others about your position.

One of the features that stands out in these texts is lexical cohesion (also referred to as collocational sets). As we have seen, this feature contributes to cohesion and also serves to identify the topic.

Practice

As you read through Texts 1, 2, 3, complete the chart for each text by filling in other lexical choices. We have begun this to give you an idea of what is required. Remember that we are looking for lexical sets (vocabulary chains or collocational sets) realized by noun groups.

Text 1	Text 2	Text 3
IMF	IMF	The World Bank and the IMF
Health in world economies	Wealthy governments	
	Debts	Short term credit crunch
Lending facility	(lending) conditions	Debtor countries
	rich countries	Strings attached
		The slashing of government budgets

Discussion

After you have completed the chart with as many of the elements of the lexical sets as you can find, compare your list to others from your group.

Then in groups discuss the following questions:

1. What words clue you into the position of the writer in each of the texts?
2. On the basis of the lexical chains you have identified, how would you characterize each writer's position?
3. Which specific lexical choices tell you most about these positions?

Views from the theorists:
Peter Teo

Lexical items

In the analysis of newspaper treatment of a particular group of recent Asian immigrants to Australia and their role in committing crimes, Teo comments on the role of collocations in contributing not only to textual but Ideational meanings:

> Lexis is not merely a static element embedded within the lexico-grammar of a text expressing a fixed and stable meaning. Instead, through a deliberate interplay of lexical items that are collocationally related or even just baldly repeated another level of meaning that supersedes the sense of each word in isolation can be created. In this way, lexical cohesion transcends its cohesive role as textual linkers and assume a role in the Ideational function of language, re-shaping and re-contextualizing meaning and experience. (Teo, 2000: 34)

5.5.2   Ideational choices

Active versus passive voice

Although you can tell a great deal about the positions of the writers from the lexical choices they have made, there are also other choices that help you identify stances. To complement the lexical choices, let's examine the question of agency in the active and passive sentences evident in the texts.

Look at the summary of the information from Chapter 2 to briefly review the difference between the active and passive voices.

Review: active versus passive voice

When the active voice changes to the passive, the form of the sentence changes, as we see below. The meaning is the same if the original actor role is retained in the passivized sentence. The emphasis, however, is different, with the focus now on the goal. If the actor role is missing then the meaning may change, because some of the information is left out, as in the last example * below.

Active	Passive
Actor is in the Subject position before the process.	Goal is in the Subject position in front of the process.
Goal is after the process.	Goal is before the process.
Example: The IMF (Actor) advises... member countries (Goal)	Examples: The IMF (Goal)... is controlled by the wealthy governments (Actor) ... * The IMF (Goal) was created in 1945...

The passive voice tends to shift the reader's focus from the actor to the goal, since the latter now comes first in the sentence and becomes the Theme of the sentence. Also, in the passive voice, the actor role may be eliminated, as in the example* above. In passive sentences, what is of particular concern is whether or not we as readers can identify who is carrying out the actions. The presence or absence of agency in passive sentences is often ideologically driven.

Practice

To get an idea of the significance of these choices, let's look at the three texts before us in terms of the questions below.

1. In Text 1 there are five examples of the passive voice. We used one of these in our example above of the passive without an identified actor. List the other four instances of the passive in the chart below. Include the actors if they are provided in the text.

    Note that a few of the passives occur in clauses that describe or modify other parts of the sentence, as in the following excerpt from Text 1a: 'Low income countries receive… assistance (that is) provided by the Fund…'

Text 1: Instances of the passive voice:
1. The IMF (Goal) was created in 1945
2.
3.
4.
5.

2. Now that you have identified these instances, let's look at active choices in the same text. These occur primarily in sentences 2 and 3 of Text 1. In the space below, identify the actors and processes that occur in the active voice in these two sentences.

Actor Role	Processes
Example: The IMF (Actor)	Advises: (Verbal)

To substantiate this claim about the characterization of poorer nations as powerless, let's look more closely at Texts 2 and 3. Focus on the material processes associated with each group: the IMF and the poorer countries.

1. Go through each text and make two lists, one for each of the groupings discussed in the article; in each list, write down the processes along with accompanying participants.
2. Write down the roles the participants are playing in each group. Once you are finished, look over the results and try to determine whether a pattern has emerged.
3. Discuss your analytical findings with your group.

Texts 1, 2 and 3

After completing the SFL analysis above you are now in a good position to reflect on the texts from a critical discourse perspective. Answer each question in one or more complete sentences.

1. Whose perspective is being represented in each of the versions? Once you have identified these perspectives, write a short paragraph in which you compare and contrast these perspectives. Provide proof from your analysis.
2. In terms of Ideational choices, how would you characterize the different positions of the writers of the three texts in terms of Ideational choices?
3. Do your analyses show the actions of the IMF in the three texts to be mainly positive or mainly negative?
4. In those texts in which there are a great number of passives, were you able to identify or guess the actors in the different actions carried out by the IMF? How did this contribute to your overall view of the activities of the IMF?
5. Compare the actor roles of the IMF with those filled by the poorer countries as they are identified in the three texts.

5.6   Text 4: National organization FDA flyer

This flyer originates in the United States National Department of Health and Human Services. The department includes what is known as the Food and Drug Administration, which is responsible for approving and legalizing drug use throughout the nation.

LOOKS CAN BE DECEIVING

The medicine you buy from outside the United States may be unsafe or ineffective.

Don't risk your health.

The U.S. Food and Drug Administration (FDA) and your community pharmacist are concerned that medicines you buy from outside the U.S. may present a health risk.

- Some imported medicines may have been made using unsafe procedures.
- Some imported medicines are fake.
- Some imported medicines may not have been checked for safety or effectiveness.
- Some imported medicines may be addictive or use dangerous ingredients.
- An imported medicine may not have information for treating side effects.
- The medicine's label, instructions and list of possible side effects may be in a language you do not understand.
- The label of some imported medicines may make claims or suggest uses that have not been approved.

Medicines you buy from outside the U.S. may be unsafe or ineffective. Don't risk your health.

If you have any questions about the use of any medicine, FDA encourages you to contact your doctor, your local pharmacist or your state board of pharmacy.

U.S. Department of Health and Human Services
Food and Drug Administration

The flyer is intended for people who buy drugs outside the U.S. because they are cheaper. The two countries which figure most prominently in the sales of drugs to U.S. citizens are Canada and Mexico, to the north and south of the United States respectively. The pervasive suggestion in the flyer is that doing so presents a risk.

Our activities will focus on the different means the writer employs to present this risk linguistically.

5.6.1   SFL analysis: Text 4

Textual choices: Coherence

Coherence, as we briefly suggested in Chapter 4, can be created in a variety of ways. One way is through exophoric reference (reference to something outside the text), in this case the magnifying glass and pills. Coherence, as defined in Chapter 4, refers to the connection between the discourse and the situation in which it occurs. A situation can, of course, include many components. We will focus only on one or two here.

Even a quick glance at this flyer reveals the prominent sketch of a magnifying glass with pills being magnified, and the pharmacy sign near the glass at the top of the flyer. We will examine the connections and the reasons for them in the analytical activities which follow.

1. After reading the text, briefly explain how exophoric reference is created in the text. Which words or phrases point outward to the picture to connect the verbal and the visual?
2. After you have made your choices, discuss them with other members of the class. Try to arrive at a consensus on the role that exophora plays in this text in order to show how texts achieve coherence with the surrounding situation.

Discussion

Practice

Cohesion

Having looked at one type of textual choice, exophoric reference, we can now begin to see how two types of cohesion, repetition and collocation, reinforce the coherence of this text.

Repetition

The flyer is an interesting text in that it has an unusual degree of reiteration of the same word, phrase or sentence.

1. To capture this more concretely, fill out the chart below with single words that are repeated more than once.
2. Next, add to the chart the one phrase that is repeated several times.
3. Finally, add to the chart the sentence that is repeated twice. Explain the form of the sentence and suggest the purpose this form serves in the text.

One word	Two-word phrase	Sentence

The repetition so evident in this text indicates how important the FDA thinks this issue is.

Discussion

Collocational or lexical sets

It is obvious as you read the text that people are being warned about the risk of buying medicine from outside the U.S. This is emphasized through the choice of collocations related to medicine.

Identify the items in the collocational set that spell out the nature of this risk and discuss it with other members of the class.

Ideational choices

One sub-category of relational process outlined in Chapter 2 is Relational Attribution. Relational Attribution processes assign a quality or an epithet to the participant with which it is associated. In the chart below an example of such a process is provided. There are many such processes in the text.

Complete the chart below with examples from the text to get a better idea of the attributes the writer associates with medicine bought outside the U.S. The first one has been done for you.

Practice

Carrier	Process	Attribute
The medicine	may be: Relational Attributive	unsafe

Interpersonal choices

We have looked so far at ways in which Textual and Ideational choices reinforce each other. There are also Interpersonal choices that further support the particular position adopted in this text.

Modality

Very noticeable is one kind of marked modality: possibility, realized by 'may'. There are in fact nine instances of this expression of possibility. This seems to indicate that the author of this flyer can only suggest the possibility of a risk even though the suggestion is strengthened by the repetition of the risk.

Application

1. Go through the text and list each instance of possibility, along with the process it modifies.
2. Then try to decide why the writer chose 'may' instead of 'will'? Discuss your response with other members of the class and try to come to a consensus about the reasons for this choice.
3. Rewrite the bullets in the box without any modality (making any necessary grammatical changes). Discuss the resulting differences in meaning.

CDA questions

In Chapter 4, we referred to Norman Fairclough's discussion of how strategic discourse is designed to get people to do something, in contrast with communicative discourse, which simply provides information. Although the flyer could be mistaken for communicative discourse, it contains several features of strategic discourse. This reveals very clearly Fairclough's point about the 'colonizing trends' of strategic discourse in ads and how '...other discourse types are influenced by advertising discourse' (Fairclough, 1989: 208).

To get a clear idea of this trend, go through the text *Looks Can Be Deceiving* in Section 5.6 and identify examples where this official government communication, directed at the public, reveals features of advertisements that we saw in Chapter 4.

1. Make a list of these features of strategic discourse. If necessary go back to Chapter 4 to review such features.
2. Using your list of strategic discourse features, can you suggest why this text seems to be using an advertising format in both looks and content when no product is being sold?
3. In Chapter 4, we looked at what Fairclough calls 'building the image' (ibid: 205). In that case there was in fact a product to be bought – Centrum vitamins. In *Looks Can Be Deceiving*, there is no obvious product, and yet there is a characterization of a category of product. What is the missing product? How is it characterized? Why? Answer in a short paragraph.
4. Whose interests are explicitly mentioned in this flyer? Do you think there are any unidentified interests that might also be represented in this flyer? Discuss your answers with other members of your class. Do you all agree?
5. How might these interests conflict with those of other communities? (Lemke, 1995: 57). And what are these other communities?

Text 5: Provincial organization: Message to employees   5.7

Message to Employees
January 2002
Dear Fellow Public Servant:

As you are no doubt aware, the government has announced a workforce adjustment strategy that will be part of the process of re-profiling the scope of government's programs and services. The strategy includes eliminating vacant positions, reducing the number of temporary workers, offering early retirement and voluntary departure packages and, as a last resort, layoffs. The Premier has asked me to convey the reasons underlying this strategy and, in particular, its impending effects on the shape and size of the provincial public service.

The government recognizes that B.C.'s public servants are dedicated, hard-working and proud of the work they do for British Columbians. The coming changes are in no way meant to reflect on you personally or professionally. Rather, they are a necessary part of redefining a Government that is too big, too expensive and not focused in the right areas. Successive governments spent beyond their means. This excess, combined with the significant fiscal challenges we're facing, means we urgently need to redefine government and ensure taxpayers get value for money in the services they receive.

The goal of the workforce adjustment is to transition the government's workforce from the practices of the past to the innovative business practices of tomorrow. Within the next few weeks, your human resources departments will provide information regarding early retirement and voluntary departure packages. Specific work force adjustments will be announced in January. Please rest assured that, if you are presented with an early retirement or departure option, you will be given time to arrive at your decision.

The Premier and Cabinet recognize that these are stressful times. Some staff will face a difficult transition. Affected employees will be encouraged to take full advantage of the assistance that will be available to them, including counselling and career transition services.

As difficult as these decisions will be for many public servants, delivering the priority services of government in an affordable and effective manner will present an opportunity to create a renewed public service. Moreover, as people take advantage of early retirement and voluntary departure options, new opportunities will open for others to advance in their careers. Continuing public servants will be part of a government that encourages creativity and innovation, responsibility, accountability and results-based work.

Whether your future lies within or outside the provincial public service, the Premier and Cabinet hope you will benefit from their efforts to create a thriving spirit of free enterprise and ensure British Columbia a prosperous future.

Yours truly,
Ken Dobell,
Deputy Minister to the Premier

http://www.bcpublicservice.ca/workforce/message.htm (April 2005)

The above text is taken from the British Columbia (Canada) provincial government website. It focuses on a particular issue, that of the workforce adjustment plan. This plan is explained and defined in a variety of ways in the discourse. The text is a memo from the Deputy Minister to the Premier of BC, designed at least in part to persuade employees of the positive aspects and outcomes of the adjustment plan. The purpose of the plan itself, however, is to reduce the number of public servants in British Columbia, meaning that many employees will lose their jobs. This inherent conflict in the message can be identified very clearly through a variety of linguistic choices.

Our analytical review activities will focus on how the writer uses these choices to lessen the negative implications of the plan.

We will look first at a different type of chain, composed not of lexical sets but of two types of participants which surface in this text, creating an 'us' versus 'them' scenario.

We will then look at the textual choices used to define 'workforce adjustment' evident in the lexical cohesion of this text. The focus will be on the contrast between the positive and negative equivalencies provided for the workforce adjustment plan.

Finally, in terms of interpersonal resources, we will look at one type of modality predominant in this message which suggests future certainty.

5.7.1   SFL analysis: Text 5

Participant chains

In the text below there seem to be two sets of participants: government officials and public servants, which we have bolded for you.

Message to Employees
January 2002
Dear Fellow Public Servant:

As you are no doubt aware, the **government** has announced a workforce adjustment strategy that will be part of the process of re-profiling the scope of government's programs and services. The strategy includes eliminating vacant positions, reducing the number of temporary workers, offering early retirement and voluntary departure packages and, as a last resort, layoffs. **The Premier** has asked **me** to convey the reasons underlying this strategy and, in particular, its impending effects on the shape and size of the provincial public service.

The government recognizes that B.C.'s **public servants** are dedicated, hard-working and proud of the work they do for British Columbians. The coming changes are in no way meant to reflect on **you** personally or professionally. Rather, they are a necessary part of redefining a **government** that is too big, too expensive and not focused in the right areas. **Successive governments** spent beyond their means. This excess, combined with the significant fiscal challenges **we**'re facing, means **we** urgently need to redefine **government** and ensure taxpayers get value for money in the services they receive.

The goal of the workforce adjustment is to transition the government's workforce from the practices of the past to the innovative business practices of tomorrow. Within the next few weeks, your **human resources departments** will provide information regarding early retirement and voluntary departure packages. Specific work force adjustments will be announced in January. Please rest assured that, if **you** are presented with an early retirement or departure option, **you** will be given time to arrive at your decision.

The Premier and **Cabinet** recognize that these are stressful times. Some **staff** will face a difficult transition. **Affected employees** will be encouraged to take full advantage of the assistance that will be available to them, including counselling and career transition services.

As difficult as these decisions will be for many **public servants**, delivering the priority services of **government** in an affordable and effective manner will present an opportunity to create a renewed public service. Moreover, as **people** take advantage of early retirement and voluntary departure options, new opportunities will open for others to advance in their careers. **Continuing public servants** will be part of a **government** that encourages creativity and innovation, responsibility, accountability and results-based work.

Whether your future lies within or outside the provincial **public service**, **the Premier** and **Cabinet** hope **you** will benefit from their efforts to create a thriving spirit of free enterprise and ensure British Columbia a prosperous future.

Yours truly,
Ken Dobell,
Deputy Minister to the Premier

Discussion

1. Make two lists labelled 'government officials' and 'public serv-
    ants'; place the bolded participants above into the appropriate list.
2. Then answer the following questions in relation to the selections.
    a) Are the participants in each list in support of, or in conflict
        with, each other?
    b) Why do you think the 'public servant' list contains several
        instances of 'you'?
    c) Which list constitutes the 'us' group and which the 'them'
        group?
    d) What are the main characteristics of the members of each list?

3. Discuss your lists with other members of the class, considering
    as well the following points.
    a) Were there any differences among your answers and those
        of others?
    b) How would you defend your choices and convince others
        of your selection?
    c) Alternatively, were other members of your group able to
        persuade you about the correctness of their list? How did
        they do so? What evidence did they use?

Lexical sets or collocations

We will focus here on the way major change can be presented in order
to make it more palatable for those concerned. In the text, there are two
sets of collocations related to the workforce adjustment plan. One set is
positive, while the other is negative.

Application

1. Go through the text and identify the positive and negative
    aspects of the plan in the two lists of collocational sets.
2. Identify the euphemisms that are being used in the positive set.
3. For each of the positive representations, provide synonyms that
    may more accurately reflect what is being proposed in the plan.

An example of such a euphemism from the text is: 'innovative business practices of today'. To represent what is really going on it would probably be more accurate to say: 'more streamlined' or 'fewer people will be employed'. Go through the text to identify other examples and suggest more neutral or more accurate synonyms.

Interpersonal choices: modality

In Chapter 3, we presented the different modals which express either probability or frequency. We also looked at Suzanne Eggins's explanation of probability, which she says occurs 'where the speaker expresses judgements as to the likelihood or probability of something happening or being' (1994: 179). When you read the communiqué, it is obvious that there is only one type of marked modality: 'will'. With this choice, the writer expresses his attitude towards, and judgment of, the future of the workforce adjustment plan. Through this selection, he seems to be presenting it as a near certainty, almost as a promise, expressed by 'will'.

CDA questions

1. To understand the force of the writer's choice, go through the text and make a list of all of the propositions that are modified by 'will'. Describe where this form occurs – in negative or positive propositions. Why do you think this is the case?
2. Explain in writing, with examples, why you think the writer is using this device and how it reveals his position and therefore that of the government. How does the choice reveal the interpersonal relationship between the writer and the readers of this text in terms of distance or power? How does the question of power relate to this form of modality?
3. Do the interests of the Government come into conflict with those of any other community such as advertisers, consumers, workers?

We will now focus on a communiqué from a large North American university (McGill University in Montreal Canada), directed at incoming students. The topic is academic integrity. The communiqué focuses on cheating and plagiarism at universities, and the university policy at McGill. (If you are curious about other university policies on this issue, there are many discussions which can be accessed by typing 'Academic Integrity' into the Google search engine.)

Academic integrity

As a McGill student, you are responsible for knowing the rules and regulations concerning academic honesty, which can be found in the Code of Student Conduct and Disciplinary Procedures. Perhaps more important, it is also your responsibility to help maintain the academic integrity of the University.

Cheating or plagiarizing by even one student hurts all students, because anything that undermines the evaluation process undermines the value of McGill's degrees. Therefore, carefully considered steps are taken to prevent students from cheating or plagiarizing and to catch those who do. Unfortunately, some students still resort to dishonesty, but any McGill student caught cheating or plagiarizing faces potentially serious consequences including, but not limited to, the possibility of conduct probation and a failure in the course; and such sanctions form a permanent part of the student's disciplinary record.

Some students try to justify cheating or plagiarism by claiming that they are pressured to outperform their classmates in order to succeed. There are two problems with this argument:

First, pressure to get good grades may explain the motivation to cheat, but it cannot justify actions that undermine the academic integrity of the University, and thereby debase the grades and degrees that students are striving for.

Second, McGill does not have a policy of "weeding out" a percentage of students. Indeed, we pride ourselves on the very high quality of our incoming students. We would like everyone who is accepted to McGill to succeed academically and to graduate with a degree. In addition, there is no policy in either Arts or Science to grade students by how they rank in a class. Therefore, focus on mastering your course material, not on competing with your classmates.

http://www.mcgill.ca/artscisao/departmental/examination/integrity/ (Accessed January 2005)

This communiqué provides another instance of organizational discourse at the institutional level, in this case, to clarify the university's policy on cheating and plagiarism. There is little doubt after reading it that this message reflects the hierarchical structure inherent in a message from the administration, aimed at incoming students.

We saw a similar expression of authority in the Workforce Adjustment message. There the writer, by virtue of his position as Deputy Minister to the Premier, took on an authoritative role in relation to the workforce. Similarly, although we do not know who wrote this text, we can assume it was someone from the office of the President or the Rector, or the Dean of the particular faculty. In other words, the text reveals several linguistic choices by which power is exerted in and through the text.

The analyses related to this text will identify the resources used by the writer to ensure that the students understand the authority embedded in this official communication. The purpose is undoubtedly to make sure that students realize the seriousness of the message about cheating and plagiarism.

We will look first at thematic development, and the patterns that surface in the text to indicate the focus of the communication. Related to these thematic patterns are the lexical sets that reflect not only the cohesive devices, but also the Ideational content of the text. As in all discourse, through each set of meanings, the writer makes choices about what experiences to communicate. These selections tell us a great deal about the intention of the communication. Thus, by examining the content through a study of themes and lexical choices we can identify the preoccupation of the writer. Interpersonally, through a study of the modality in this text, we become familiar with the stances of the writer.

5.8.1   SFL analysis: Text 6

Textual choices: thematic development

We learned in Chapter 4 that Topical Themes can be any element that realizes Ideational meanings: circumstances, participants or processes; Textual Themes, on the other hand, are realized primarily by connectors such as 'and' or 'however', also called conjunctions. As we saw in Chapter 4, interpersonal Themes make explicit a writer or speaker's stance towards the information in the clause. These Themes can be realized by adverbs such as 'unhappily', or by adverbial phrases such as 'more disastrous', to express evaluative meanings.

Read the text below again. Note that we have numbered the clauses for ease of reference.

Practice

1) As a McGill student, you are responsible for knowing the rules and regulations concerning academic honesty, 2) which can be found in the Code of Student Conduct and Disciplinary Procedures. 3) Perhaps more important, it is also your responsibility to help maintain the academic integrity of the University.

4) Cheating or plagiarizing by even one student hurts all students, 5) because anything that undermines the evaluation process undermines the value of McGill's degrees. 6) Therefore, carefully considered steps are taken to prevent students from cheating or plagiarizing and to catch those who do. 7) Unfortunately, some students still resort to dishonesty, 8) but any McGill student caught cheating or plagiarizing faces potentially serious consequences including, but not limited to, the possibility of conduct probation and a failure in the course; and such sanctions form a permanent part of the student's disciplinary record.

9) Some students try to justify cheating or plagiarism by claiming that they are pressured to outperform their classmates in order to succeed. 10) There are two problems with this argument:

11) First, pressure to get good grades may explain the motivation to cheat, 12) but it cannot justify actions that undermine the academic integrity of the University, and thereby debase the grades and degrees that students are striving for.

13) Second, McGill does not have a policy of 'weeding out' a percentage of students. 14) Indeed, we pride ourselves on the very high quality of our incoming students. 15) We would like everyone who is accepted to McGill to succeed academically and to graduate with a degree. 16) In addition, there is no policy in either Arts or Science to grade students by how they rank in a class. 17) Therefore, focus on mastering your course material, not on competing with your classmates.

1. Identify the thematic choices and thus the patterns that surface in this text. Enter these in the chart below. Focus on main clauses, which are indicated by the numbers inserted beside each clause. The first clause has been done for you. In one case, clause 3, there is another type of interpersonal theme realized by the phrase, 'Perhaps more important', which we have not yet considered; it also is designed to express the writer's stance and is known as a mood adjunct, which we will look at in later chapters.

Interpersonal Themes	Textual Themes	Topical Themes
		'1) As a McGill student, you' (two Topical Themes here – one realizing circumstance and the second, a participant).
3) Perhaps more important,		it

2. Discuss each type of identified Theme and the purpose it serves in this discourse. For example, the first Topical Theme identified in clause 1 provides the setting and thereby identifies the referent for 'you'. That is, it refers only to McGill students.

Lexical sets

As we have seen in other sections in this chapter, different lexical sets or collocations reveal not only textual, but also Ideational choices. They also indicate the content on which the author focuses.

1. To get a clearer idea of the writer's perspective on this issue, identify and list all the lexical items that make up what you could label an 'academic integrity' set. How is academic integrity being defined here?

2. Use these ideas to discuss McGill's position on academic integrity.

Interpersonal choices: modality

We have seen in our work on other texts that writers often use modality to explicitly indicate their positions on issues they write about. For example, 'Medicines you *may* buy outside the U.S. *may* be unsafe or ineffective.'

1. As you go through the text, underline the modals that you find.
2. What is the role of each of the modals you have found? That is, how does each colour the proposition in which it occurs?
3. What other forms of modality might have been used that would present a different stance towards the information being conveyed?

1. After analyzing the text, how would you summarize the writer's perspective? That is, what does your analysis tell you about the

type of position presented here? To paraphrase Lemke (1995: 57), what kinds of people would write such a discourse?

2.   Two sets of interests are represented in this communiqué. What are they? Are they in conflict?

3.   As a student, how do you react to such a memo? Discuss this question with other students in your class.

4.   How did your analyses inform your discussion of these questions? Be specific in your answers.

Application

In this chapter, we have reviewed ideational, textual and interpersonal meanings through four texts. You have had several opportunities to practice identifying, describing and discovering the meanings of the choices in each of the texts. In the last activity of this chapter, you will be the ones to choose the text to analyze, from the website provided below. You will notice when you go to this site that some of the texts are a bit different in style, with several of the following features evident:

A more personal tone;
Marked modality;
Synthetic personalization;
Imperatives and alternative means of realizing commands.

1.   Go to http://www.internalmemos.com/memos/ and select one memo to analyze. (Access is free to any memo without a green dollar sign.) Copy it so that others can share it.

2.   Then carry out an Ideational analysis focusing on processes and participants, and an interpersonal analysis looking at mood selections and/or modality choices.

3.   Look at your discourse from a textual point of view. Identify the textual choices that surface more than once: anaphoric reference, lexical sets or collocations, ellipsis, repetition, exophoric reference, or themes.

4.   Summarize your analytical findings and critically discuss their implications.

The following analysis is intended to give you an idea of how you might write up your findings about findings in a text in terms of nominalizations and we/us participants.

Read the following example of a critical discourse analysis.

Harrison and Young on phasal analysis

In this analysis Harrison and Young carry out a phasal analysis, that is, the analysis of a strand of discourse in which there are marked similarities of choice among the three metafunctions. In the following analysis the researchers focus on nominalizations and we/us choices designed to make the recipient group more cohesive.

The text analyzed was a memo sent to members of an Assistant Deputy Minister's staff in The Canadian Department of Health. The memo was sent during a huge realignment of staff and facilities.

Phase 3: Concealment

Phase 3 contains clauses that reveal the ADM's adherence to a management style that is more reflective of the old capitalism than those of Phases 1 and 2. Phase 3 includes 13 clauses that provide staff with information on what Iedema (1997) called 'Guidance':

> *The area of institutional Guidance is concerned with planning and rationalising future actions and directions (whereto and why), with determining who (or rather what kind of people) should do it, with deciding what exactly needs to be done, and how it needs to be done. (p. 3)*

This phase contains the hot issues around the realignment – hot because they involve major decisions that will affect employees' futures and because these issues, particularly in a new organization, involve extensive negotiation. The ADM's high level of discomfort with guidance issues is apparent in his concealment of agency and intent by (a) embedding Ideational processes in relative clauses and (b) using nominalizations (i.e., verbs that are transformed into nouns), which not only eliminate agency but also time through the loss of tense. In the following example, we have italicized the nominalizations and used // marks to delineate the relative clauses:

> *The purpose of these meetings was to develop a shared understanding of the issues and challenges // [that] we face in bringing together the various components of the Branch, the Branch and Programme systems and processes // [that] we need to construct, // and the linkages // that will need to be strengthened or created across Canada, both with staff and with stakeholders. //* Harrison, Young (2005)

In Phase 3, the high number of nominalizations and nonhuman agents as participants in the clauses (e.g., challenges, purposes, responsibilities, goals, commitments) effectively removes people from the activities and plans. The only human agents are, significantly, the inclusive we/us. Whereas in Phase 1, the ADM used the exclusive we/us to provide distance in order to counterbalance the intimacy of reaching out to staff, he does the reverse in Phase 3, in which he used the inclusive we/us to provide human intimacy to counterbalance the distance of the impersonal participants.

(Harrison and Young, 2005: 64–65)

Chapter 5
Further readings

Readings on organization and discourse

Fairclough, N. (2001) *Language and Power*. We have talked about Fairclough's work in other chapters. Of particular note here is his discussion in the second edition of his final chapter, 10, in which he looks at the question of organizational discourse primarily from the perspective of social change. He provides several theoretical discussions about organizational discourse and several interesting and useful analyses. For those interested in more information about the work of Fairclough and others on the issue of neoliberal and organizational discourse in general, we recommend you go to the following website: http://www.cddc.vt.edu/host/lnc/papers/fair_lnc.htm or to his own website for other links on this topic: http://www.ling.lancs.ac.uk/staff/norman/norman.htm

Grant, D. and Hardy, C. (2004) *Introduction: struggles with organizational discourse*. This introduction, as well as an article by Fairclough, appears in the special issue of *Organization Studies* 25(1).

Munby, D. K. and Clair, R. P. (1997) *Organizational Discourse in Discourse as Social Interaction Discourse Studies: a multidisciplinary introduction. Volume 2*. (Edited by T. A. van Dijk) This article is key to the discussion of organizational discourse from a CDA perspective.

SFL readings

Butt, D. et al. (2000) *Using Functional Grammar, An Explorer's Guide. Second Edition.* Since this is a review chapter, we have already provided further readings on each of the analytical tools we have covered in each of the preceding chapters. However, should you want a quick review of the major areas covered in Chapters 1–5, we would suggest you read Chapters 3–6 of Butt et al. in which they very clearly explain each of the metafunctional components we have introduced and have reviewed.

CDA readings

Lemke, J. (1995) *Textual Politics Discourse and Social Dynamics.* In Chapter 3, Lemke talks about thematic development and then analyzes two conflicting discourses with very different thematic patterns. The questions he raises following his discussions are particularly interesting. We would recommend you read the entire chapter, but pay particular attention to pages 44–57.

Chapter 6 contents

Visual and verbal modes of communication

This chapter introduces multimodal analysis and examines the interplay between visual and verbal modes of communication. You may wonder why a book on language looks at visual means of communication. Perhaps the best way to explain this is to quote some of the researchers working with this mode. They make it clear that in our society, the visual mode has greatly increased – often replacing the verbal mode. Furthermore, these researchers suggest that few meaning-making situations involve only one mode; much more common today is the interplay of modes in a wide variety of communicative situations.

To introduce the ways in which meanings are conveyed visually in today's world, we begin with an art critic's view of the importance of the visual:

Views from the theorists:
E. H. Gombrich

The visual

> Ours is a visual age. We are bombarded with pictures from morning till night. Opening our newspaper at breakfast, we see photographs of men and women in the news, and raising our eyes from the paper, we encounter the picture on the cereal package…
>
> Picture books, picture postcards and colour slides accumulate in our homes as souvenirs of travel, as do the private mementos of our family snapshots.

> No wonder it has been asserted that we are entering a historical epoch in which the image will take over from the written word. In view of this claim it is all the more important to clarify the potentialities of the image in communication, to ask what it can and what it cannot do better than spoken or written language. (1982: 137)

Now we will look at similar appraisals by linguists.

Kress and van Leeuwen (1996), prominent analysts of visual and verbal modes, examine visual communication from yet another perspective. They focus on how different meanings are made by each mode, and the interplay between them. They suggest that a transformation in communication has led to a greater reliance on the visual over the verbal, especially in science. They also question whether everything that is communicable verbally is also communicable visually, and further, whether in certain situations, one mode is better than the other.

Lemke extends Kress and van Leeuwen's view, saying that:

> … meanings (in scientific communication) are made by the joint co-deployment of two or more semiotic modalities, and such co-deployment of resources is likewise needed for canonical interpretation. …no verbal text can construct the same meaning as a picture, no mathematical graph carries the same meaning as an equation, no verbal description makes the same sense as an action performed. (1998: 110)

Teo, in his analysis of posters in Singapore (which we will examine later in this chapter), echoes this in his discussion of Goodman's (1996: 39) point about the increase of multimodal texts when he says that:

> …it has been argued that modern texts are becoming not only increasingly multimodal but also increasingly visual, as new technologies make it possible to bring visual forms of communication (photographs, book covers, videos, etc.) into contact with traditional print media. (Teo, 2004: 193)

The role of the visual mode in itself, as well as in relation to the verbal mode, suggests its importance, and the need to increase multimodal literacy. To do this, it is particularly useful to analyze both visual and verbal modes of communication.

Throughout this book, we examine how language expresses and conveys different meanings and, through these exchanges, exerts influence and power. In this chapter we will continue to look at verbal communication, but we will also focus on the visual modes of interacting. We will continue to use the SFL approach to analysis to show how this has been applied to other semiotic modes.

Lemke, Kress and van Leeuwen, and O'Toole make clear that the visual mode, like the verbal, has to be able to make meanings in terms of the three familiar metafunctions: the Ideational, the Interpersonal and the Textual. Although some of the researchers use slightly different labels for the three metafunctions, their actual descriptions of each function in relation to the visual mode are very similar.

Before beginning to work with these different approaches to the visual mode, let's review Halliday's concept of the three metafunctions – functions of a very general kind, according to Halliday (1978: 21). These are described in Butt et al.

> The **Ideational** Metafunction is used '… to encode our experience of the world; it conveys a picture of reality.' (Butt et al., 2000: 39)

> The **Interpersonal** Metafunction is used to '… encode interaction and show how defensible we find propositions. Thus it allows us to encode meanings of attitudes, interaction and relationships…' (ibid: 39)

> The **Textual** Metafunction is used '…to organize our…meanings into a linear and coherent whole. Thus, it allows us to encode meanings of text development…' (ibid: 39)

Chapters 1–4 focused on these three metafunctions, and Chapter 5 provided a review of all three. In the three charts which follow, we can now examine a similar approach to the analysis of the visual mode. Each chart provides comparable explanations of the metafunctions in relation to visual analysis as seen from the perspectives of Lemke, Kress and van Leeuwen, and O'Toole. We will also provide a fourth chart adapted from O'Toole, which itemizes approaches to the analysis of each metafunction in pictorial depictions.

Metafunctional components (Lemke, Kress and van Leeuwen, and O'Toole)

Lemke: Representational Function	Kress and van Leeuwen: Ideational Function	O'Toole: Representational Function
Every meaning – making act constructs a *presentational* state-of-affairs that construes relations among semiotic participants and processes... In language this is the so-called representational or propositional function. In visual depiction this is the *figural or representational* function... (1998: 93)	The visual like all semiotic modes have to serve several communicational and representational requirements, in order to function as a full system of communication. We have adopted the theoretical notion of 'metafunction' from the work of M. Halliday for the purpose of dealing with this. (1996: 40)	One of the three major functions in painting and sculpture... whereby the artist structures a work or its details in such a way as to represent aspects of the real world... (1994: 278)

Lemke: Orientational Function	Kress and van Leeuwen: Interpersonal Function	O'Toole: Modal Function
In visual depiction, every image takes an orientational stance which positions the viewer in relation to the scene (e.g. intimate, distant...) establishes some sort of evaluative orientation of the producer/interpreter toward the scene itself... (ibid: 94)	... any semiotic system has to be able to project a particular social relation between the producer, the viewer and the object presented. (ibid: 41)	One of the three major functions in painting and sculpture... whereby the artist structures a work or its details in such a way as to engage the attention of the viewer and draw them into the world of the work. ... At an abstract semiotic level, this function is equivalent to Halliday's **interpersonal** function for language... (ibid: 278)

Lemke: Organizational Function	Kress and van Leeuwen: Textual Function	O'Toole: Compositional Function
... every meaning-making act constructs a system of *organizational* relations defining wholes and parts of them... Depiction deploys *compositional* resources to organize the visual into elements and regions and to link disjoint regions by such features as colour and texture. (ibid: 94)	Any semiotic system has to have the capacity to form texts, complexes of signs which cohere both internally and with the context in and for which they are produced. Here too, visual grammar makes a range of resources available: different compositional arrangements to allow the realization of different textual meanings. (ibid: 41)	One of the three major functions in painting and sculpture and other arts whereby a work is structured and its details linked and related in such a way as to make it seem a perfect whole... (ibid: 278)

Practice

1. After reading through each of these descriptions, compare them to Halliday as quoted by Butt et al. earlier in the chapter. Focus on the similarities among the researchers. Write these down in note form.
2. Next, explain each metafunction as a compilation of the explanations offered above. Being able to capture the essence in your own words ensures that you can work with them in subsequent analyses.
3. Compare your explanations to others in the class. Discuss any significant differences among these explanations.

In his book *The Language of Displayed Art* (p. 25), O'Toole provides a further set of analytical tools: a table based on metafunctional criteria. This table indicates what features to focus on under each metafunctional component when carrying out analyses of figural depictions. A simplified and adapted chart based on O'Toole's categories is presented below.

Functions		
Representational	**Modal**	**Compositional**
Narrative themes Actions, events, agents, patients etc. Act, stance, gesture, clothing	Rhythm, gaze, perspective, prominence, characterization	Gestalt: Framing Horizontals Verticals Diagonals Relative position of object(s) or people in work Parallelism or opposition

6.2   Overview of Chapter 6: multimodal analyses

We will be using our adaptation of O'Toole's categories, as well as other resources based on and drawn from Lemke, Kress and van Leeuwen, to carry out all the multimodal analyses in the rest of the chapter. We will consider four visual and verbal texts – two news stories with accompanying photographs, and two websites. With each analysis we will add analytical tools.

For each text, we will begin with an analysis of the visual mode. We will follow this with an analysis of the verbal mode.

In this chapter, then, the focus is on the interplay between these two modes of communication. We will be commenting on four ways in which each mode can contribute to meaning:

1) by providing information that is essential for understanding information in the other mode;
2) by providing information that supplements information in the other mode;

3) by providing redundant information that repeats information in the other mode; or

4) by providing information that is different from information in the other mode.

Image 6.1: Newspaper report (Photo: Rod McIver)

STUDENTS BLAST FEE-HIKE PROPOSAL

Pilot Project would let schools increase tuition to cover full cost of education

Becky Turner, a business administration student at Winnipeg's Red River College, and delegate to the Canadian Alliance of Student Associations annual meeting in Ottawa, stands next to a 'wall of debt' erected on Parliament Hill yesterday, composed of postcards signed by students with the amount they owe for their education.

6.3.1 Background to Text 1

In order for the visual and verbal analyses to make sense, it is necessary to contextualize the information. We will be examining the concepts of context of situation and context of culture more thoroughly in Chapter 7. However, to understand what is happening visually and verbally in this news story, we need to understand two pieces of information. The first deals with the context of situation of the story itself. The second deals with the context of the culture in which such stories take place. The latter is a broader concept than the former.

To understand this photo, viewers have to recognize that the photo is taken on Parliament Hill, the seat of the federal Government of Canada. Parliament Hill itself is in Ottawa, the capital of Canada. To understand the broader context of culture, beyond this particular story, we need to know that the story concerns the Canadian education system. Traditionally, university students have paid only about 25 per cent of the actual cost of their education. The remainder of the cost has been paid by the federal and provincial governments. So in Canada, the real financial burden has not fallen on the students. The significance of the new proposal, therefore, is that students will have to pay the entire cost of their education – an additional 75 per cent in fees.

It is against this background that the story takes place, and it is this background that creates the significance of the proposal and of the protest.

The purpose of the questions below is to indicate how the roles of the visual and the verbal differ depending on the genre. In the news stories which follow, it will become evident that the pictures play a very important role in the story; they may tell their own story, but it is necessary to include the verbal in order to understand what is really happening. It is also possible that a photo may tell one story and the verbal another. Or the verbal may be needed to complete the story begun in the photo. In websites, on the other hand, the role of the visual often seems to be less significant, since for technical reasons, most well-designed websites are primarily text-based. Visuals are often used more to create an ambiance than to add significantly to the information contained on the website.

Consider the questions below concerning the role of the photo in the story that follows. Discuss them with other members of your class before you go on with the analysis.

1. Is the information redundant in each mode or does each mode provide new and different meanings?
2. Does the verbal message reinforce the visual one or vice versa, or does it offer contrasting information?
3. Is the verbal message necessary in order to understand the visual?
4. Who or what are the most prominent participants in each of the modes?

6.3.2   Visual analysis: Text 1

With the analytical tools provided by the chart below, we can now begin to carry out a multifunctional analysis of the visual, and then, with related tools, of the verbal texts which accompany the photo.

O'Toole's metafunctions

Functions	Representational	Modal	Compositional
	Narrative themes Actions, events, agents, patients etc. Act, stance, gesture, clothing	Rhythm, gaze, perspective, prominence, characterization	Gestalt: Framing Horizontals Verticals Diagonals Relative position of object(s) or people in work Parallelism or opposition

Representational meanings

Using the chart above as our guideline, let's examine the ways in which representational meanings are made in the photo. In terms of the narrative theme, which O'Toole suggests is the actual content of the pictorial depiction, it is obvious that the young woman forms the nucleus of the picture as she gazes at the wall. Her act calls attention to the construction of the wall although without the verbal text we do not know what its significance is, only that the wall is an important part of the story. What we can see as part of the theme are the postcards which form the wall. On each postcard are people's names and amounts of money.

Practice

Look at the picture again. What constitutes the narrative theme – that is, what's happening in the picture? Compare your response with our answer below.

Our answer

The narrative theme involves the construction of the wall by other young students as the young woman gazes at it. The photo mainly contains two kinds of processes, material processes in which the young men are building the wall, with the young men in the role of actors and the wall, the goal. The young woman, on the other hand, simply looks sadly at the wall, expressing her mental reactions. Her look is, in a sense, a commentary on the actions carried out by the young men. Her expression of sadness tells us her evaluation of what we later learn is meant to be a 'wall of debt.'

As we've seen, the students are involved in material processes, but the action is set against a background of what Kress and van Leeuwen call a 'conceptual pattern', in which the focus is on a timeless essence, in this case the Canadian Parliamentary buildings. In this framing, the Peace Tower seems to loom over the actions of the students, and seems to suggest symbolic power.

Practice

How do the young woman's stance and gesture contribute to the representational meaning? Compare your response with our answer below.

Our answer

The young woman adopts a stance (or the photo journalist has her adopt it) in which she seems overwhelmed by the size of the debts as she leans against the wall; the stance echoes and reinforces the sadness evident in her eyes. It also emphasizes the poignancy of the issue as she calls attention to it through her gaze and leaning position against the wall.

Modal meanings

Although the young woman plays a prominent role in the photo through her central placement in the foreground (something we will talk more about when we discuss the compositional meanings), her gaze is not directed at the viewers but at the wall of cards. She engages our sympathy through her stance, but she does not seek to interact with viewers and to thus engage us in the evaluation of what is going on in the photo. On the other hand, the perspective of the photo is such that we are on the same level as the young woman. We do not look up to her; we relate to the woman as equals. This in itself engages us in place of a gaze that is not directed at us.

The sympathetic characterization of the young woman seems designed to win over viewers to the plight she is in and on which she seems to be commenting.

Rhythm is created in the photo through the various elements established in relation to each other. The cards form a wall. Each card connects to the others, creating a rhythm among them from the recurring dollar amount on each card, the first names that appear on each card, and the repetition of the cards themselves.

Compositional meanings

When we consider the photo in terms of the overall gestalt, it is clear that there is a contrast between the vertical and the horizontal or diagonal elements in the photo.

Practice

Identify the strongest vertical, horizontal and diagonal elements in the photo. Compare your response with our answer below.

Our answer

The vertical, horizontal and diagonal elements contrast with each other, and with the vertical Peace Tower in the background. The flat perspective and static positioning of the Peace Tower also contrasts with the dynamic foreground action of erecting the wall. The wall itself is a horizontal structure with a strong perspective conveyed by the diagonal lines formed by the gaps between the cards. One wonders whether the contrast is designed to challenge the pending decision of Parliament. In O'Toole's sense, there is an opposition between these two main elements: the wall and the Peace Tower. The opposition reinforces the representational meanings where the activities of the students contrast with the timeless and authoritative essence of the Peace Tower.

A further contrast is presented by the immobility of the young woman, gazing at the wall, in contrast to the activity of the young men, constructing more of the wall.

Cohesion is achieved by the cards on the wall. In other words, there is an interplay among the cards that forces us to direct our eyes to discover the different amounts distributed along the wall, and even to learn the first names of the people involved.

6.3.3   Verbal analysis: Text 1

Let's move on to a brief analysis of the verbal text so that we can determine what information it adds, what other participants if any are prominent, and how it contributes to the overall message of the story.

We will only look at the headline, the sub-heading and the caption; they contain the core information we need to fully understand the story. The actual story is 17 paragraphs long, but through these short texts alone we can begin to understand the role of the verbal and the visual. In later analyses we will examine longer verbal texts along with visual depictions in the two websites we examine.

Before we begin an analysis of the three texts below, labelled A, B, C, let's consider the role that the verbal text could play here.

First, answer each of the questions below. Then discuss your answers with other members of the class. Next, write a short summary of your answers. You can later examine and evaluate this summary in light of the analysis carried out on the texts.

Discussion

1. What is the role of the headline, sub-heading and caption in relation to the image?
2. Does each different verbal text play a different role?
3. Would we be able to understand the visual meanings without the explanation of the verbal ones?
4. Which verbal ones are necessary and which are not?

A (headline)

STUDENTS BLAST FEE-HIKE PROPOSAL

B (sub-heading)

Pilot Project would let schools increase tuition to cover full cost of education

C (caption)

Becky Turner, a business administration student at Winnipeg's Red River College, and delegate to the Canadian Alliance of Student Associations annual meeting in Ottawa, stands next to a 'wall of debt' erected on Parliament Hill yesterday, composed of postcards signed by students with the amount they owe for their education.

We can now carry out a metafunctional analysis of the three texts together, since they are short.

Our analysis

Ideational meanings

If we look at the three mini texts, labelled A, B, C, the main participants are immediately identifiable as those in first position in each of the texts: Students; Pilot Project; and Becky Turner. 'Students' in the headline are carrying out two kinds of processes: in one sense they are the sayers in the verbal process of 'blast', and the phenomenon is the 'fee-hike proposal'. However, because of their actions, evident in the photo, they are 'blasting' not just verbally but materially, by erecting a wall of cards. In other words, their protest is not simply verbal, but also material. They are simultaneously carrying out actions against a goal, the 'proposal', as they build a wall. The construction of the wall is the material process, and the wall itself is the goal. We have goals on two levels: the first is in the action itself, where the goal is the result of the action; and secondly, in a larger sense, the goal is the proposal against which they are 'blasting' or acting. The reader/viewer knows clearly who is doing what, to whom, and where.

However, in the sub-heading, Text B, it is interesting that the actor roles are filled by different participants. These roles are not filled by a person or a group of people, but by the 'project' itself. The sub-heading reads: 'Pilot Project would let schools increase tuition to cover full cost of education'. From our past analyses you should be able to recognize that such abstract nouns can serve the purpose of obfuscating the one or ones responsible for the action. We do not know who proposed this action of the fee hike. Although the 'project' does not occur in a passive sentence which hides agency, here we see another means by which agency is avoided: the selection of the abstract noun 'pilot project'. Projects normally have initiators and people responsible for them; the fact that none are mentioned certainly seems to have a purpose, as we shall discuss in the CDA section. Interestingly as well, the one process type here is a relational process: 'increase', being used as a material process. But again, no one is responsible for the increase.

Text C has only one material process, 'stands', and only one named actor: Becky Turner. She 'stands next to the wall' – identifying and situating her rather than telling us what she is doing. The inclusion of her name under the photo tells viewers who she is. It also identifies her role as not only a student but also as an official delegate to the Canadian Alliance of Students. Her role in the Association gives her a certain status. It also explains what a young student from another part of the country is doing in Ottawa. Interestingly, although there are other people involved in the erection of the wall, they are not named; Becky stands next to the wall, 'erected on Parliament Hill yesterday.' The other students remain unidentified through exclusion.

Interpersonal meanings

In Text A, although the choice of process type and verbal realization is primarily a matter of ideational choices, the selection of the word 'blast' has interpersonal meanings as well. The term is not neutral; the writer may have chosen 'protest', 'stand against' etc, but the selection of 'blast' suggests that this is a strong action and one perhaps that is not approved of. This is an interpersonal decision, a way of interacting and interjecting the journalist's or the paper's stance towards the action. The journalist probably did not choose this headline; rather the sub-editor may have done so, bearing in mind space limitations. In either case, the selection of certain lexical choices can indicate attitude. We will explore possible ideological implications in our CDA section but we raise the point here to ensure that you begin to see this type of choice as more than chance.

In Texts B and C, which modal (if any) is evident? Why do you think it was chosen? Compare your response with our answer below.

Practice

Our answer

The selection of the modal 'would' in Text B suggests a sense of near certainty in the hypothetical case. It does not say 'will', which is much more definite and is used for situations that are in place. The project under discussion here is proposed; it is not yet a reality, so 'would' is more appropriate. It adds to the hypothetical nature of the sub-heading and calls attention to the 'proposed' nature of the statement, that is, a proposed, as opposed to enacted, fee hike.

In Text C, there is no modalizing of propositions. There is only simple description of what is; but the posing of the student, as we saw in our visual analysis, is certainly an expression of the attitude of the journalist, who places her prominently in the centre of the picture and in the foreground, looking sadly at the wall. The pose itself is the statement of the journalist's attitude towards the event. But the statement in the caption is a straightforward description of what we see.

Textual meanings

With your experience in analysing verbal texts, you should be able to identify and describe some of the more central textual resources through which the texts achieve cohesion.

Practice

1. Go through the texts and identify the lexical chain that connects the texts to each other.
2. Which lexical items, taken together, form a lexical or collocational set?
3. How does this serve ideational as well as textual purposes?
4. Could you make a case for more than one lexical set? If so, what would you include in each set? What purpose does it serve to identify different lexical strands? That is, what thematic focuses do these strands reveal?

Application

1. Now that you have carried out a metafunctional analysis of the verbal texts, compare the results of this analysis with those of the visual text we analyzed earlier.

2. Discuss in writing the similarities or differences in the messages
    in the two modes of communication.
3. Do the two modes of communication provide redundant infor-
    mation? Or does each mode offer new information?

---

1. One can only surmise that the photographer or the journalist
    asked the young woman to pose as she is in the photo. In light of
    our work throughout the book and in this chapter, it is interest-
    ing to ask the following questions in relation to this pose:

    a. How else could the photo have been framed?
    b. How else might the young woman have directed
       her gaze?
    c. What other elements in the photo could have been
       foregrounded and backgrounded?
    d. Why is the young woman the most salient participant,
       rather than the male students erecting the wall?

2. After answering all of the above questions, discuss what the
    photo and texts tell us about the ideological views of the jour-
    nalist towards this topic.
3. Is the conceptual essence of the Peace Tower in the photo
    designed to counter the narrative happenings of the students? If
    so, why? If not, why not?
4. Would you say that this photo challenges the existing system of
    power? (Adapted from Shapiro, 1988: 130.)

CDA questions

6.4   Text 2: The baggage handler

6.4.1   Background to Text 2

This photograph accompanied a Canadian news story from the *Vancouver Province* newspaper, reprinted in the *Ottawa Citizen* on 12 January 2005.

Image 6.2: Newspaper report (Photo: John Moorhouse)

In the analysis of each of the modes we will be adding analytical tools adapted from Jay Lemke's website on multimodal analysis. We have simplified and edited Lemke's questions.

These questions provide an additional set of analytical tools to supplement those offered by O'Toole's chart. After you have had a chance to work with Lemke's tools, it will be evident that his questions are based on similar metafunctional considerations. For example, when we ask questions about content and participants under representational meanings, these questions closely resemble O'Toole's focus on narrative themes, and actions, events, agents etc. Lemke's approach, then, is not different from O'Toole's, but rather a closely-related one that will reinforce what you learned from O'Toole's chart of features.

We will first examine the visual and verbal components of the story separately. We can then discover how much of the story is contained in the photo itself, how much in the verbal accompaniments, and to what extent the two modes depend on each other.

After both analyses, we will revisit the image to see how our perception of it has changed with the inclusion of the information from the verbal mode.

For the visual analysis that follows, we pose questions for each of the three sets of meanings and then provide our responses.

6.4.2   Visual analysis: Text 2

Representational meanings

1. How can we describe the content of the image? Are there participants?
2. Are there any happenings in the image as a whole?
3. What actors and processes are represented? Are the actors animate beings or objects?
4. Where is the image set?

Our responses

1. How can we describe the content of the image?

The photo shows a man sitting (or kneeling?) behind a large, soft-sided suitcase, in an outdoor, snowy setting which is not immediately identifiable. On his right is a large, more or less representational statue of a male figure carrying a large suitcase. (Despite its prominence in the photo, the significance of the man's suitcase is not immediately apparent.) The man is dressed appropriately for the wintry weather. The statue, on the other hand, is nude.

The statue appears to be more than life-size when we compare it to the trees in the background. Around the base of the statue is a rectangular object on a metal stake. On closer examination, this appears to be a real suitcase.

Are there participants?

The photo has two participants: the man with his suitcase in the left foreground, and the statue with its suitcase in the mid-ground on his right.

2. Are there any happenings in the image as a whole?

At first sight, there seems to be nothing happening in the photo. The man is not looking at the statue. Despite the prominence of his suitcase, he is not doing anything to or with it – he is merely leaning on it.

The statue is carrying its suitcase in one hand. The other hand is a clenched fist. The clenched fist suggests some emotion, but we do not yet know what it is. And we cannot without the accompanying verbal text.

3. What actors and processes are represented?

There are two actors, one animate and the other inanimate: the man and the statue. There are several suitcases in the photo, the goals of the actions undertaken by the actors. In one case, the man is leaning on the suitcase, a material action with a Goal; in the other, the statue is holding a suitcase, again a Goal for the action. There is another process, relational, indicating placement of the suitcase on a bench or some such structure, behind and to the left of the statue.

4. Where is the image set?

All we can tell from the photo is that it is set outside, and that there are a few trees, and a mountain in the background. Viewers do not know precisely where the statue is located; it seems to be in a park-like setting. We assume that the setting is somewhere in an urban environment, because of the concrete steps behind the statue in the foreground. This perception is confirmed by the partly obscured vehicle in the background on the right. We do not know the location of this urban space.

Modal meanings

1. How does the image position the reader in terms of intimacy or distance?
2. How does the creator express his or her attitudes in relation to the following features: repetition of items in the image, the relative prominence or scale of these items, and centrality of aspects of the image?

3. What is the stance of the creator of the image?
4. Who is the intended viewer and how do we know this ?

Our responses

1. How does the image position the viewer in terms of intimacy or distance?

The human element (the man) is fairly close, while the statue is in the middle distance. Given the height of the statue, the photo is taken from as close as possible. The gaze of the statue is over the heads of the viewers, and does not engage us directly, partly by reason of its large scale, but more because of its turning away slightly, to look into the distance. Because of the perspective from which the photo is taken, we have to look up to it. The man, on the other hand, looks directly at us and seems to be interacting directly with the viewers who are at the same level as his gaze. This is thus a more intimate relationship, especially compared with the statue, which, by virtue of its size and the perspective of the photographer, is more distant.

2. How does the creator express his or her attitudes in relation to the following features: repetition of items in the image, the relative prominence or scale of these items, and centrality of aspects of the image?

Despite the fact that there is no interaction between the man and the statue, we understand from the inclusion of the two figures that the story will probably be about a relationship of some kind between the man and the statue. The man kneels with a suitcase to the left of the statue, which also has a suitcase. The similarity seems explicitly designed to indicate a relationship between the two.

This relationship is expressed in the photo by means of repetition and contrast. The most obvious repetition is that of the suitcase. Both the man and the statue have them. Further, there is another suitcase which appears at the base of the statue. The different perspectives from which the man and the statue are presented highlight the contrast in the positions of the man and the statue. The man is kneeling or sitting; the statue is standing. The man's suitcase is supporting him; the statue's suitcase is being carried. The man is fully dressed in outdoor clothing; the statue is nude. The man appears serene and faintly amused; the statue is serious, and expresses some tension in its clenched fist.

The dominant element in the photo is the man's suitcase. It is the element that is closest to us. It partly obscures the human figure of the man. The type of material from which it is made has a strong repeated pattern which makes it catch the eye. This relative prominence, together with the three-fold repetition of the suitcase motif, tells us that the concept of luggage is in some way central to the meaning of the photo, although as yet we don't have enough information to see exactly how.

3. What is the stance of the creator of the image?

This photo is clearly posed: nobody normally kneels in the snow behind a suitcase, beside a statue. The posing of a subject is often an indication of the stance taken by the photographer.

Barthes's comments about meanings in photographs offers us an additional perspective.

Views from the theorists:
Barthes

Photographs and connotational meaning

The photograph, according to Barthes, 'transmit[s] ...the scene itself, the literal reality' (17)... This direct representation (the 'what it is') is the photograph's *denoted* message. In addition, a photograph also conveys 'a *connoted* message, which is the manner in which the society to a certain extent communicates what it thinks of it.'

Barthes lays out six 'connotation procedures' or processes whereby a photograph takes on a connoted meaning. 'These are: trick effects, pose, objects which index certain things, photogenia, aestheticism, and syntax, where photographs exist in a series.'

In Barthes' terms then, we can therefore assume from the pose that this photo carries a second-order connotational meaning as well as a denotational meaning. And so, when we carry out our analysis, we also are looking for the stance towards the particular representation to see the angle that the photographer and the journalist have taken with the story.

The stance of the photographer is conveyed mainly by the human element in the picture: the man with the suitcase. He is kneeling in the snow. Only his head, shoulders and arms are visible; the rest is hidden behind the large suitcase which dominates the picture. This position is unconventional, to say the least. He obviously finds something amusing in the situation, since he is smiling slightly. His almost conspiratorial expression suggests that the viewer will also find humour in the photo. The photographer too seems to think that the situation he is representing is faintly ridiculous, and shows this through his presentation. That is, the positioning of the man, and the man's expression, clearly indicate the photographer's stance of amusement.

The statue, on the other hand, is portrayed purely denotationally. The photo conveys simply that 'this is what the statue looks like and this is where it is.'

From this duality of stance the viewer knows that the statue is to be taken seriously; the man's function seems to be tied to the comment he has to make. All that we know from simply looking at the photo is that the man and his suitcase are the dominant elements by virtue of being closer to the viewer and relatively larger in scale. Therefore the story may concern the comment rather than the statue.

4. Who is the intended viewer and how do we know this?

The intended viewer of this photo is primarily a reader of the newspaper in which the story appears – in this case, the *Vancouver Province* – and secondarily a reader of the other regional or national newspapers that also carry the story. We don't know a great deal about this viewer just from the photo. We can assume that the statue and its location are familiar to the local readership. But the identity of the man in the photo may not be familiar, even to local readers, although we can assume that since the photo and accompanying story have reached the national press, there has already been considerable publicity attached to the statue and the man.

Compositional meanings

1. What is/are the most salient visual element(s) in the image?
2. Are there parallels within the image and if so, how does this contribute to cohesion?
3. How are the elements in the image positioned to relate to each other?

Our responses

1. What is/are the most salient visual element(s) in the image?

One way to get at this answer is to think about where your eye is drawn to first. Lemke suggests that there are pathways or vectors that lead to these elements.

The photo has two figures: one is human, one human-like. The human figure holds the same object as the statue – a suitcase. He forms a mass in the lower left of the picture which is solid and dark. The figure of the man is compact: his arms are in front of and close to his body, while his leaning forward on the suitcase foreshortens his position and makes his head appear close to his shoulders. This human element contrasts with the right side of the photo: the statue is of an elongated human figure with its arms held straight beside its body, creating an elongated and airy atmosphere. The suitcase held by the statue itself seems to point back towards the man and in fact the man almost seems to be touching this suitcase.

2. Are there parallels within the image and if so what does this contribute to cohesion?

The photo achieves cohesion through the motif of the suitcase, which is repeated in the hands of the statue and on the ground beside the figure. This repetition provides a link between the two figures and also between the two sides of the picture. The suitcase in the foreground also contains a strong horizontal line along its top edge, which is paralleled by the man's arm. Horizontals also occur in the edges of the steps behind the statue on the left-hand side of the picture.

3. How are the elements in the image positioned to relate to each other?

The vector created by the man's left arm seems to point to the statue over his left shoulder, thus connecting the two elements. Furthermore, the two sides are related through the strong vertical bands on the man's large suitcase, which echo verticals of the statue, the edges of its suitcase, the metal stake and the trees. In contrast to these predominantly straight lines, the mountain in the background supplies a curve which frames the photo by creating a backdrop for the figures, human and inanimate, and encloses the two contrasting areas of darkness and airiness.

6.4.3 Verbal analysis: Text 2

The photograph is accompanied by (or accompanies) a caption, a headline, a sub-heading, and an eight-paragraph text. We will once again focus only on the first three sections and not analyze the actual story. We gain the needed information from the headline, the sub-heading and the caption (Texts A, B, C).

A (headline)
No nudity please, I'm British Colombian

(Note: The headline is a humorous reference to a long-running British theatrical show called *No Sex, Please, We're British.*)

B (sub-heading)
Penticton mayor says he was 'duped' by art committee over naked statue.

C (caption)
Curtis Collins, director of the Art Gallery of the South Okanagan and member of Penticton's public art committee, says he never hid from the city the fact that the statue would be naked.

Ideational meanings

It is interesting that most of the processes are verbal or mental and relational: 'says' (2) is a verbal process, 'was duped' is mental reaction; 'I am' and 'statue would be' are relational. This is not a story about actions, but about who said what to whom, and who was responsible for the naked statue being erected in a traffic circle in a small city in the interior of a large province: British Columbia. The participants are identified through relational processes; but what they are quoted as saying is the crucial element.

Interpersonal meanings

Interpersonally, the most obvious attitudinal meaning comes across in the word 'duped' and the title itself, playing on the title of a popular British show. The stance of the journalist is obvious from these choices; he tells the story with his tongue firmly in his cheek.

Textual meanings

Textually, the basic aspects of the story are clearly defined by the collocational sets 'nudity', 'naked', 'naked statue'; and 'art committee', 'art gallery' and 'statue'. It is evident that this is a story about a statue selected by an art committee, and that the furore is about the fact that the statue is naked.

Application

Although we have carried out only a very brief analysis of the verbal text, we can begin to consider the roles of the verbal and the visual by answering the following questions. Answer each question on your own in writing. Then compare your answers with others in the class.

1. What is the role of each verbal text in relation to that of the visual one?
2. Are all the verbal texts necessary to understand the visual one?
3. Has your understanding of the visual meanings changed now that you have read the verbal texts? In what ways?
4. On his website (http://michaelhermesh.com), the artist said this about his statue: 'It's about man and baggage, there's no other things in between those… In one hand, he's carrying the actual physical baggage that slows people down. In the other hand, he's carrying internal baggage.' Can you now explain why the photographer posed Curtis Collins with a suitcase?
5. Did you need the artist's statement as well as the verbal texts to properly understand the second-order connotational meaning of the photo?

CDA questions

The furore about the statue in the small city of Penticton is about nudity. The mixed reaction to the statue tells us something about the cultural values of the viewers.

1. Do you share the negative reactions to the nudity of the statue? If so, why? If not, why not?
2. Do you think the issue is a serious one? What are its serious and humorous sides?
3. What is the position of the journalist towards this story? How do you know? Could the journalist have taken another position towards the story? If so, what could it have been? Do you think his position represents the mainstream one or not?
4. The interpretation of this story and the side that we take '…depends critically on where we situate ourselves among the discourse viewpoints of our community' Lemke (1995: 55). Based on that view, how would you answer the following questions:

    a. What kinds of sub-communities would be against
        the nudity?
    b. What are the interests of these communities?
    c. What kind of people would find the nudity acceptable?
    d. What kind would not? (Adapted from Lemke, ibid: 57)

Our next set of examples is drawn from two university websites, in particular from their sections for prospective students. The focus will again be on developing analytical expertise of the visual as well as the verbal.

Photos and pictorial depictions in newspapers, as we have seen, provide actual information. On websites, however, visual elements often do not so much tell us something as create an ambiance; the visuals are not there for the sake of adding information, unlike newspaper photos. Nevertheless, it is important to begin to understand how this ambiance is created and what other purposes are served by the visual components. The analyses will extend your ability to discover how each mode contributes to your understanding of different multimodal sites.

Text 3: McGill University website   6.5

Image 6.3: McGill University website (Photo: Marci Denesiuk)

6.5.1   Visual analysis: Text 3

Representational meaning

We will begin our analysis based on O'Toole's categories from Section 1 of this chapter. We will focus on the relevant elements listed under each metafunctional category, and thus provide extended definitions and explanations as well as new analytical tools.

Let's begin with O'Toole's 'narrative theme', which refers to what is going on in a photo such as the one on the McGill website. It is similar to asking what the events are, what is happening, who is involved and where the event takes place. This narrative theme is close to what Kress and van Leeuwen describe as narrative patterns, which they define below and contrast with conceptual patterns.

Kress and van Leeuwen say the following about both types of patterns:

> When participants are connected by a vector, they are presented as *doing* something to or for each other. From here on we shall call such vectorial patterns *narrative* ... and contrast them to *conceptual*. When conceptual patterns represent participants in terms of their class, structure or meaning, in other words in terms of their generalized and more or less stable and timeless essence, narrative patterns serve to present unfolding actions and events, processes of change... The hallmark of the visual 'proposition' is the presence of the vector: narrative structures always have one, conceptual structures never do. (1996: 56–57)

The photo seems to be a combination of narrative and conceptual patterns: some elements suggest a conceptual timeless construct and others a pattern of activities. The foreground is taken up with a tree in bloom, adding to the overall feeling of wellbeing in the photo. The tree is a static entity, as is the building framed by the tree, providing a sense of timeless essence. But this is in contrast to the happenings involving students who are interacting with each other, talking, gesticulating or reading. So there is a combination of narrative and conceptual patterns in the photo. The narrative shows vectors connecting students who are talking to each other or reading. These vectorial patterns are of course missing from the conceptual patterns created by the tree and the building.

We can see another way to analyze the visual elements by looking at a short section of Teo's analysis of posters in Singapore.

Teo, in his visual analysis of posters in Singapore, carries out a full ideational analysis (representational in O'Toole's terms).

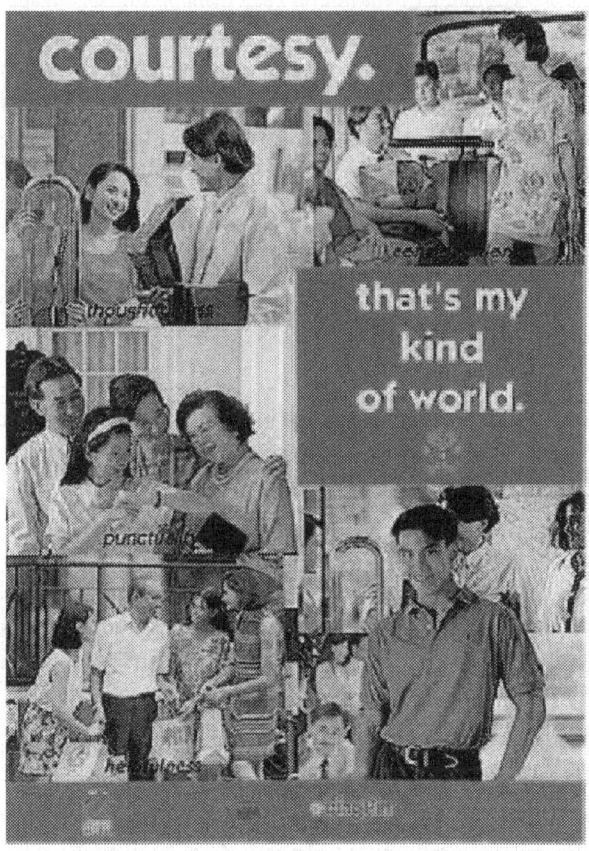

Example of a
visual analysis

Image 6.4: Poster (Courtesy of Singapore Kindness Movement)

Read the following example of an ideational analysis of a poster.

> Turning now to the ideational meaning of the poster, we observe that, unlike the two previous posters examined, the Courtesy poster is a snapshot or, more accurately, a montage of four snapshots, depicting various 'happenings' located in various settings. For the sake of convenience, I

shall refer to these individual snapshots by the 'captions' which appear at the bottom of the images. Moving anti-clockwise from the top right-hand corner, we have, firstly, the 'consideration' scene which shows a seated man in a bus pointing ('Material' process) to a vacant seat next to him, presumably inviting ('Material') a lady who is standing to have the seat. The 'thoughtfulness' scene depicts what looks like an office setting where a lady is smiling ('Behavioural') at a man, presumably in appreciation for helping ('Material') her with some files. The 'punctuality' scene portrays what one can only presume to be a family, comprising grandmother, parents and daughter, who is looking ('Mental') and smiling ('Behavioural') at a watch on her wrist. The fourth scene, entitled 'helpfulness', depicts three ladies who seem to be helping ('Material') an elderly man with some bags. (2004: 204)

Going back to the pictorial depiction in the McGill website we can now look at modal meanings.

Modal meanings

Refer to the McGill image again. The viewers of the scene can easily see the people in the photo, but the most prominent element is the tree in the foreground; people are backgrounded, as is the building. The tree is more prominent.

In the second column of O'Toole's chart, there are particularly relevant elements: gaze, perspective or angle, and rhythm. It is immediately evident that the students are gazing, not out at the viewers, but rather at each other. The perspective of the photo is such that we as viewers are on the outside looking in, as it were, at students interacting with seeming ease and a relaxed attitude. On the other hand, they face away from the viewer, which creates a distancing effect. So in one sense, there are conflicting messages, reinforced by the angle of the photo which places the students above the viewer. Kress, Leite-Garcia and van Leeuwen suggest that 'Relations of power are coded by the position of the viewer in vertical relation to the object; if the object is more powerful we look up to it, if we are more powerful we look down on it…' (1997: 276).

It is possible that the students in the photo, by virtue of attending a prestigious university, attain and carry with them a certain power, especially in relation to prospective students, who would naturally look up to them.

Looking further at the photo, its rhythm is constructed by the repeated interactions of small groups of people. The repetition seems designed to illustrate how casual social interaction is at McGill, evidenced by students meeting and chatting outside a building that is probably the library.

Since sites such as these are intended to attract prospective students, it is not surprising to find elements that will attract these students. Whether they do so ultimately rests with the verbal as well as the visual meanings conveyed, but it seems certain that showing the students seated, standing, and interacting with each other is designed to portray a positive image of students at McGill.

This website is, after all, an extended form of advertising; it is not only about conveying information, but about persuading viewers of the value of McGill. This it does through the photo, showing the ease of contact and the position of power of its participants, placed above the viewer. Both are designed to convince students to investigate the McGill website further. It is another example of strategic discourse.

Compositional meanings

The photo achieves cohesion in ways similar to the cohesive elements in verbal texts. We focus on how the parts are linked to each other to connect different elements in the photo. The difference here is that we analyze compositional meanings in terms of what O'Toole calls parallelism and gestalt. The latter is formed by elements such as framing, horizontals, verticals and diagonals.

The most salient object in the photo is, of course, the tree, whose vectors frame a part of the building and draw our eye to the section within the V shape. It also serves to focus on the separate groups interacting and converging around the V, further connecting different parts of the image to each other. This recurrence of the groups within and on either side of the V creates a parallelism between groups, which ties them to each other in different parts of the photo.

In terms of the gestalt of the photo, the tree serves to frame the photo, dividing the groups into two sets; the building forms the backdrop in the photo, cutting off anything behind the library, further framing the interactions of students in a defined space. In addition, the tree provides the vertical, and the building and the wall the horizontal, boundaries for the photo. Cohesion is therefore achieved through similar means to those we see in verbal texts, the difference being that visually it is through means such as parallelism and gestalt.

Coherence seems to centre around the building in the photo. The image serves to tell us that libraries take on a particular importance as the place where students gather, study, read and discuss, as well as socialize, in a university. The connection with the building is to the outside world of the viewers and not among the elements of the photo itself.

6.5.2 Verbal analysis: Text 3

Accompanying the photo is the verbal text that adds to and reinforces messages in the visual. There are several different texts on the website; we will focus only on the section immediately below the photo after the caption.

We will carry out a brief metafunctional analysis of the verbal text so that we can compare the information conveyed in the two modes and see the relations between the two meaning-making modalities. The analysis will be brief, because by this time you are familiar with metafunctional discussions and descriptions of verbal modes of communication.

Ideational meanings

In terms of ideational meanings, of immediate note is the thematic patterning established by the choice of participants in first position. These Topical Themes have been bolded in the text below. Not surprisingly, the Topical Theme positions (also of course a matter of textual considerations) are filled by the unique characteristics of McGill University.

Welcome to McGill.

Why do students from over 150 countries come to McGill?

- **Our reputation** is built on strong academics. **McGill's 21 faculties and professional schools** offer programs in some 300 areas of study.

- **Our outstanding faculty** bring the latest research directly to their students.

- **Our Montreal setting** has it all. Lively and cosmopolitan, **Montreal**'s the second-largest French-speaking city in the world. Although **McGill** is an English university, **over 20% of our students** are francophone.

- **The name McGill** sparks recognition worldwide and **our graduates** are prominent in every field of endeavour.

- **Our active alumni network** provides graduates with contacts around the globe.

(Copyright McGill University)

1. As you go through the text, fill in the chart below the processes with which the above participants – animate and inanimate – are involved. These, combined with participants, contribute to what Lemke calls 'thematic formations' which are patterns of representational meanings. You have carried out this kind of analysis many times before as you considered who was doing what to whom in what circumstances, all ideational considerations.

Practice

Reputation	
McGill's faculties and professional schools	
Outstanding faculty	
Latest research	
(to) students	
Montreal setting	
Montreal	
McGill	
The name McGill	
Our graduates	
Our active alumni network	

2. Once you have identified the processes, suggest a rationale for these choices.

3. Are they congruent with the purpose of the verbal text? If so, how? If not, why not?

Interpersonal meanings

This small text begins with two particularly interesting choices.

The first is the 'welcome' in the imperative form followed by the rhetorical question. Of more than 10 websites we examined, only McGill explicitly welcomes viewers to its site. The purpose seems to be to establish connections with the viewers – potential students. The welcome is designed as a direct form of address to make viewers feel that McGill does in fact want them and is directing its information to them.

The rhetorical question that follows the welcome is used to get viewers' attention; a question is asked but viewers know that they are not supposed to answer it, although they can mentally suggest some answers. The question is there rather to focus attention on why students from around the world come to McGill, information provided in the form of bullets to make it even clearer.

Interestingly, there is no marked modality here. Every statement occurs in the simple present tense without any modalizing, which gives the text an air of sureness, of '… what is real in the world' (Teo, 2004: 204). In other words, there is no question of probability, only of certainty about its message.

Textual meanings

As you read through the text a few times you will notice two particularly prominent choices. One is repetition, and the other is an especially congruent collocational set, given the purpose of the text on this kind of website.

---

1. List the repeated words or phrases. Discuss possible reason(s) for these repeated lexical items.
2. List of the lexical items that together form the most prominent collocational set in the piece. Check your list with others in the class. Are there differences between your list and theirs? What other selections might have been made and could be included in your collocational set?

Discussion

3. What textual purpose does the collocational set serve? What ideational purpose does it serve? Discuss your answers.

Application

Although we have only carried out a very brief analysis of the verbal text, your experience in analyzing texts in this chapter gives you the expertise to examine the relationship between the visual and the verbal modes of meanings. Answer the following questions. (If you have trouble answering a question, refer back to the analyses of the photo stories in the newspapers and our answers there.)

1. Is the information redundant in each mode or is it new or different from the message being conveyed in the other mode?
2. Does the verbal message reinforce the visual one or vice versa, or does it offer contrasting information?
3. Who or what are the most prominent participants in each of the modes?
4. Are the process types similar or different in the verbal and visual modes?
5. What relationships do the verbal and visual modes seek to establish with their viewers?
6. Write a short paragraph based on your answers to 1–5, in which you discuss what each mode has contributed to your impression, and your evaluation of this website.

Once you have written your answers, compare them with other members of the class. Pay particular attention to the points of difference and similarity in your answers and those of others.

CDA questions

We have not yet explored the critical perspectives in these visual and verbal texts, but we can now begin to reflect on the findings of the analyses and discuss why choices were made and how they may have been influenced by ideological purposes.

To do so we raise questions similar to ones you have considered before, but now your answers will be more complete because of your experience with visual and verbal modes.

On the basis of your general knowledge about websites such as the one we have examined, it should be evident that each university in its 'Prospective Students' sections emphasizes those aspects that each considers core to its values and attractive to students. As you answer the following questions, consider the messages conveyed in terms of the social forces behind the choices.

1. Given what you now know of the visual and verbal modes, what relationships does each mode seek to establish with the viewers in the website we have analyzed?
2. What does the website for prospective students from McGill suggest about universities in our society? What are the dominant cultural values inherent in this website? And are they evident in each of the modes? To answer this question you may want to reconsider Fairclough's view on ads, which we discussed in Chapter 4 in relation to how advertisers seek to build relations with consumers, build images and build the consumer.
3. One of the contrasts you may have identified in the Application section above is that the main participants in the visual and verbal modes are somewhat different. How would you account for the difference? What ideological decisions might have resulted in these differences in each mode?
4. An obvious follow-up question is to ask who each mode is directed at. If the participants are different in the different modes then there may also have been different viewers at whom the messages were directed.
5. Have the combined analyses of the two semiotic codes provided you with further insights? If so, describe how.

6.6   Text 4: Columbia University website

Image 6.5 A (left) and B (right): Columbia University website for prospective students (Photo: Arjun Mehra/Columbia University Digital Knowledge Ventures)

Let's begin our representational analysis by asking some questions that differentiate this visual from the one we have just been analyzing – in fact, there are two separate visual semiotic messages here. For the purpose of our discussion, we will label the Image A on the left and Image B, on the right. We will deal with them separately first. Then we will talk about the possible relationships and connections between the two.

We begin with Image A. Let's focus our attention on the image through questions adapted from Jay Lemke's list for multimodal semiotic analysis to complement O'Toole's approach. As we have seen in our work with the second newspaper story and photo, these questions provide another way to carry out a metafunctional analysis.

6.6.1   Visual analysis: Text 4

For further practice with visual analysis we offer the following sets of questions on each of the metafunctional components of visual analysis.

Representational meanings

The first set of questions is on representational meanings. Look at Image A and answer the following questions.

1. How would you describe the content of the image? Are there participants? Are there any happenings in the image as a whole?
2. What happenings occur within the newspaper image itself?
3. What actors and processes are represented?
4. Are the actors animate beings or objects?
5. What are the concrete entities evident?
6. Where is the image set? That is, what are the circumstances of and within this image?

Now answer the same questions regarding Image B.

Modal meanings

The second set of questions is on modal meanings. Look at images A and B and answer the following questions.

1. How does each of the images position the reader in terms of intimacy or distance?
2. How does the creator express his or her attitudes in relation to the following features: repetition of items in the images, the relative prominence or scale of these items, and centrality of aspects of the image?
3. What is the stance of the creator of the images?
4. Who is the intended viewer and how do we know this from the features that appeal to or are aimed at a particular type or category of viewer?
5. Is there a shift or difference in presentational content between the two images?

Compositional meanings

The third set of questions is on compositional meanings. To answer the questions below, look at images A and B again. Answer the set of questions for each image first before comparing them. Then discuss your responses with others. Together with one other student, write your analytical explanations of the compositional meanings of both of the images.

1. What is/are the most salient visual element(s) in each image? One way to get at this answer is to think about where your eye is drawn to first. Lemke suggests also that there are pathways or vectors that lead to these elements.
2. Looking at O'Toole's chart, how is the gestalt – the overall structure leading to a sense of wholeness – achieved?
3. Are there parallels within each image? If so, what do they contribute to cohesion?
4. How are the elements in each image positioned to relate to each other?
5. Do any elements in the images rely for interpretation on the context in which they occur? Which ones?
6. How does this connection add coherence for you as the viewer?

Our findings

This section is designed to give you an idea of how you might present and write up the findings of your analysis.

We have analyzed each of the functional elements to identify the ways in which each set of meanings is made. The question now to consider is how each connects to others in the images. Looking at Representational, Modal and Compositional meanings individually is necessary to begin to understand how these elements are responsible for different meanings. Putting them together then reveals how each contributes to the overall message of the visuals.

Representationally, we identified the main objects in the images, focusing on the content of the images. Looking first at Image A we saw that the photos as well as the hands provided the only animacy of the images with no actors or processes evident. Even the gaze in the photos is not directed at the viewers. Furthermore, there is no connection of participants by vectors so there are no narrative patterns in Kress and van Leeuwen's terms. This seemed to lead to a distancing effect, but when we examined the Modal meanings we found this countered by the photos under the heading of 'orientation'. The photos, caricatures of students going to or through orientation, are designed to appeal to student viewers, thus establishing a relationship that counters the distancing of the representational meanings. Also, in terms of modal meanings, there is a shift in perspective and stance when we turn to the image on the right, in which the sole focus is on the seats in a lecture hall. This shift takes on textual and compositional meanings as well. Through the choice of placement on the left the creator assumes the student viewers are familiar with university orientation programs; they further understand that as the new students they may feel awkward, as do those in the stylized pictures. But the image on the right is the new information, namely that the central part of learning takes place in lecture halls, thus shifting the creator's stance from light to serious.

Both images rely for their interpretation on the connections they establish with their viewers. Coherence relies on students knowing that orientations take place at universities and that they will be expected to participate in orientation activities. By the same token, they know that lecture halls play a central role.

Even this brief discussion illustrates the necessity of carrying out a thorough analysis before you can begin to interpret choices that have been made.

6.6.2   Verbal analysis: Text 4

As you will notice from the website, we have once again selected only the small verbal text which follows the visual depiction under the title of 'Prospective Students'.

> From a one-room classroom with one professor and eight students, Columbia University has grown to include more than 4,000 faculty members and 23,000 students. Over the years, 64 of Columbia's graduates and faculty have received the Nobel Prize. Today Columbia is what President Lee Bollinger has called 'the quintessential great urban university' – attracting students and faculty from 150 countries to engage with each other and with the cultural, scientific, and business enterprises that make New York City one of the most exciting cities in the world.

© Columbia University

Our findings

Ideationally, not surprisingly, the main participants are similar to those of McGill, namely, faculty members, graduates and students. But contrary to the previous website text, there are in fact very few actual activities presented that do not occur in unembedded clauses. Only three do: 'include', 'have received' and 'is'. The first and the last are relational processes; the one material process places the graduates in a position of 'receiving' (a rather weaker form of achieving, obtaining etc...) the very impressive Nobel Prize. The other verbal groups are in the heavily embedded clause beginning with 'attracting'. The emphasis here seems to be on both size – with the growth from 1 to 4,000 professors over time – and the impressive prizes won by graduates. Only one actual person is identified: the President, Lee Bolinger. But the focus is primarily on Columbia's history.

The focus on size seems further reinforced through the use of the phrase with which this text opens: 'one-room classroom', in direct contrast to the image of the lecture hall in the photo, emphasizing the size of classes and the number of students who now attend Columbia. Is the contrast intentional, to emphasize the growth of the university? We cannot know for sure, but the connection between these two elements is certainly suggested. In terms of content, the focus is on growth and stature, maintaining a kind of consistency between the visual and verbal modes of meaning, with underlying timelessness and the essential nature of the university emphasized in the content of each mode.

Interpersonally, there are very few of the interactive elements that we saw in the McGill website. Mood variation is not evident, nor is any marked modality; in fact, very little indicates the attitude or stance of the writer of this text. It seems that interpersonally, there is a kind of distancing taking place here, similar to what we saw in the visuals. No interactive elements are visible. No potential student is addressed directly; the only individual named is the President, who, by virtue of his position, is very much removed from the prospective students. With such combined and persistent patterns of distancing, one wonders if this section is directed at the parents rather than at potential students, and whether it aims to impress rather than to establish contact or connection with a student viewer.

Textually, the thematic resources reinforce the focus on the process of growth of the university. You may notice the emphasis on circumstances in this text. Each sentence begins with a topical element realized not by participants but by circumstances: 'from a one-room classroom', 'over the years' and 'today'.

Now that you have analyzed two websites, you will be able to respond to the questions which follow, focusing on critical dimensions of the choices you have identified.

1. Are the cultural assumptions inherent in the visual and verbal modes the same?
2. Is there any difference in those assumptions from those of McGill? That is, how does Columbia visually and verbally present itself to students, compared to McGill?
3. What are the dominant cultural values inherent in this website?
4. Are the main participants in the visual and verbal modes the same or different?
5. How would you compare the verbal and visual messages of both websites in terms of their central messages? That is, who are they appealing to and why?
6. What are the ideological assumptions of each of the websites? How do they resemble or differ from each other?

Critical discourse analysis

You have by now carried out a number of critical analyses. Comment on the two statements below: the first by two well-known researchers on multimodal analysis who we have quoted throughout this chapter, Kress and van Leeuwen (1996: 45); the second from a researcher who has analyzed photos in depth.

> Pictorial structures do not simply reproduce the structures of 'reality'. On the contrary, they **produce** images of reality, which are bound up with interests of the social institutions within which the pictures are produced, circulated and read. They are ideological.

1. Review your work in this chapter on critical discourse analysis. Respond to the above statement with 1–2 pages of your own explanations in relation to the photo stories as well as the multi-modal messages in the websites in this chapter.

The second statement comes from a discourse analyst, Michael Shapiro, who says that if we want to understand the importance of photographs we need to look at them:

…on the basis of their tendency to either reproduce dominant forms of discourse, which help circulate the existing system of power, authority and exchange or to look at them on the basis of their tendency to provoke critical analysis, to denaturalize what is unproblematically accepted… (1988: 130)

2. Do you think that in Shapiro's terms, the photos in the stories and the pictorial representations in the websites we have examined reproduce or challenge existing systems of power and authority? Respond to this question in a page or two.

Chapter 6 Glossary

Conceptual representation: Kress and van Leeuwen's term for representing participants not in terms of their actions but in terms of their class or structure, emphasizing their essence.

Compositional meanings: O'Toole's term for textual meanings in visual depiction; focus is on overall composition of picture.

Modal meanings: O'Toole's term for interpersonal meanings in visual depiction; focus is on ways in which elements of the picture interact with the viewer.

Mode of communication: A means by which we exchange meanings; this can be done through language or pictures or gesture or other symbolic means. Each means is a mode of communication.

Multimodal analysis: an approach to analysis that analyzes visual as well as verbal means of communication.

Narrative pattern: Kress and van Leeuwen's term for representing actions and events and processes of change. This is in contrast to conceptual representation above.

Narrative theme: O'Toole's term for what is happening or the story being told in the picture. This is one of the elements of his analysis.

Semiotics: Semiotics refers (in a somewhat oversimplified definition) to the signs that we make and through which we exchange meanings. We can do so through language, drawing, through signs on doors such as the sign of a line through a cigarette to indicate 'No smoking'. Each means is a mode of communication, a type of sign-making through which we exchange meanings.

Visual communication

Kress, G. and van Leeuwen, T. (1996) *Reading Images: the grammar of visual design*. This book is central in the literature on the analysis of visual communication. Especially relevant to our discussions in this chapter is their Chapter 1, in which they set out the relationship between verbal and visual modes of meaning.

Lemke, J. (1998) *Reading Science Critical and Functional Perspectives on Discourses of Science*. The chapter 'Multiplying meaning: visual and verbal semiotics in scientific text' sets out the basic descriptions of the metafunctional components in relation to visual communication. In this chapter Lemke explores the different ways in which visual means of communication contribute to overall meanings in particular in scientific texts.

Jay Lemke on his website extends his discussion of analysis of visual means of communication (http://www-personal.umich.edu/~jaylemke/mxm.htm). For a metafunctional analysis of visual modes of communication go to http://www-personal.umich.edu/~jaylemke/guides/multimedia_semiotic_analysis_questions.htm. This page on multimodal meanings is particularly useful; Lemke provides a very thorough and useful set of questions as guidelines for visual analysis.

Shapiro, M. (1988) *The Politics of Representation: writing practices in biography, photography and policy analysis*. The chapter 'Political rhetoric of photography' provides a different but related methodology for analysis. Although Shapiro's focus is on photography, his methodology and insights are very useful in the approach we have outlined in this chapter.

Chapter 6
Further readings

Chapter 7 contents

Spoken language and power

We have been examining a wide variety of discourse types throughout this book. In Chapter 6 we also looked at the connections between visual and verbal means of communication. In this chapter we will look at different forms of dialogic discourse: informal conversation, a media interview, and two types of oral courtroom discourse. Each discourse is unscripted; the transcripts of the conversations and interviews are written after the fact. Each of the texts began as unscripted, although not always unplanned, exchanges, particularly in the case of the courtroom samples. While unscripted, these courtroom discourses take place in a predetermined framework in which lawyers and judges question witnesses, or potential jurors. Although there is a ritual form to these courtroom conversations, each of the samples we will be examining consists of spontaneous or semi-spontaneous utterances.

We will also look at the bi-directional influence of context on discourse in a variety of situations. Our main concern is with the nature of the registers – varieties of language – that emerge in situations in which the spoken mode predominates. We are interested in discovering how language and power interact in conversations, in interviews, and in courtroom exchanges. The purpose is to show, as we have done in other chapters, the interplay between discursive choices and power. The additional focus here is on how registerial constructs influence this relationship, especially in terms of Textual and Interpersonal choices. In terms of the latter we will introduce Appraisal Theory, a recent development within SFL.

We will continue to carry out analyses within the SFL model because it allows us to identify both the discursive patterns in different varieties of spoken interaction and the contextual constructs that influence these patterns.

7.2   Context of situation

We begin with a discussion of the constructs that together inform situations and influence language. We then go on to examine the way this influence plays out in discursive choices in each of the samples of spoken discourse that constitute our data.

The idea of context of situation originated, not from a linguist but from an anthropologist, Branislaw Malinowski, who many years ago carried out anthropological studies of Trobriand Islanders. In the course of his studies of their language and habits, he came to realize that without knowing the context in which the language he was describing took place, what they were saying meant little. He said that: '… a word without linguistic context is a mere fragment and stands for nothing by itself, so in reality of a spoken living tongue, the utterance has no meaning except in the context of situation' (1946: 307, as quoted in Eggins, 1994: 51).

Over the years a linguist named J. R. Firth extended this idea of context in terms of the predictability of language in different contexts (Eggins, ibid: 52). After Firth's extension, Halliday and others developed the theory further into what has come to be known as register theory.

Register refers to a variety of language which varies according to use in different situations. The situation itself consists of three constructs:

1) **Field** accounts for what language is being used to talk about, accounting for the content of what is being said in different contexts;

2) **Tenor** explains the types of interactions between interactants carried out through language in the situation;

3) **Mode** has to do with the nature of language itself, whether it is spoken or written, or spontaneous, or planned discourse. Each mode – spoken or written – and its sub-categories has certain characteristics that determine discursive choices in different situations.

When we examine these three constructs we can begin to see what influences the actual choices evident in a particular language event, and how each of these selections in turn reflects and influences each context. The concern is not with just any features of a situation, but only with those that are relevant to discursive choices. The correspondence between the situation or context of a language event and the linguistic choices are outlined below:

Contextual or situational constructs	Language choices: semantic level	Language choices: lexicogrammatical level
Field →	← Ideational →	Transitivity
Tenor →	← Interpersonal →	Mood, modality and attitudinal elements
Mode →	← Textual →	Theme, cohesion and coherence

The Field of discourse is realized in the Ideational choices of processes, participants and circumstances; the Tenor, accounting for the role relationships between interactants, is found in Interpersonal meanings expressed through Mood, attitudinal and modality choices; and Mode, accounting for whether the interaction is spoken or written, influences Textual selections through cohesion, coherence and theme/rheme patterns. However, these language choices not only reflect but also influence the situation. The concept of register, then, is bi-directional, with influence shifting back and forth between the situation in which the language event occurs and the language choices themselves.

Views from the theorists:
Eggins

An explanation of
Halliday's position on
register constructs

A very succinct overview of registerial constructs is provided below in Eggin's explanation of Halliday's theory of the registerial constructs:

> Thus, the claim Halliday makes is that each type of meaning is related in a predictable, systematic way to each situational variable. It is therefore no accident that we single out the three register variables of field, mode and tenor as the aspects of the situation significant to language use. Their status derives from the fact that they are linked to the three types of meaning language is structured to make: the experiential (or in our terms the ideational) the textual and the interpersonal. We can see that language is structured to make these three kinds of meanings because we find in the lexico-grammar the three main grammatical resources of Transitivity, Theme and Mood. (Eggins, 1994: 78)

As we analyze each of the texts of this chapter we will get a much clearer idea of the role of register in the discursive choices in each type of spoken interaction outlined below.

We will:

1) analyze two conversations among graduate students, focusing on the influence primarily of Tenor in terms of Appraisal Theory, which provides an extended framework for the analysis of Interpersonal meanings.
2) examine another casual conversation among friends discussing citizenship and private education. In this section we will also use Appraisal Theory to examine valuation going on in the conversation. As well, we will focus on the role of Mood choices.
3) study Mood as well as modality in the third text – an interview of Tony Blair – looking at how Tenor influences specific Interpersonal choices. At issue here is the exertion of discursive power by the interviewer, who challenges not only the power of the Prime Minister but also the PM's knowledge.
4) look at another type of spoken interaction: that of the courtroom. We will study the influence of situation on discursive choices in terms of persistent control exerted through questioning by lawyers of a witness in one case, and of a potential juror in the other case. The power exerted is particularly evident in terms of Tenor and Mode.

The first transcript is of a dinner table conversation, one of several verbal interactions by graduate students who taped a long series of such conversations as part of a project for a course they were taking.

1	Kevin:	So is America a symbol of a gatekeeping country?
2	Dayna:	I don't know – when we talked about it, it seemed to make sense.
3	Lynne:	You know, to me it almost seems opposite – for the fact that, isn't that what the whole American Revolution was about?
4	Kevin:	Keeping people out?
5	Lynne:	No, I mean getting away from the gatekeeping, rules, regulations, and being free?
6	Mary:	In a way; England wanted to impose restrictions on America that many felt were unfair such as taxation without representation.
7	Kevin:	So, is America a gatekeeping country now, or is it an open-gate country?
8	Mary:	Well, according to Jeff Smith, we definitely have gates to go through. We can't avoid it. For example, Doctor Brooks, how many 'gates' did you have to enter to be a doctor? We can't be doctors.
9	Kevin:	You can if you go through the same gates as I did. I'm going through many gates; factor in the INS (Immigration and Naturalization Service).
10	Mary:	There you go!
11	Dayna:	Are you becoming an American citizen?
12	Kevin:	No, I'm on my two-year probationary status. That means that because I married an American, they want to give us two years to see if I really want to apply for citizenship.
13	Dayna:	They want to see if you're really married.
14	Mary:	Do you want to become a U.S. citizen?
15	Kevin:	I had no intentions of changing citizenship because the U.S. requires you to give up your other citizenship – there's an example of Americanism and gatekeeping because many countries allow you to have both citizenships.

http://www.ndsu.nodak.edu/ndsu/kbrooks/MVE/transcripts/americana.html
(Accessed September 2005)

7.3.1   Analysis: Text 1: Casual conversation

In the first excerpt, the background to the discussion is provided as the group decides what to talk about and why. We will carry out a brief registerial analysis of the background discourse for you and then ask you to do the same for the actual sample discourse which follows; this will allow you to investigate the language choices that result from the situational constructs.

Looking at the background discourse in terms of these constructs, those factors that are directly relevant to linguistic choices; we will consider the questions which help us identify each of them. These questions focus on the different aspects of the discourse that identify and reflect the context of the discourse. Our questions are adapted from Butt et al. (2000: 185).

In order to identify the field of discourse, we consider the following two questions:

1) What activity is taking place?
2) How do we know this? Another way to put this is to ask what is there in the discourse that tells us this?

To discover the answers to these questions, we examine the discourse itself in terms of Ideational choices of processes, participants and circumstances. That is, to understand the activity here, constituted by talk, we look at who is doing what to whom, where and when and how. The field of discourse concerns gatekeeping and citizenship. Carrying out a very brief Ideational analysis we would come up with a list of processes which are mainly Relational, appropriate to the situation in which terms and concepts are being identified and explained. The participants are graduate students. In terms of circumstances, we do not know where this conversation takes place, nor when. But because of the nature of the activity it is not important.

In fact, once we have identified the topic of the conversation, which here conflates with the field (because the whole of the activity consists of talk about citizenship), we can then move on to the second construct, Tenor.

This type of casual verbal encounter, like the next conversation we will be looking at, often occurs just to establish and maintain social relations between people. Of particular importance are the relationships between participants which we examine in terms of the following questions:

3) What is the relationship between the interactants in the conversation?
4) Is there a social distance between them or not?
5) Is the relationship between them equal or not?
6) How do you know from examining the discourse?
7) How are items appraised? Positively or negatively?
8) Are there appraised motifs running through the discourse? How do you know? What is there in the discourse that tells you so?

To answer questions 3–6 we begin by examining Mood choices. If we look at the utterances, we see an almost even mixture of questions and responses; that is, people are equally engaged in asking and answering questions.

This equal distribution of questions and answers is one indication that the relationship between the interactants seems to be an equal one. If one person asks all of the questions, this might indicate an inequality because one who asks is usually in a position to expect answers, indicating a powerful position, as we see later in the chapter. But here each participant asks or answers in about the same proportion – there is a balance among all of the interactants in general, which you can see by looking back at the sample again. Kevin, the only male in this segment of the conversation, seems to speak more than anyone else, with Mary coming behind – however, we would have to study the whole discourse over a period of days to see if that was a pattern that indicated power being exerted on a consistent basis. When we encounter the next segment, the pattern is reversed and Kevin speaks the least. So, it is always a good idea not to jump to conclusions on the basis of only one short sample.

In considering appraisals of items and motifs in the discourse (questions 7 and 8), a fairly unified approach to the topics is evident. In fact, one of the ways in which we know that the relationship between the participants is an equal one, and that there is little social distance between them, is that their evaluation of the topics is similar. This suggests that they not only come from similar communities but as a result share views and appraise them similarly. We can see this in the background sample as well as the one you will be analyzing.

To fully understand how appraisals of topics occur, we will briefly expand on and exemplify the definitions presented in the chart below for the main aspects of Appraisal Theory, a new approach to the study of interpersonal relations.

Appraisal Theory

Appreciation	Affect	Judgement
Speakers' reactions to and evaluation of reality	Speakers' expression of emotional states, both positive and negative	Speakers' judgements about the ethics, morality or social values of other people

(From Eggins and Slade, 1997: 125)

Although Appraisal Theory has many sub-categories we will focus only on the 3 basic types briefly defined above. This will serve to introduce the main categories of Appraisal in this chapter.

Let's look further at each of these sub-categories of Appraisal: appreciation, affect, and judgement.

Appreciation covers the ways speakers or writers express their likes and dislikes and personal evaluations of people and events. They do so usually through either lexical choices or whole clauses. To elicit this type of appraisal we would ask: 'What do you think of X'? The focus here then is on evaluation of an item or idea. As you read the short selection below, pay particular attention first to the bolded words to get a better idea of the evaluations that are going on here.

1   Kevin: So is America a symbol of a **gatekeeping country**?

2   Dayna: I don't know – when we talked about it, *it seemed to make sense*.

3   Lynne: You know, to me it *almost seems opposite* – for the fact that, isn't that what the whole American Revolution was about?

4   Kevin: Keeping people out?

5	Lynne:	No, I mean getting away from the gatekeeping, rules, regulations, and being free?
6	Mary:	In a way; England wanted to **impose restrictions** on America that many felt were **unfair** such as taxation without representation.
7	Kevin:	So, is America a **gatekeeping country** now, or is it an **open-gate country**?
8	Mary:	Well, according to Jeff Smith, we definitely have **gates to go through**. We can't avoid it. For example, Doctor Brooks, how many 'gates' did you have to enter to be a doctor? We can't be doctors.
9	Kevin:	You can if you go through the same gates as I did. I'm going through many gates; factor in the INS.
10	Mary:	There you go!
11	Dayna:	Are you becoming an American citizen?
12	Kevin:	No, I'm on my two-year probationary status. That means that because I married an American, they want to give us two years to see if I really want to apply for citizenship.
13	Dayna:	They want to see if you're really married.
14	Mary:	Do you want to become a U.S. citizen?
15	Kevin:	I had no intentions of changing citizenship because the U.S. requires you to give up your other citizenship – there's an **example of Americanism and gatekeeping** because many countries allow you to have both citizenships.

The second form of Appraisal is called Affect, and expresses emotions and feelings. Affective appraisals are typically expressed through adjectives. If you want to elicit this type of appraisal you would ask: 'How did or do you feel about X'? What is being expressed are primarily attitudes towards some event or person or object as in: *He's **very happy** about the choices*; *he's **particularly sad** about the result*. There are no examples of Affect in this text.

The last sub-category we will deal with concerns Judgement, usually about people's behaviour in terms of social values and ethics. The question to ask in relation to Judgement is 'How would you judge that behaviour?'

'His actions were those of a *really nasty guy!*' In the sample above, early on in the discourse there are two such judgements that we have italicized, and one later in response to a statement made by Kevin, also italicized: *it seemed to make sense* and *almost seems opposite*

So, in terms of Tenor considerations, we can summarise choices through appraisals of propositions and ideas. The interactants seem to be in agreement with each other in their appraisal of the idea of gatekeeping despite the fact that at the beginning, Lynne had a different view of America. In terms of the questions posed at the beginning of our discussion, although there is a hint of negative appraisal of the idea of gatekeeping, at the end it becomes more acceptable, although still resisted by Kevin who will not seek American citizenship. Gradually, as each person gives his or her opinion, a consensus builds about the need to gatekeep, evident in their evaluations. Affective appraisals are not apparent in the above piece of discourse, perhaps because their appreciation expressed in different statements obviates the need for further evaluation. There are, however, two examples of judgements as we've seen.

Moving on to our last situational construct, Mode, we can characterize spoken discourse here with the following features:

- interactive
- two or more participants
- face to face
- in the same place at the same time
- language as action
- using language to accomplish some task
- spontaneous
- casual: informal and everyday

(Adapted from Eggins, 2004: 92)

Of course, not all the discourses in this chapter contain all of the characteristics above, but each of the samples contains more than one.

Let's examine the Mode of this discourse further in terms of the following questions:

9) Is the discourse a monologue or a dialogue?
10) Do you think it was originally spoken or written? How do you know?

11) How would you summarize the main thrust or point of the discourse? What resources in the discourse did you use to identify this?

The answer to question 9 is obvious because of the interactive nature of the sample discourse, with several people contributing comments throughout the discussion. In some cases, people do not finish their statements because they are interrupted or have questions or statements finished by other speakers, as in the exchange below:

Lynne:	You know, to me it almost seems opposite – for the fact that, isn't that what the whole American Revolution was about?
Kevin:	Keeping people out?

It seems equally obvious that this is not a script that is being read but one that was originally spoken in a face-to-face situation and that has been transcribed. We know that it was originally spoken because of features that are typically found in spoken discourse. There are two such features. First, there are Continuity adjuncts which Eggins discusses below:

> This category includes the continuative and continuity items, particularly frequent in casual talk, such as *well*, *yea*, *oh*, where these items occur to introduce a clause, and signal that a response to prior talk is about to be provided. … They merely signal that the speaker will be saying more. (2004: 164)

Views from the theorists:
Eggins

Continuity adjuncts

Also evident here are two lexical sets – one that runs through the whole of the discourse sample and another that is found at the end; the first is gatekeeping and the second, citizenship. These sets identify the main thrust of the sample. What has occurred here is the repeated use of the term 'gatekeeping'. It is an evaluative term of appreciation but its repetition influences cohesion. This is very evident in the underlined words in the excerpt below.

1	Kevin:	So is America a symbol of a <u>gatekeeping country</u>?
2	Dayna:	I don't know – when we talked about it, *it seemed to make sense*.
3	Lynne:	You know, to me it *almost seems opposite* – for the fact that, isn't that what the whole American Revolution was about?

4	Kevin:	Keeping people out?
5	Lynne:	No, I mean getting away from the <u>gatekeeping, rules, regulations</u>, and being free?
6	Mary:	In a way; England wanted to impose restrictions on America that many felt were unfair such as taxation without representation.
7	Kevin:	So, is America a <u>gatekeeping country</u> now, or is it an <u>open-gate country</u>?
8	Mary:	Well, according to Jeff Smith, we definitely have <u>gates to go through</u>. We can't avoid it. For example, Doctor Brooks, how many '<u>gates</u>' did you have to enter to be a doctor? We can't be doctors.
9	Kevin:	You can if you go through the same <u>gates</u> as I did. I'm going through many <u>gates</u>; factor in the INS.
10	Mary:	There you go!
11	Dayna:	Are you becoming an American <u>citizen</u>?
12	Kevin:	No, I'm on my two-year <u>probationary status</u>. That means that because I married an American, they want to give us two years to see if I really want to apply for <u>citizenship</u>.
13	Dayna:	They want to see if you're really married.
14	Mary:	Do you want to become a <u>U.S. citizen</u>?
15	Kevin:	I had no intentions of changing <u>citizenship</u> because the U.S. requires you to give up your other <u>citizenship</u> – there's an example of Americanism and gatekeeping because many countries allow you to have both <u>citizenships</u>.

Now that we have had an introduction to the kind of findings that registerial analysis and Appraisal Theory offer, we can begin to apply these principles to the second sample. This immediately follows the first one in the original data.

1	Dayna:	Have you ever been to a naturalization thing? I was in a choir that sang in one once in high school. We were like the special music. It was really incredible to watch all those people give up their own country. I couldn't believe it! I didn't know you had to do that. I mean this whole thing – you basically say 'I denounce my country, all of my loyalty, all of my list of seven things I put forth onto American soil, blah, blah, blah, blah.' It's pretty incredible!
2	Lynne:	Wow, that's powerful!
3	Dayna:	It was kind of – I couldn't believe we got to go there and do that. I remember looking at people who were giving it up like from England and thinking 'What are you doing?' I mean, I can understand why someone from North Korea tries to get out, but England? It was really weird!
4	Lynne:	Wow! That's amazing! What's the draw?
5	Mary:	FREEDOM! Remember Braveheart?
6	Lynne:	Oh, Canadian, Joe Canada – the job?
7	Kevin:	Yeah.
8	Lynne:	You would denounce your country because of a job?
9	Kevin:	Oh, no. I'm just saying in terms of being here. I don't know why somebody from England would necessarily take that citizenship.
10	Dayna:	You wouldn't be here now if you and Betsy wouldn't have gotten married?
11	Kevin:	Yeah, I'll be moving into my five-year period and then after that, I could apply for citizenship if I wanted to, but I don't know if I want to do that.
12	Lynne:	So you are just like a resident alien now?
13	Kevin:	You got it!

7.4.1   Analysis: Text 2: Casual conversation

Because this discourse sample is part of the same conversation as the first one, we do not have to establish further the context of situation in which this sample occurs. But we will again focus on realizations of Tenor which are particularly evident in terms of Appraisal: Appreciation and Judgement and Modality and Mood.

Discussion

1. Go through the discourse and underline the lexical and clausal elements that realize Appreciation.
2. Next, circle those elements which realize Judgement.
3. One you have completed this, discuss your choices with other members of the class. Was your categorization of Appraisal types the same as other members of your group? If not, after discussion did you agree with others or did they change their choices to agree with yours? What made you or others change their minds?
4. How did the addition of Appraisal categories augment your insights into Interpersonal meanings?

Modality

Another noticeable set of interpersonal meanings is Modality as we've seen. Before we look at the actual types that are evident in this discourse sample it may help to look over and briefly discuss different expressions of Modality. The list of possible resources is drawn from Eggins and Slade (1994: 107) in their analysis of casual conversation.

Expressions of Modality

Type	Meaning	Examples
Probability	How likely? How obvious?	May/will/must; perhaps, maybe, of course, surely I'm sure/certain; in my opinion; it is sure/certain/likely/probable (Interpersonal Metaphors)
Usuality	How often? How typical?	usually, sometimes, always, never, for the most part, seldom, often
Obligation	How required?	will/should/must; required to/permitted to
Inclination	How willing?	will; gladly, willingly, readily
Capability	How able?	can; is able to; capably, ably

On the basis of this list it will be obvious that there are two main types of modals in this conversation, with two instances of one other type.

1. Based on the list above, identify the modals and classify them into their correct categories according to the list.
2. Then outline in writing the roles these modals play in this discourse. That is, how do they express the speakers' opinions and stances toward each other and/or towards the content they are discussing? You might include in your discussion a few words about which participant modalizes propositions the most and how this helps to identify the participants' stances towards what they are saying.

Mood

Complementing these two Interpersonal choices is another which is typical of conversations: Mood variation with statements interspersed with questions which seem designed to keep the conversation going. All contribute, with Lynne asking slightly more questions than others do. We have looked elsewhere at the purpose that questions serve and talked about them as possible indicators of power. It is important to remember that context very strongly influences purpose. After reading over the conversation, it did not seem to us that the questioning was designed to indicate or exert power. Rather, in casual conversations such as this, one way those participants maintain contact throughout is to question. When questions are asked, engagement with the other is maintained.

Also of interest is how different participants further the conversation through exclamation. In this short sample three exclamations reinforce the evaluative appraisals that we have seen.

Lynne prefaces two of her evaluative comments with 'Wow!' which is of course another way in which to express appreciation. Mary's one exclamation: 'Freedom!' also serves as a commentary on the discussion – her evaluation of the topic of naturalization.

Finally, Kevin ends this sample with 'You got it!' in agreement with Lynne's comment that precedes it. The comment terminates the conversation and shows how agreements allow closure of a topic. Through talk, the participants have settled their differences of opinion and have reached a consensus that was lacking at the beginning. This is not atypical of verbal interactions; in fact, Gunther Kress, whose work we have referred to elsewhere in the book, has said that 'In dialogue the constitution of texts in and around difference is most readily apparent' (1985: 14). The participants started out with differences of opinion that became resolved through talk. Of course, this is not always the case, as we shall see in the court case sample we will analyze later. Although one of the purposes of talk is to resolve differences, this is not always accomplished.

7.5   Text 3: Casual conversation

We now move on to another sample of casual conversation to more fully explore this registerial variety.

1	Kate:	uhm, here the uh, the it is just unbelievable what it costs now Roy to send the kids
2	Steven:	It's crazy. What does the tuition depend on?
3	Anne:	twenty-five thousand
4	Roy:	About, about twenty a little over twenty thousand yeah
5	Miriam:	Can you can you get scholarships or?
6	Steven:	tuition alone?
7	Anne:	Yeah.
8	Lynne:	That's not living?
9	Miriam:	But that's a private school
10	John:	room and board
11	Kate:	That's not including room and board?
12	Steven:	…for an undergrad
13	Kate:	Oh my god so what would be the uh
14	Steven:	the…cost
15	Roy:	I don't know. So does a BMW a year
16	Kate:	a BMW a year
17	Anne and John:	(LAUGHTER)
18	Kate:	God
19	Miriam:	But that's for a private school, right that's not a…

20	Roy:	Yes…It's not high enough.
21	Anne:	Not high enough?
22	Kate:	Roy
23	Roy:	that's right
24	Debbie	(LAUGHTER)
25	Anne:	(GULP) Excuse me?
26	Kate:	It's ridiculous
27	Roy:	Today was payday
28	Kate:	It's ridiculous
29	Roy	I get paid out of this
30	Steven:	Do you think the education is worth it?
	…	
31	Roy:	What?
32	Steven:	Do you think the education is worth it?
33	Roy:	Sure
	…	
34	Roy:	As long as those people are willing to pay it why should we reduce the price?
35	Kate:	uh It just makes me mad I don't know why
36	Miriam:	mh – it makes me mad too
37	Anne:	what does one you…
38	Steven:	but that's not what I'm asking
39	Kate:	there is too much money it's just too much money
40	Roy:	That's what you get. Everything is worth exactly what people are willing to pay

(Adapted from Locher, 2004: 158ff)

7.5.1 Analysis: Text 3: Casual conversation

We will begin by looking at the context of situation and at the relevant constructs that influence the language choices: Field, Tenor and Mode.

The field of activity is constituted by a conversation among three women and two men about the cost of private education and whether it is worth this cost. The intention again seems to be to resolve the difference of opinion about the costs and value of private education. The fact that they do not resolve their differences of opinion does not detract from the activity. The conversation itself constitutes the whole of the activity occurring here; it is what brings these people together. The circumstances of this conversation are neither very apparent nor do they seem relevant. We do not know where the conversation occurs, nor other circumstances, but this does not seem in any way to constrain our understanding of the conversation. The Field of activity here is expressed mainly through Ideational choices of attributive relations. The values associated with many of the items are evaluations and as such have interpersonal implications. These selections of process types influence interpersonal as well as Ideational meanings.

Application

Moving on to expressions of the Tenor of this situation – the social relations of the participants, the attitudes towards each other and the discussion – it is evident that other interpersonal resources are in place to reinforce those we referred to above.

1. Go through the transcribed conversation which follows and underline the resources that help you to identify relationships among interactants.

1	Kate:	uhm, here the uh, the it is just unbelievable what it costs now Roy to send the kids
2	Steven:	It's crazy. What does the tuition depend on?
3	Anne:	twenty-five thousand
4	Roy:	About, about twenty a little over twenty thousand yeah
5	Miriam:	Can you can you get scholarships or?
6	Steven:	tuition alone?
7	Anne:	Yeah.
8	Lynne:	That's not living?
9	Miriam:	But that's a private school
10	John:	room and board
11	Kate:	That's not including room and board?

12	Steven:	…for an undergrad
13	Kate:	Oh my god so what would be the uh
14	Steven:	the…cost
15	Roy:	I don't know. So does a BMW a year
16	Kate:	a BMW a year
17	Anne and John:	(LAUGHTER)
18	Kate:	18.Kate: God
19	Miriam:	But that's for a private school, right that's not a…
20	Roy:	Yes…It's not high enough.
21	Anne:	Not high enough?
22	Kate:	Roy
23	Roy:	that's right
24	Debbie	(LAUGHTER)
25	Anne:	(GULP) Excuse me?
26	Kate:	It's ridiculous
27	Roy:	Today was payday
28	Kate:	It's ridiculous
29	Roy	I get paid out of this
30	Steven:	Do you think the education is worth it?
		…
31	Roy:	What?
32	Steven:	Do you think the education is worth it?
33	Roy:	Sure
		…
34	Roy:	As long as those people are willing to pay it why should we reduce the price?
35	Kate:	uh It just makes me mad I don't know why
36	Miriam:	mh – it makes me mad too
37	Anne:	what does one you…
38	Steven:	but that's not what I'm asking
39	Kate:	there is too much money it's just too much money
40	Roy:	That's what you get. Everything is worth exactly what people are willing to pay

2.   What is the relationship between the interactants in the conversation?
     a. Is there a social distance between them or not?
     b. Is the relationship between them equal or not?
     c. How do you know from examining the discourse?

3.   When you answer the next two questions you will become particularly aware of how appraisals and the appraised motifs come to be expressed through the evaluations in attributive processes. Identify these values by circling those revealing the appraisals of the different participants towards the idea of the cost of private education.
     a. How are items appraised? Positively or negatively?
     b. Are there appraised motifs running through the discourse? Again, how do you know? What is there in the discourse that tells you so?

Now, focus on Mode to get a more complete idea of the register in this conversation.

4.   a. How would you summarize the main thrust or point of this discourse?
     b. What resources in the discourse did you use to identify this?

CDA questions

You probably have noticed in working through this discourse that several questions and discursive points are raised but are not answered. Also apparent in this short sample is the fact that the difference of opinion is not resolved. Although there is cooperation in the continuance of the conversation, there is also a persistent resistance to the positions expressed by some of the interactants.

1.   Go through the sample and identify the two positions that are being contested.
2.   Identify the participants involved in each of the positions.
3.   Quote the utterances of the conversation which most succinctly express each stance.
4.   The two positions represent different values and perhaps even different sub-communities to which some of the participants

belong. Discuss the ideologies that may form the basis of each of the positions, ideologies that may have become common sense assumptions. What are the ideological bases for the differences of opinions evident in this discourse? How might they have become common sense assumptions?

We have been examining casual conversations. Now we turn to an interview, to find out how it resembles or differs from our previous free-flowing discursive samples. Interviews may be scripted or even prerecorded, but even when they are spontaneous they follow a recognized format in which the interviewer asks the questions and the interviewee answers. The interviewer is thus placed in a position of power and controls the verbal interaction.

Despite the fact then that the interview we will examine is unscripted, it is a form of semi-spontaneous discourse because it is an interview. That is, there is a sense of formality present here that was absent in the casual conversations above, and of the discoursal 'rights' and obligations' of the interview register (Fairclough, 1989: 69). Although there is no fixed sequence, the interviewer is the one who gets to pose the questions and to challenge the interviewee and so pre-determines the sequences. But it is interesting to watch how the interviewee attempts to challenge the power of the interviewer by resisting both the format and the positioning of the interviewer.

Text 4: Political interview　　7.6

BBC News' Transcript of Andrew Rawnsley's interview with the Prime Minister:

Andrew Rawnsley: Prime Minister, after nearly eight years in power, you're announcing yet another attempt to deal with asylum and immigration. Does that mean you accept that many people in Britain think that your government has lost control of the numbers of people coming in to this country?

Tony Blair: I don't think it's that, but I think that because of the nature of the world we live in to-day, you've got to keep going back to this issue, because the circumstances change ...

Andrew Rawnsley: Well, one big concern among many voters is the people who apply for asylum, fail to get it and stay in Britain, neverthe-less. The Conservatives say there are around a quarter of a million people in Britain who shouldn't be here. Do you accept that figure?

Tony Blair: No, I don't accept that figure.

Andrew Rawnsley: So what is the figure?

Tony Blair: But it's, but it's true

Andrew Rawnsley: Do you know what the figure is?

Tony Blair: There is a backlog of asylum claims and actually, when we came to power, the backlog I think was over sixty thousand, it's now down significantly.

Andrew Rawnsley: How many people are in Britain illegally at the moment, as we speak tonight?

Tony Blair: Well, as we've always said, and indeed as I think Michael Howard said when he was Home Secretary several years ago, the fact is you can never be exactly sure because if they're illegal …

Andrew Rawnsley: What's your guess?

Tony Blair: Oh, I don't think it's sensible to guess. But if you've got, if you've people who are here illegally, by their very nature, it is difficult to pin-point individual people. However …

Andrew Rawnsley: (overlap) So you don't know is the answer. You don't know how many, even roughly, how many people are in Britain illegally at the moment.

BBC Radio 4 *The Westminster Hour with Andrew Rawnsley*

Practice

Before we analyze the political interview above, read it through again and write a brief description of the context of situation based on our work in this chapter. Briefly characterize the field, the tenor and the mode, with the awareness that this is a broadcast political interview by the British Broadcasting Company in Britain in 2005 with the Prime Minister, Tony Blair. At the time of this interview Blair has been in office for 8 years and is dealing with a persistent political issue: political asylum and immigration. With this information and the actual discursive choices in the interview, you will be able to identify the main characteristics of the context of situation.

7.6.1 Analysis: Text 4: Political interview

You will have noticed that one of the most prominent discursive choices is the intensive and persistent questioning of Tony Blair by Andrew Rawnsley. Although it is normal to have the interviewer in the role of questioner, what is perhaps a bit surprising is the persistent demand for information. The fact that the interviewee is the Prime Minister does not seem to influence the intensity of the questions. Evident here is a reversal of roles. Andrew Rawnsley as an individual would not normally be in a position to quiz the Prime Minister as he is doing, but by virtue of the fact that he is the interviewer it is expected; the role allows him to mercilessly go after Blair to get answers to his questions. In other words, because of the context of situation, he takes on a certain authority that allows him to do so.

Blair is caught in a dilemma because he wants to use the broadcast as a vehicle for politics, as Fairclough has suggested in relation to an interview with Thatcher in the 1980s (1989: 190–191). He has strategic purposes; he is not interested simply in conveying information but in selling himself as the best candidate, the interview coming as it does before the British elections in 2005. Blair's responses are a form of strategic discourse; he is trying to convince the listeners of this program to vote for him again.

So his motivation for accepting to be interviewed is to get airtime, to get a chance to convince potential voters to vote for his party. But the interviewer persistently and none too gently asks question after question about this one issue and colours the issue itself so that Blair has to fight to defend his government; he has to convince the public that the interviewer's representation and interpretation of the facts are not correct. Examining how the two positions about a fundamental difference of both knowledge and power are expressed through discursive means is precisely the task of a critical discourse analyst.

There are specific ways in which Rawnsley tries to get Blair to answer questions on a particular representation of information. The framing of the questions, as well as the persistent interpretation of events, creates an effect very similar to that of a lawyer framing questions and interpreting facts from his or her own perspective.

The interviewer, Rawnsley, frames the questions not only in a negative way but selects lexicalizations of the events being discussed so as to create a particular 'lexical landscape' (Cotterill, 2004: 527). That is, through lexical choices Rawnsley takes on and conveys a particularized stance towards the issues of political asylum and immigration.

CDA questions

Through our critical analysis we can begin to understand fully the contestation of power and how participants can resist an interviewer's discursive power.

Part A

Below is the discursive sample of the interview again, this time with selected questions and answers bolded. We will focus on how Blair, the interviewee, responds to the questioning and framing of Rawnsley, given the constraint imposed by the negative landscape created by Rawnsley.

As you go through the sample which follows, answer the questions which follow each section.

> 1. Andrew Rawnsley: Prime Minister, after nearly eight years in power, you're announcing yet another attempt to deal with asylum and immigration. **Does that mean you accept that many people in Britain think that your government has lost control of the numbers of people coming in to this country**?
>
> 2. Tony Blair: **I don't think it's that, but I think that** because of the nature of the world we live in to-day, you've got to keep going back to this issue, because the circumstances change…

    a.   Does Blair answer with authority? What is there in his response that qualifies his answer and makes it seem less certain?

b. What other possible answers could Blair make to the negative framing of Rawnsley's question?

c. What are the implications for voters of Blair's qualifiying statements?

3. Andrew Rawnsley: Well, one big concern among many voters is the people who apply for asylum, fail to get it and stay in Britain, never the less. The Conservatives say there are around a quarter of a million people in Britain who shouldn't be here. **Do you accept that figure**?

4. Tony Blair: **No, I don't accept that figure.**

5. Andrew Rawnsley: **So what is the figure**?

a. Once again, does Blair have other choices with which he could respond to Rawnsley's question in 3?

b. How does Rawnsley's question in 5 position Blair differently than in 3?

c. Is it less or more confrontational than in 3?

6. Tony Blair: **But it's, but it's true**

a. Interestingly, Blair's response in 6 does not really address the question that Rawnsley asks in 5. He is using the time-honoured media strategy of answering the question he would have preferred to have been asked. What question do you think Blair is actually responding to in 6?

7. Andrew Rawnsley: **Do you know what the figure is**?

8. Tony Blair: There is a backlog of asylum claims and actually, when we came to power, **the backlog I think was over sixty thousand, it's now down significantly**.

a. Once again, Rawnsley poses the same question in 7 as he has posed in previous ones. How does Blair respond this time? How does it resemble or differ from his response in 2?

b. How do you think his response has strengthened or weakened his image with listening voters?

9. Andrew Rawnsley: **How many people are in Britain illegally at the moment, as we speak tonight**?

10. Tony Blair: Well, as we've always said, and indeed as I think Michael Howard said when he was Home Secretary several years ago, **the fact is you can never be exactly sure because if they're illegal** …

    a.   In question 9 Rawnsley actually asks a more loaded question by associating those seeking asylum with illegality. Do you think Blair's answer confirms or denies that illegality?

    b.   Does Blair come across here with more assuredness, the same amount or less than in previous answers? What is in the language here to help you to decide?

11. Andrew Rawnsley: **What's your guess**?

12. Tony Blair: **Oh, I don't think it's sensible to guess**. But if you've got, if you've people who are here illegally, by their very nature, it is difficult to pin-point individual people. However …

    a.   How does Blair's answer reinforce or challenge the position that Rawnsley has created for him throughout the interview?

    b.   Do you think his response justifies the conclusion that the interviewer draws in 13? Is Rawnsley's conclusion similar to or different from yours? If it is different, explain how this may stem from the fact that you belong to a different community than he does. If it is the same, discuss the community you seem to share with the interviewer.

    c.   Briefly discuss in writing the role modality plays in positioning Blair throughout this segment of the interview. If Blair had chosen other expressions of modal meanings, or none at all, would his position at the end of the interview be stronger or weaker?

13. Andrew Rawnsley: (overlap) **So you don't know is the answer. You don't know how many, even roughly, how many people are in Britain illegally at the moment.**

Part B

Now let's examine Rawnsley's role as interviewer and the ideological considerations that underlie his position and his positioning of Blair in this interview.

1. Go through the text and identify the questions with which he challenges Blair in this interview. Make a list of these.
2. Identify again the negative questions or those that carry a negative connotation.
3. Go through each of the questions and create a second list, this time one that focuses on the lexical set developed in his questions.
4. Discuss in writing the ways in which the questioning itself, combined with the lexical set, provides a particular framework for the issue being discussed in the interview. How does this combination position Blair in terms of possible and actual responses?
5. Explain in writing the relationship between language and power here. One way to do this is to evaluate the implications for voters that result from the interviewer's framing. That is, how would you as a listener be influenced by this interview in terms of your voting decision?

Text 5: Courtroom discourse, jury selection   7.7

7.7.1 Analysis: Courtroom discourse

In the next two samples of spoken discourse, you will notice that the role of lawyers in some ways resembles that of interviewers. They are the ones who lead and determine both the content and the form of the responses of potential jurors in the first case, and of witnesses in the second case. But there is in a sense even more prescription here because of the ritual nature of this type of spoken discourse. There are questions and answers that are asked rather formally following the format of courtroom practice. Although there is no script in either of the discourses we will examine, there is an expected pattern of interaction established by the legal system. The witness or the juror can expect to be asked questions, and is often forced to answer questions he or she may not want to answer; further, the lawyer may press and guide responses so that it is difficult to resist certain representations determined by the lawyer's framing of the questioning (Cotterill, 2004: 514). The role of the lawyer is that of the narrator of the story that unfolds in any given case, with prosecution and defence each shaping the story to their own ends. As well, Cotterill further suggests, lawyers frame the events through negative questioning which she explains below.

Views from the theorists:
Janet Cotterill

Negative questioning

Cotterill examines the ways in which lawyers control a witness's testimony. At one point in her work she focuses on negative questioning, which is particularly relevant to our discussion. She is referring to a specific trial concerning a domestic violence attack on a woman.

> Having persuaded the witness to admit that this was indeed a 'desperate situation', the lawyer goes on to construe her (the witness) as inconsistent in this context; her reluctance to extricate herself from the situation… is portrayed as unreasonable or irrational behaviour, since she is shown as having rejected the opportunity… (to escape the situation). The phrasing of the initial question in this way '*Had you not thought* about going to…' portrays this possibility as entirely common-sensical and therefore implicitly evaluates the witness's apparent lack of willingness to pursue this option…
>
> The force of the lawyer's challenge to her behaviour is strengthened by its construction as a negative… yes/no question: '*Had you not* thought about going to…?' Implying that the logic of such an action is self-evident… (2004: 528–529)

We will once again focus on the Tenor relationships in this situation in terms of Interpersonal selections of Mood and Modality because in this register realizations of Tenor are particularly prominent. We will also examine the difference between the two parallel discourses that take place in sample 5, between the court and lawyers on the one hand, and between the lawyers or the court and the potential jurors on the other.

The sample you are about to read takes place in a particular type of courtroom setting in which jurors are being selected for a trial of a suspected bomber who sent bombs through the mail for almost 20 years. He killed and injured many over the years and was finally caught in 1995. His name is Theodore Kaczynski and further information about him can be found on the web at http://www.unabombertrial.com/ which we examined in April 2005.

The Unabomber was tried in 1997 in the United States by a jury; jury selection took more than a month. A jury consists of 12 people; a jury pool may consist of several hundred. Potential jurors were questioned to determine whether they were suitable to serve on the jury for his trial. The questioning, in the judge's words, is designed to determine several things, among which are whether the jurors have heard anything about the suspect, if they have formed an opinion about guilt, if they have strong feelings for or against the death penalty and so on. These are the aspects that determine the suitability of a juror to serve on a jury. The prosecution and the defence have, of course, different concepts of 'suitability', particularly in a murder trial.

Below is the interview with one potential juror; as you can see by the number, 241, there have been examinations of many such people to determine suitability.

The following interactants take part in the first sample discourse which follows:

> Q: not immediately identifiable, but it seems that it is Mr. Lapham, which we can determine from utterances 4 and 5.
> A: potential Juror 241
> Ms Clarke: Attorney for the Defense
> Mr. Lapham: Attorney for the Prosecution.

Read the discourse below to get an overall idea of the content before we begin questions and further analysis.

> 1. Q. Do you think you would have any problem undertaking that weighing process?

> 2. A. I don't think so.

> 3. Q. And if you found, based on your weighing of those factors, that the aggravating factors outweighed the mitigating factors, under those circumstances do you think you could impose the death penalty?

> 4. MS. CLARKE: He's asking for a prejudgment on this case, given the text of the question.

> 5. MR. LAPHAM: I didn't give any facts. How can I be asking for a prejudgment?

6. THE COURT: Why don't you just state that you're not asking for prejudgment. You don't have to say you haven't give any facts. That's arguing with counsel that made the objection. I don't really need that.

7. MR. LAPHAM: I apologize, Your Honor.

8. THE COURT: All right.

9. Q. BY MR. LAPHAM: If you were undertaking this weighing process, and if you believed, based on your view of the factors and the evidence in the case that the aggravating factors outweighed the mitigating factors – and I'm not asking about the facts and circumstances of this case – would you – could you return a verdict of death?

10. MS. CLARKE: Your Honor, the question is could you, not would you.

11. THE COURT: He said could you. He said would you at first, but he corrected himself.

12. PROSPECTIVE JUROR NO. 241: I think I could.

13. Q. BY MR. LAPHAM: Do you have any hesitation about that?

14. A. Again, I don't think so. Right now I don't think I would.

15. Q. Okay. I want you to understand –

16. THE COURT: Wait a minute. I don't know what the last answer means. What do you mean?

17. PROSPECTIVE JUROR NO. 241: I keep saying not ever being there, I don't know, but I think I could.

18. THE COURT: Okay.

19. Q. BY MR. LAPHAM: Okay. Well, I just want you to understand how the process works.

20. THE COURT: It's been explained how the process works. I don't want you to explain that again.

21. MR. LAPHAM: I was going to explain the oath that she would take.

22.THE COURT: Okay. I didn't know that. I'm sorry.

http://www.unabombertrial.com/transcripts/121097.html (Accessed April 2005)

Practice

1. Having read through the sample, use what you have learned about registerial constructs to write a short description of the Field, Tenor and Mode of this register. Identify the language choices that helped you with your description.
2. Describe the differences that are evident in this sample compared to the previous ones. How, in other words would your description help someone understand that this is a courtroom discourse? What are the features in particular that indicate this?

In order to get a better idea of the nature of the two parallel conversations that occur in this discourse, we have abstracted those parts that belong to the court/attorney text, labelled Text A; and those that form the one between lawyers, the court and the potential jurors, labelled Text B.

Text A

4. MS. CLARKE: He's asking for a prejudgement on this case, given the text of the question.

5. MR. LAPHAM: I didn't give any facts. How can I be asking for a prejudgment?

6. THE COURT: Why don't you just state that you're not asking for prejudgment. You don't have to say you haven't give any facts. That's arguing with counsel that made the objection. I don't really need that.

7. MR. LAPHAM: I apologize, Your Honor.

8. THE COURT: All right.

10. MS. CLARKE: Your Honor, the question is could you, not would you.

11. THE COURT: He said could you. He said would you at first, but he corrected himself.

20. THE COURT: It's been explained how the process works. I don't want you to explain that again.

21. MR. LAPHAM: I was going to explain the oath that she would take.

22. THE COURT: Okay. I didn't know that. I'm sorry.

Let's look at parallel Text A first in terms of interpersonal choices. In utterances 4–8, there is an argument between the attorneys for the prosecution and the defense. Ms. Clarke accuses the prosecution of asking the potential juror to make a prejudgment, and the latter denies this. Interestingly, the Judge takes Ms Clarke, the defense lawyer, to task for arguing with the prosecution. He does so through interpersonal choices. Notice in line 6 that there are three ways in which he makes it clear that he does not approve of the prosecution's arguing.

First, the Judge (the court) makes a suggestion, which we can take as a command; it is not congruently in the form of a command, but rather in the form of a statement to soften the fact that it is really an order. Second, he chastises the prosecution by suggesting that he not argue with Ms Clarke. In terms of Appraisal Theory that we have looked at earlier, his comment, 'I don't really need that.' is clearly a negative judgement of the activity, the arguing between counsels. And Mr. Lapman takes it as a negative appraisal; this is clear in his apology which follows. It is also clear that the Court – the Judge – is in the powerful position, commenting on behaviour and then getting an apology.

In 10–11, the question is not about whether the juror is inclined to act in a certain way but whether he is capable of making a particular decision when faced with particular evidence. The selection of this juror depends in great part on this capability as we will see in the questioning in parallel Text B.

Moving on to parallel Text B, we will focus on three features particularly prominent here: interpersonal metaphors, modality choices and Mood selections.

Text B

1. Q. Do you think you would have any problem undertaking that weighing process?

2. A. I don't think so.

3. Q. And if you found, based on your weighing of those factors, that the aggravating factors outweighed the mitigating factors, under those circumstances do you think you could impose the death penalty?

9. Q. BY MR. LAPHAM: If you were undertaking this weighing process, and if you believed, based on your view of the factors and the evidence in the case that the aggravating factors outweighed the mitigating factors – and I'm not asking about the facts and circumstances of this case – would you – could you return a verdict of death?

12. PROSPECTIVE JUROR NO. 241: I think I could.

13. Q. BY MR. LAPHAM: Do you have any hesitation about that?

14. A. Again, I don't think so. Right now I don't think I would.

15. Q. Okay. I want you to understand –

16. THE COURT: Wait a minute. I don't know what the last answer means. What do you mean?

17. PROSPECTIVE JUROR NO. 241: I keep saying not ever being there, I don't know, but I think I could.

18. THE COURT: Okay.

19. Q. BY MR. LAPHAM: Okay. Well, I just want you to understand how the process works.

Interpersonal metaphors refer to a metaphoric way of expressing modality. Instead of choosing a modal to express probability, the speakers here do so through a clause: 'do you think' or 'I do/don't think'. You will also notice that many of these metaphoric clauses precede two types of modals: 'would' and 'could', with the latter much more prominent.

1. Go through parallel Text B and underline every case of interpersonal metaphor in the juror's responses. Circle the instances of modals that follow many of these interpersonal metaphors.
2. On the basis of the potential juror's modalized responses do you think he will be selected as a juror? Would you select him if you were counsel for the defense? For the prosecution?
3. Discuss your answers with other members of the class.

Practice

Also important in this parallel text are the questioning patterns in this parallel text, mainly absent from the former one. The purpose here, of course, is different from that of the exchanges between lawyers and the court. Here the juror is being questioned quite thoroughly by the prosecution. The most important basis for selection of the juror by the prosecution seems to be whether the juror could vote for a verdict of death.

1. In order to identify the persistent questions, go through the text and simply underline the questions that the prosecution attorney keeps asking.
2. You will have noticed that there are several examples of Interpersonal metaphors in the questions. What purpose do they serve in the prosecution's questions? How would you compare them to those in the potential juror's responses?

CDA questions

1. Having gone through the two parallel conversations and analyzed them in terms of realizations of the Tenor in this situation, how would you explain the power relations evident here? How do you know?
2. How would you describe the distance between the interactants? Does it resemble or differ from that of the first two discourses? From the third discourse? Does the distance between the interactants in this sample affect the power expressed here? How?

In the sample discourse below, the scene is again that of a courtroom in which a witness is being cross-examined by the prosecution. This time it is the murder trial of a man called Arlo Looking Cloud. Looking Cloud was accused of killing a woman named Anna Mae Aquash almost 20 years earlier. The trial only occurs at this point because evidence about the murder has only recently become available. From a discursive perspective it is particularly interesting because of three features that are prominent and that surface frequently in such courtroom discourse. They are choices that reflect the context which is generating the discourse. Before analyzing the discourse in detail, read it over to get a general idea about the thrust of the message and the intentions behind the questioning of the witness.

Trial of Arlo Looking Cloud for the murder of Anna Mae Aquash (2004)
Witness
The United States of America vs. Fritz Arlo Looking Cloud
Court Trial Transcripts
February 2004
Rapid City, South Dakota
(END OF PAGE 356)

THE COURT: Cross-examine.
CROSS EXAMINATION BY MR. RENSCH:

1. Q. Do you distinctly remember every conversation you had with him?

2. A. Not enough to be able to separate them and itemize them.

3. Q. You have also said that he has consistently told you what happened through the years, haven't you, sir?

4. A. Yes.

5. Q. What does the word consistently mean to you?

6. A. I could quote Webster's definition, but I believe it should mean the same thing to both of us, it happens often.

7. Q. Go ahead and quote whatever you would like, tell us what consistently means.

8. A. It happens often, it stays the –

9. Q. It agrees with the same?

10. A. It happens often the same.

11. Q. In your quote of Webster's dictionary it means stays the same, doesn't it?

12. A. I said I could quote the Webster's dictionary.

13.Q. Well, quote it then.

14. A. I don't. Consistent, you had asked me for a definition of the word consistency.

15. Q. I asked you for the word consistency. You have said to people that Arlo Looking Cloud consistently told you the same thing over the years, have you not, sir?

16. A. Yes.

17. Q. If you say that someone consistently tells you the same thing over the years, that means their story isn't changing, doesn't it?

18. A. No.

19. Q. It doesn't. Tell us how someone can consistently say to you the same thing over the years and change their story.

20. A. Well, we have a conversation about the same subject that happens more than once, we consistently have the same types of questions, same types of inquiries, we focus on the same object, but the answers are often different.

21. Q. How can someone consistently say the same thing to you while saying something different?

22. A. Because all the different answers are consistently the same.

23. Q. All the different answers are consistently the same. That is what you are telling this jury?

24. A. Yes.

http://web.telia.com/%7Eu71502499/arlo/#feb2004 (Accessed April 2006)

Typical in such courtroom situations of course is the questioning of witnesses; there are features of questioning evident here that we have not yet discussed. The first concerns Question tags which follow statements; if the preceding statement is negative, the tag is positive; if the preceding statement is positive, the tag is negative. There are four examples of these negative tags in the sample discourse below:

> 3. Q. You have also said that he has consistently told you what happened through the years, **haven't you, sir?**

> 11. Q. In your quote of Webster's dictionary it means stays the same, **doesn't it**?

> 15. Q. I asked you for the word consistency. You have said to people that Arlo Looking Cloud consistently told you the same thing over the years, **have you not, sir**?

> 17. Q. If you say that someone consistently tells you the same thing over the years, that means their story isn't changing, **doesn't it**?

Question tags

First, let's look at how the tag is created and how it connects to the statement it follows. We can then discuss the functions tags serve in general and here in this discourse. You will notice that each follows a statement. In each case the statement is positive so each of the tags is negative. Each of the tags refers back to elements in the statement. In 3, the reference is to 'you have said'. In 11, it is to the clause 'it means stays the same'. In 15, the tag again refers back to 'you have said', and in 17 it refers back to 'that means…'.

Generally, such tags seek confirmation from the person being addressed; they also place the addressee in a position where he or she usually has to agree with the point. That is, the way the speaker states his or her position and positions the addressee so that they have to agree. Posing the question in this way presupposes agreement. If someone says to you, 'You know what I mean, don't you?' it is assumed that you will say 'Yes, I do', or 'Yes, of course' to this negative question. It would be much rarer (although possible) for you to say 'No, I don't', 'No, of course not' because the natural response to a negative question is a positive answer.

So, in this discourse the lawyer so positions the witness that he has little choice but to agree with the lawyer's version of the meaning of a word. By so doing, by leading the witness as he does through question tags and other means, the attorney presents his version of events, his narrative. The witness is in a sense coerced into a particular position in relation to this version, this story. If he does not agree, or if he looks as though he does not agree, then doubt is cast on his veracity or reliability as a witness.

Repetition

In fact, this is only one of the means by which the attorney leads this witness, by framing the questions, by creating a thread of discourse, and weaving a specific version of events that leads to a special lexical landscape (Cotterrill, 2004: 527). Second, the repetition of one word by the lawyer creates a very particularlized version of a story from this witness. If we examine the discourse again, this time with the repeated item bolded you will see how the lawyer proceeds to build a distinct interpretation of the word that shapes and positions the witness.

1. Q. Do you distinctly remember every conversation you had with him?

2. A. Not enough to be able to separate them and itemize them.

3. Q. You have also said that he has **consistently** told you what happened through the years, haven't you, sir?

4. A. Yes.

5. Q. What does the word **consistently** mean to you?

6. A. I could quote Webster's definition, but I believe it should mean the same thing to both of us, it happens often.

7. Q. Go ahead and quote whatever you would like, tell us what **consistently** means.

8. A. It happens often, it stays the –

9. Q. It agrees with the same?

10. A. It happens often the same.

11. Q. In your quote of Webster's dictionary it means stays the same, doesn't it?

12. A. I said I could quote the Webster's dictionary.

13. Q. Well, quote it then.

14. A. I don't. **Consistent,** you had asked me for a definition of the word **consistency.**

15. Q. I asked you for the word **consistency**. You have said to people that Arlo Looking Cloud **consistently** told you the same thing over the years, have you not, sir?

16. A. Yes.

17. Q. If you say that someone **consistently** tells you the same thing over the years, that means their story isn't changing, doesn't it?

18. A. No.

19. Q. It doesn't. Tell us how someone can **consistently** say to you the same thing over the years and change their story.

20. A. Well, we have a conversation about the same subject that happens more than once, we **consistently** have the same types of questions, same types of inquiries, we focus on the same object, but the answers are often different.

21. Q. How can someone **consistently** say the same thing to you while saying something different?

22. A. Because all the different answers are **consistently** the same.

23. Q. All the different answers are **consistently** the same. That is what you are telling this jury?

24. A. Yes.

Example of a CDA analysis: lexical choices

Let's see what Cotterill has to say about a questioning based on a particularized narrative about one lexical item and then examine how it relates to the attorney's cross examination of the witness in the sample discourse above.

Janet Cotterrill discusses lexical landscapes. Specifically, she talks about how certain lexicalizations:

> …can express far more than a straightforwardly neutral denotational meaning, and as such can be exploited by cross-examining lawyers in court. The majority of these 'negotiations' take place at a fairly local level and can be identified at particular moments of the transcript. However it is also possible [as we see in our sample discourse] for trial lawyers to manipulate certain lexicalizations across extended stretches of testimony or in clusters within a segment of evidence, to create *lexical landscapes*… If lawyers can construct a particular lexical landscape within which to elicit testimony, both through the lexical representations themselves and through the more subtle exploitation of connotational and semantic prosodic properties of lexicalizations they select, the jury may be more likely to incorporate these versions into a schematically satisfying version of events. (2004: 527–528)

CDA questions

We have examined earlier in this chapter how an interviewer leads the interviewee through particular representations of information, specifically through interpersonal choices. By identifying how, in his cross-examination, a lawyer demands information through questions of different sorts and through commands, you will discover how he presents his own version of the story. By doing so he exerts power over the witness and the listening jury.

1. Go through the discursive sample (reproduced again below for convenience) and circle all of the different types of questions. Identify whether they are polar or wh- interrogatives. Next, underline all of the commands in the sample. Then also circle

the tag questions twice to get a complete idea of how these resources provide the means by which the lawyer cross-examines the witness to get the information he seeks.

1. Q. Do you distinctly remember every conversation you had with him?

2. A. Not enough to be able to separate them and itemize them.

3. Q. You have also said that he has **consistently** told you what happened through the years, haven't you, sir?

4. A. Yes.

5. Q. What does the word **consistently** mean to you?

6. A. I could quote Webster's definition, but I believe it should mean the same thing to both of us, it happens often.

7. Q. Go ahead and quote whatever you would like, tell us what **consistently** means.

8. A. It happens often, it stays the –

9. Q. It agrees with the same?

10. A. It happens often the same.

11. Q. In your quote of Webster's dictionary it means stays the same, doesn't it?

12. A. I said I could quote the Webster's dictionary.

13. Q. Well, quote it then.

14. A. I don't. **Consistent,** you had asked me for a definition of the word **consistency.**

15. Q. I asked you for the word **consistency**. You have said to people that Arlo Looking Cloud **consistently** told you the same thing over the years, have you not, sir?

16. A. Yes.

17. Q. If you say that someone **consistently** tells you the same thing over the years, that means their story isn't changing, doesn't it?

18. A. No.

19. Q. It doesn't. Tell us how someone can **consistently** say to you the same thing over the years and change their story.

20. A. Well, we have a conversation about the same subject that happens more than once, we **consistently** have the same types of questions, same types of inquiries, we focus on the same object, but the answers are often different.

21. Q. How can someone **consistently** say the same thing to you while saying something different?

22. A. Because all the different answers are **consistently** the same.

23. Q. All the different answers are **consistently** the same. That is what you are telling this jury?

24. A. Yes.

2. Which of the questions constrains the witness most? Which constrains him least in the sense that they are more open-ended?
3. In which question tags does the witness accept the positioning imposed by the tag by responding appropriately? Which question tag does he resist by not responding as expected? How does he do this? What is the outcome of the resistance?
4. How do the commands reinforce the positioning of the witness that emerges from the lawyer's questions?
5. How does the lawyer lead the witness with his questioning about the word 'consistent'? What is the version of the word 'consistent' that the lawyer wants the jury to come away with? Does the lawyer's repeated questioning of the witness about the meaning of the word 'consistency' lead to doubt about the witness's testimony? Do you think this results from the lawyer's interpretations or lexical landscaping of this word?
6. What is the meaning or interpretation of 'consistent' that you as the reader come away with? Is it the same as the witness's?

Critical discourse analysis

Now that you have analyzed different types of discursive samples you should be in a better position to examine how power is conveyed in spoken interactive situations.

1. Look back over our explanations and your responses through-out the chapter. Discuss in writing the relationship between language and power as explicitly expressed in different types of spoken discourse. You should focus on the influence of registe-rial constructs on discursive choices, concentrating on those that clearly reflect and realize power. For example, in lawyers' cross-examination, there is persistent questioning of witnesses, expressing the differentiation in power between the lawyer and the witness. It is important to discuss not only how power is reflected in linguistic selections, but how specific choices express different aspects of power, depending on the particular context of situation.

2. Either tape-record a casual conversation with your friends or record a political interview from the radio or TV. Transcribe a short excerpt and analyze it in terms of power expressed in spoken language through interpersonal resources.

Appraisal Theory: an approach to the study of interpersonal assessment and evaluation of attitudinal meanings. In this chapter we briefly cover three sub-categories:

Appreciation: speakers' reactions and evaluations of reality;

Affect: speakers' expression of emotional states, positive and negative;

Judgement: speakers' judgements about the ethics, morality or social values of other people.

(Definitions based on Eggins and Slade, 1997: 125)

Chapter 7 Glossary

Context of situation: the immediate situation in which a discursive event occurs. It is described in terms of three constructs:

Field which refers to the activity taking place;

Tenor which accounts for the relationships between interactants and the information being conveyed in a situation;

Mode which refers to whether the discursive event is spoken or written.

Lexical or narrative landscape: a term Cotterill uses to explain how lawyers in courtrooms focus on certain lexicalizations and thus create certain representations and narrative scenarios.

Negative questions: include questions such as 'Had you not thought of doing x?' Continued use of such questioning techniques can create certain representations of information according to Cotterill.

Register: Explains how varieties of language differ according to the use to which they are put in different contexts. Features of varieties are identifiable in terms of the Field, Tenor and Mode.

Chapter 7
Further readings

SFL readings

Butt, D. et al. (2000) *Using Functional Grammar, An Explorer's Guide.* The book provides, in Chapter 8, a very thorough and accessible discussion of registerial variables.

Eggins, S. and Slade, D. (1997) *Analysing Casual Conversation.* This book covers many features of casual conversations and other forms of spoken discourse. Of particular interest in Chapter 3 is their discussion of the grammatical patterns of conversation. In terms of interpersonal meanings they outline different types of modality and in Chapter 4 they introduce Appraisal Theory.

CDA readings

Cotterill, J. (2004) 'Collocation, connotation, and courtroom semantics: lawyers' control of witness testimony through lexical negotiation.' This article carries out a very interesting analysis of lexical choices that create what she calls a lexical or narrative landscape.

Fairclough, N. (1989) *Language and Power*. Chapter 7 provides a very thorough analysis of an interview with Margaret Thatcher, then the Prime Minister of England. His analysis complements those in this chapter on the political interview and the courtroom discourses.

Chapter 8 contents

Language in modern trends

In Chapter 8, we end the book with a discussion of some of the current trends in discourse, showing how the SFL analytical tools are still relevant in this new context to help us to understand the power and ideological basis for each trend. We examine features such as modality, Mood, process type and participant roles as we look at and analyze these new trends which reflect and construct the many changes in contemporary society.

We will focus on four major discursive trends of the late twentieth and early twenty-first centuries to find out how language and power interact in the creation of current social changes. The discussion of the trends is based primarily on the research of two linguists: Lemke (1995), and Fairclough (1989; 1993; 1995; 1997; 2001).

The first trend is **Technicalization,** which refers to the introduction of technical language and the language of experts into the social policy domain. Although several theorists discuss this phenomenon, we will limit our discussion to Lemke's interpretation because it seems to us a particularly clear and accessible discussion of this trend.

Lemke claims that that one of the dominant current political strategies is '...the transformation of discourses of expert knowledge into discourses of social policy' (1995: 58). That is, political strategists use technical knowledge to underwrite social changes in areas such as education, welfare and social security. Lemke suggests that '... the political advantage of this *technocratic* strategy to those who practice it is that it presents policy as if it were directly dictated by matters of fact... and deflects consideration of *values* choices and the social, moral and political responsibility for such choices' (ibid: 58). Further, the policies are presented in technical language directed primarily at those with a certain expertise.

The problem arises when the audience to whom these policies are being presented is a lay audience, not an expert one. Technicalization gives the policies an air of legitimacy, but discursive choices prevent the lay audience from fully comprehending the discourse. One such discursive choice that renders the language inaccessible is condensation.

Condensation is achieved through nominalization. As we have seen in previous chapters, processes which are normally realized by verbs can also be realized by nominal groups. Nominalization involves the process itself and may even include participants in the form of modification in the nominal group, e.g., 'The Spanish war', 'The Croatian battle'. In neither case do we know who the agent or the patient is, nor where or when the activity occurs.

Condensation creates a problem for people who lack sufficient knowledge of relevant thematic formations to fully process and understand the information presented. Thematic formations occur when the same patterns of words and the presentational meanings they help to express '... occur from text to text in slightly different wordings, but recognizably the same, and each wording can be mapped onto a ... semantic pattern that is the same for all' (1995: 42). With this awareness of the same or related meanings, readers can process new information presented in a condensed form that assumes that readers do in fact have this understanding. Without it, they cannot do so.

A second aspect of technical language is that it tends to use mostly third-person forms; in other words, there is almost no dialogue in which there is an 'I' speaking to a 'you'. So technical language is monologic. Pronouncements of policy are made in non-interactive discourse without the elements that would engage interactants in dialogue about the particular policy. As a result, there is no possibility of questioning the policy.

The second discourse trend we will look at is **Conversationalization.** Conversationalization is in many ways the opposite of technicalization, in that it transfers the features of personal conversation into public domains. Current public speech, therefore, often seems more casual and more accessible. Most people are familiar with the conversational style, whereas they are less so with technical language. The process of conversationalization involves applying and using discourse practices from ordinary or private life in public discourse.

According to Fairclough and Mauranen (1997), features that are common in casual conversation include more frequent first-person pronoun usage, subjective marking of modality, fewer monological discursive practices and more dialogical ones, for example questions and replies rather than orders. Interestingly though, Blommaert (2001) suggests that the effect is not a lessening of power but an increase, because the boundaries between public and private discourse are blurred; there is, in a sense, an infiltration of the private by the public.

The third trend, **Marketization**, refers to the infiltration of discursive elements of the commodities market (where items are bought and sold) into other discursive realms such as politics and education. Generally, what is happening is a restructuring of discourse based on a market model where things are bought and sold. The result is that information within domains such as education is presented not for communicative purposes but for strategic ones like those we saw in Chapter 4 in relation to the language of advertising. There the purpose was to get people to act, to buy products. Similarly, many of the discursive practices of education are designed to attract consumers (students) by promoting educational facilities, universities and institutes as if they were simply another product. Marketization has infiltrated education to such an extent that the language often resembles a sales pitch, as we shall see when we come to this trend.

The fourth trend is the discourse of **Globalization.** This trend incorporates what Fairclough (2004: 106) calls 'global space-time': events are presented in the simple present tense, thus acquiring a particular air of inevitable reality; as well, actions are presented without agency, and there are often nominalizations of processes. The discourse of globalization ends up presenting globalization as more complete than it is, and as benefiting everyone.

This discursive trend plays a prominent role in the political speeches of New Labour, primarily exemplified by British Prime Minister Tony Blair. The process of globalization itself has been described as

> … the increasing interdependence and integration of social, cultural, political, and economic processes across local, national, regional, and global levels. People, artifacts, symbols, goods, and services are exchanged more rapidly, frequently, and intensively, facilitated by the Internet, airline travel, wireless networks, and migration.

(Doreen Starke-Meyerring, lecture, Carleton University, March 2005)

The discourse of globalization, then, is particularly relevant because much of the information and many of the aspects of the process are created by and conveyed through language.

8.3   Technicalization

We begin with **Technicalization**, examining the features we have mentioned along with others that distinguish it. We will list and discuss the primary features of this trend. We will then go on to exemplify these features in a number of discourses.

1) An important feature of technicalized language is condensation. This results from putting a great deal of information into modified nominal groups instead of the more congruent realization through verbal processes. The actors who originally carried out many of the verbal processes are absent from the resulting nominalizations. Also absent in nominalizations is the sense of time. As a result, the condensed language leaves out references to when actions might have taken place, and who carried them out.

2) A second feature of technicalization is the lack of concrete actions. These are replaced by abstract processes, partly due to the many nominalizations. Many of the verbal groups are there to simply join the nominal groups together.

3) A third feature of technicalization is the frequent lack of animate actors who carry out the processes. Instead, we see propositions such as the following: 'Studies show that…', in which the actor carrying out the process is non-human. This

makes it even more difficult to engage with the proposition and to question it; there is no one to question about the information being conveyed.

4) Technicalization also involves a predominance of third-person forms over first- and second-person pronouns. This makes the discourse noticeably distant.

5) Agentless passives further contribute to the distancing and abstract nature of technicalization.

6) Value labelling is also found in technicalization. Value labelling is designed to persuade readers of the value of an event or an item. 'A certain set of values is put into place to reflect the stance of the writer, rather than an independent evaluation of a project or event' (Lemke, 1995: 73).

Lemke has called this trend of technicalization monologic, because it displays few of the interactive features found in dialogic discourse. In monologic discourse, abstract processes and the lack of interactive features such as first-person references make it difficult to interact with, or to enter into dialogue about, the policies being promoted. Most prominent in this trend are pronouncements designed to be accepted without discussion. In dialogic discourse, on the other hand, first- and second-person pronouns are frequent, making audiences feel that they are being directly addressed and included in the discussion. Passives occur with identifiable agents about whom people can argue and whom readers can evaluate. Information is presented in more congruent verbal forms representing actions and accompanying participants.

8.3.1 Technicalization: Text 1

We will examine three short texts exhibiting features of technicalization. The texts are excerpted from the Cato Institute's *Handbook for Congress*, a policy recommendation to the 107th United States Congress. The report is a long one, but one short section is devoted to the issue of welfare reform, pages 323–329.

In it are recommendations about further welfare reform that the Congress should consider. The recommendations are based on the Heritage Foundation's review of President Clinton's reform of welfare in 1996. (The Heritage Foundation is a conservative think tank that provides research policy information.)

Excerpt 1

> Although caseloads declined by 47 percent between 1996 and 1999, most people who have left the rolls have been short-term recipients who have benefited from the nation's booming economy. **Policymakers, four years into reform, continue to face the critical task of tackling *long-term dependence* and its *host of associated pathologies,* including *long-term joblessness, criminal behavior,* and *multigenerational dependence*.**

(*Cato Handbook for Congress, Policy Recommendations for 107th Congress* p. 323. Emphasis added. www.cab.org/pubs/handbook/handbook107. htm Accessed March 2005)

Let's focus only on the bolded section of this quote; in it you will see several examples of italicized nominal groups, a prominent feature of condensation. These nominal groups, by virtue of being strung together in a list, seem to be connected and related to each other: *long term dependence, associated pathologies, long-term joblessness, criminal behavior* and *multigenerational dependence*. The association of the nominal groups in the same sentence strongly suggests an interrelationship of criminal behaviour with long-term dependence.

This type of condensation results not only from the use of nominalization, but also from the making of connections between welfare recipients and crime. This is a form of what Lemke calls value labelling, where the writers make value associations that do not necessarily reflect anything but their own opinion or stance. These associations rely on other research that may or may not have been proven, but is certainly not provided. The reader has no way of evaluating the validity of the connection without being familiar with related thematic formations. Here the result is that condensation effectively hides a number of ideological assumptions, such as that dependence breeds criminal behaviour. Dependence also seems to lead to long-term joblessness. But these values, originating in a particular ideology, cannot easily be identified because readers are not sufficiently acquainted with other related themes to be able to judge.

Familiarity with other texts and related themes is what Lemke (1995) calls intertextuality, which refers to the connection between texts. The point is that, without the background knowledge to flesh out information that has been condensed, readers or listeners may accept any implied association as a fact, and also the ideological assumption behind it.

In Excerpt (2) from the Cato Institute report, we can see another feature of technicalization: the lack of animate agency. This feature, combined with abstract as opposed to concrete processes, is well-illustrated in the following.

Excerpt 2

> **Welfare reform** *has been* largely *unsuccessful* in moving <u>long-term unemployed, difficult-to-place individuals</u> off cash assistance.

(*Cato Handbook for Congress, Policy Recommendations for 107th Congress*. p. 325. Emphasis added)

Here we see the lack of animate agency evident in the nominal group: 'welfare reform'. Note that it is not a person or a group of people who have been unsuccessful, but an anonymous act, an inanimate reform. One of the difficulties with this discourse choice is that it implies that no animate being is responsible for the change. Therefore the reader or the listener cannot challenge the change; there is no one to argue with.

The same absence of animate agency is evident in Excerpt (3).

Excerpt 3

> **Studies** show that those who remain on the rolls four years into reform have less education, fewer basic skills, less previous job experience, and a longer history of welfare receipt than people who left the rolls early on.

(*Cato Handbook for Congress, Policy Recommendations for 107th Congress*. p. 325. Emphasis added)

'Studies' is another example of an abstract, non-human actor. 'This gives the ubiquitous 'studies show' … formula in which the process 'study' minus its (fallible) human Actor is reified and made to do what the same or some other human Actor actually does' (Lemke,1995: 60). The reification process further contributes to the inability of readers to argue against the policy, since it is presented as a given; further, without an animate being doing the acting, it removes any possibility of engagement, since there is no one with whom to engage.

A further linguistic choice evident in these excerpts is the limited number of 'processes of direct action' (ibid: 60). Instead, what we see are processes in which there is no action; they are either abstract or relational processes. These play an evaluative role, but do not actually explain what is going on in the sentence. For example, in excerpt (2), the main verbal group 'has been unsuccessful' is a relational process, but it does not tell us what is actually happening here – rather it evaluates the non-finite verbal group 'in moving'. As we have seen before, one important aspect of the non-finite form is that the reader cannot argue with it because there is no tense. This is another way in which technicalization removes the possibility of engaging with the policy being discussed.

The last element in Excerpt (2) shows what can happen when discursive communications are primarily composed of nominal groups. In the following example, note the modification of 'individuals':

<u>long-term unemployed, difficult-to-place individuals,</u>

Nominal groups that can be added to and specified with an infinite number of epithets are one of the linguistic resources used for condensation. The two nominalized verbal forms in the description of individuals – 'unemployed' and 'difficult to place' – are being used as modifiers in the nominal group. But these terms themselves are nominalized forms of the verbs: 'employ' and' place'. Here they are being used as modifiers, providing a categorization of individuals to which other epithets can be added. Once writers have chosen a nominalization, they are free to modify ad infinitum, which contributes to the density of the selection. It also allows writers to select modifiers that express ideological positions that are not explicitly expressed, but are hidden in the condensed nominal group. For example, '<u>long-term unemployed, difficult-to-place **individuals**</u>', is a nominal group with one head (bolded) and two complex modifiers.

The final feature of condensation evident in these texts is the lack of first- or second-person pronouns; these are replaced by third-person forms, further distancing the reader and contributing to the monologic nature of technicalized discourse. Dialogic interaction usually involves instances of 'I' and or 'we', and the second-person form 'you', allowing people to engage with one another. People are addressed directly and know that they can interject, comment, question, and so on. But in technicalized discourse, these elements are missing, replaced by third-person forms only. The following sentence from the Cato Institute's report exemplifies this features along with the others we have been discussing. The third person references are bolded.

> Although **caseloads** declined by 47 percent between 1996 and 1999, **most people**… have been short-term recipients.

Practice

The paragraph which follows is another excerpt from the Cato Institute's report on welfare. It exemplifies most of the features introduced above that are common in technicalized discourse: nominalization, inanimate agents/actors, agentless passives, lack of concrete actions, third-person forms, and lack of dialogic elements.

Excerpt 4

> As the debate over welfare reform has progressed beyond caseload numbers, disturbing information has emerged about individuals' fate after they exit the rolls. On a positive note, most people who leave welfare for work experience gains in well-being. As the nation's caseloads have plummeted over the last four years, more single parents and their children have advanced out of poverty. Studies indicate that the combined income from full-time work at a minimum wage job and supplemental supports such as federal and state EITC, food stamps, Medicaid, and child care and housing assistance should allow families to enjoy a higher level of financial well-being than when they were on welfare. Thus, warnings of an impending 'crisis' for recipients when they exit the rolls have been overblown.

(*Cato Handbook for Congress, Policy Recommendations for 107th Congress.* p. 325)

1. Identify examples of each of the technicalization features above and list them. For example: third-person references: 'caseload numbers', 'most people'.
2. When you have finished, compare your list with others in the class.

Technicalization is also evident in the discourse surrounding another political issue: Social Security reform in the United States. Since George W. Bush became president in 2000, he and other members of his government have been talking increasingly about the need to privatize Social Security. He claims that there will not be enough money in the system to continue to pay the benefits it has paid in the past. Bush and his colleagues suggest that the only way people will be able to get Social Security benefits for their retirement is to start investing privately, at least in part, in bonds instead of contributing only to Social Security. A subset of the issue has to do with whether or not the present Social Security system is economically disadvantageous for one segment of the population, namely low wage-earners and, more specifically, Black American wage-earners.

We will focus on the linguistic resources employed to persuade people of the merits of each side of this issue: whether or not Social Security, as a system of saving and providing for workers in the U.S., can and should continue.

We will also gain insights into the significance of the thematic formations on which condensed discourse is based. As you will remember, these thematic formations assume the ability to connect a text to other related texts, which in turn depends on our familiarity with the topic. This is what Lemke refers to as 'intertextuality': the connection between texts, a connection we rely on to make sense of what we read and hear.

For example, when we come across the issue of the privatization of Social Security, we do so with varying degrees of familiarity, and varying degrees of proficiency in connecting the discussion to other things we have read and heard. The problem with using technicalized discourse to discuss Social Security is that in order to understand it, we have to be familiar with the technical texts on which it is based. That is, for complete comprehension, we have to be familiar with the intertextual (between texts or discourses) thematic patterns on which the discourse relies.

Views from the theorists:
J. Lemke

Condensation in technical language

According to Lemke, intertextuality also concerns the idea that all texts that we read and hear are read and heard in the light of other texts we have interacted with as a result of belonging to a particular grouping of people. We all belong to different communities and each of these determines the types and range of meanings that we exchange, and the stance or position we take towards these meanings.

...All meaning is intertextual. No text is complete or autonomous in itself: it needs to be read, and it is read in relation to other texts. *Which* other texts? Each community, each discourse tradition, has its own canons of intertextuality, its own principles and customs regarding which texts are most relevant to the interpretation of any one text. (1995: 41)

Our understanding of these texts:

... depends critically on where we situate ourselves among the discourse viewpoints of our community. Which intertexts do we use to interpret these texts? What kinds of relations do we make between them? What discourse patterns do we construct that seem to us validly invariant from one text to another? (Lemke, 1995: 55)

As Lemke suggests, we each have a particular orientation, which stems from the communities of which we are a part. For example, when we read something about the 'hot topics' of abortion or homosexuality, our reaction to and understanding of them is formed by the communities we are from, the communities with whom we share meanings and positions.

These intertextual thematic formations are missing in the condensations of technicalized discourse, which makes it almost impossible for people to process the information completely, or even correctly. Intertextuality is missing in technical discourse because it was originally directed towards a technical and scientific audience which has the intertextual knowledge. Now the discourse has been taken over for technocratic purposes in support of social policy, and is directed at the general public who lack the thematic formations needed to process it.

Lemke talks about how we interpret discourses based on what we know of related ones. But he says, in technical discourse '...the degree of condensation, that is the number of unexpressed thematic items and relations that are needed to make sense of those that are expressed, is much greater than for other discourse types' (ibid: 62).

He claims that the main problem in highly condensed discourse is that readers and listeners do not have access to the '...appropriate formations and the issue of *which* formations the text proposes as being adequate for... expansion (ibid: 63).

For example, using the language of financial experts in a policy statement aimed at people who do not have this expertise means that the audience to whom it is directed cannot process the condensed information. This is particularly evident in the texts that follow.

8.3.2   Technicalization: Text 2

In 1997, The Heritage Foundation, a conservative think-tank, came out with a policy paper examining the whole issue of Social Security and the ways in which similar programs are being handled in other countries. The President's decision to privatize Social Security was based at least in part on this and other similar papers. The Heritage Foundation maintained that the system as it exists is failing and therefore needs to be privatized, as in other countries around the world:

> America's Social Security system is in serious trouble. Payroll tax rates have been increased 17 times in the past 40 years, yet promised benefits exceed projected revenues by trillions of dollars. Moreover, Social Security has become an increasingly bad deal for American workers who must pay record high taxes to a system that provides only meager levels of income for their retirement years. Even worse, there is no way to fix the current system to remedy these problems....

> The only answer to these seemingly intractable problems is to privatize the Social Security system.

(Daniel J. Mitchell, The Heritage Foundation, 1997: 1)

Discussion

Having examined some of the features of technicalization, look through the two small excerpts above and list examples of the use of the following resources: third person references, lack of interactive features, agentless passives, relational and thus evaluative process types.

1. Discuss with other members of the class the purpose these resources are serving.
2. Try to reword the technicalized parts of this discourse to make it more accessible.
3. Compare your rewording with that of others in the class.

Moving on to another section of the Heritage Report, again in relation to Social Security, there is a further feature of technicalization: value labelling. The writers suggest that the Social Security plan is bad for some workers, especially Blacks:

> Social Security is an especially bad deal for certain demographic groups. Two-earner couples are hit particularly hard. Black males, because of their low life expectancy, also are big losers.

> Workers with lower life expectancies, for instance, would be far better off with private savings plans that they could pass on to their children and grandchildren. (ibid: 1)

4. Examine the statements above and identify the examples of value labelling here.
5. In writing, discuss their purpose.

Having worked your way through these excerpts, you will be familiar with the two main points, the first of which has to do with the contention that Social Security cannot continue to pay the benefits that it has been paying, and therefore must be privatized. This is an issue that has surfaced again and again in Bush's years as President and that received focus in his 2004 Economic Report. In addition to this main issue, the Heritage report also suggests that Social Security does not even provide a good return on workers' investment. Both points are contested by the left-leaning Economics professor and journalist Paul Krugman in his editorial commentary on 1 February 2005 in the *New York Times*.

8.3.3 Technicalization: Text 3

Below is Krugman's first point:

> Schemes for Social Security privatization as outlined in the 2004 Economic Report of the President, invariably assume that investing in stocks will yield a high annual rate of return, 6.5 or 7 percent after inflation, for at least the next 75 years. Without that assumption, these schemes can't deliver on their promises. Yet a rate of return that high is mathematically impossible unless the economy grows much faster than anyone is now expecting.

(*New York Times*, 1 February 2005)

It is interesting that even here, when the journalist attempts to make transparent the points outlined rather opaquely in the Heritage Report, there are elements of technicalization.

Application

1. In the excerpt above, what features of technicalization are evident?
2. Write down the purposes these features seem to serve.
3. Rewrite this text with fewer features of technicalization so that it is more accessible.
4. Dicuss in writing whether Krugman could have expressed his ideas in a less opaque way. What would the effect have been on you as the reader?
5. Compare your response with others.

CDA questions

The technicalization features we have studied so far are summarized below:

- Condensation through nominalization
- Absence of concrete actions
- Absence of animate/human actors
- Predominance of third-person forms
- Agentless passives
- Value labelling

1. Read the following excerpts from Paul Krugman's editorial, *Little Black Lies*, *New York Times*, 28 January 2005.

This week, in a closed meeting with African-Americans, Mr. Bush asserted that Social Security was a bad deal for their race, repeating his earlier claim that 'African-American males die sooner than other males do, which means the system is inherently unfair to a certain group of people.' In other words, blacks don't live long enough to collect their fair share of benefits …

First, Mr. Bush's remarks on African-Americans perpetuate a crude misunderstanding about what life expectancy means. It's true that the current life expectancy for black males at birth is only 68.8 years – but that doesn't mean that a black man who has worked all his life can expect to die after collecting only a few years' worth of Social Security benefits. Blacks' low life expectancy is largely due to high death rates in childhood and young adulthood. African-American men who make it to age 65 can expect to live, and collect benefits, for an additional 14.6 years – not that far short of the 16.6-year figure for white men.

(Copyright © 2005 by The New York Times Co. Reprinted with permission.)

2. Underline any examples of technicalization in the excerpts.
3. Circle the features Krugman has used in place of technicalization.
4. How do these features contribute to the dialogic nature of the piece?
5. Does this make the piece more or less persuasive?

Conversationalization 8.4

As we suggested earlier, conversationalization is in some ways the opposite of technicalization. In conversationalization, features of casual conversation are being co-opted into public domains such as speeches and interviews. In conversationalization, discourse practices from ordinary or private life are applied to public discourse. Common features of conversationalization involve the following elements (adapted from Fairclough and Mauranen, 1998):

1) Anecdotes or stories about the particular issue being raised – in other words, narrative format and context of parts of the discourse are used to illustrate and simplify the information;
2) Frequent use of singular and plural first-person pronouns;
3) Informal chatty manner of speaking, with elements such as repetitions, colloquial speech and short sentences which often mark conversations. Also, questions posed to the audience to further involve them;

4) Subjective marking of modality, or what Eggins (1994: 181) calls metaphors of modality such as *I think, I would like.*

5) Inclusion of personal observations and reactions such as 'I am very happy', 'I was surprised', again an expression of a stance towards statements similar to those in (4) and totally missing in technical language.

6) Increasing similarity of political interviews to conversational exchanges.

Interestingly, Blommaert (2001: 5) suggests that the effect of conversationalization is not a lessening but an increase of power, because the boundaries between public and private discourse are blurred, with an infiltration of the public into the private. That is, power is often increased because the private-public boundary is transgressed. The result is what Blommaert refers to as an invasion of the private sphere.

So although conversationalization may appear to equalize power relationships, it does not do so, as Blommaert notes; these relationships simply exert power through conversational means by mixing the private with the public. Control is equally exerted through stories and other conversational features, just as it is through technicalization. In other words, in both discursive trends elites continue to exert influence by virtue of their positions of power.

To reveal the influence exerted by powerful elites through conversationalization, we will look at a short narrative by Tony Blair, several excerpts from speeches and interviews with President Bush, and selections from a speech by James Wolfensohn, the former President of the World Bank.

8.4.1 Conversationalization: Text 4

Early in his career as leader of the Labour Party, Tony Blair spoke at the Labour Annual Conference in October 1996. He was explaining to the group that while campaigning during the 1992 general election, he spoke to a man who admitted that he would be voting for the Tory party. Blair uses this story to suggest why people voted for the Tories and what is needed to gain votes for the Labour party.

Here is the story in Prime Minister Tony Blair's words:

> I can vividly recall the exact moment that I knew the last election was
> lost … I was canvassing in the Midlands, on an ordinary, suburban
> estate. I met a man polishing his Ford Sierra. He was a self-employed
> electrician. His Dad voted Labour, he said. He used to vote Labour, too.
> But he'd bought his own house now. He'd set up his own business. He
> was doing very nicely. 'So I've become a Tory', he said. He wasn't rich.
> But he was doing better than he [presumably his dad] did, and as far
> as he was concerned, being better off meant being Tory too.

http://www.prnewswire.co.uk/cgi/news/release?id=43481 (Accessed December 2005)

If you were to hear this story, you would probably have no trouble processing the information, because the linguistic resources Blair has selected are very similar to ones used in private conversations.

The numbers below refer to the list of conversationalization features listed in Section 8.4.

To begin, the narrator sets the scene (1). The story then focuses on the main protagonist – a man who is described and identified both by his occupation and his lineage. His political views become known through his father's political position and the changes that have caused this man to vote not Labour – the apparent tradition in the family – but Tory. The crux of the story has to do with the accomplishments of the man, his material advancement in the world – owning a car and his own house, supposedly an advancement over his father. For these reasons, the man is now voting for the Tory party.

Notice the short sentences often found in oral narratives, making it easier for the listeners to follow the story (3). Note also the three instances of the familiar first-person singular form used in telling stories (2).

Blair uses this short story to make points about why change is needed in the Labour Party platform, in order to attract future voters like the man in the story. Evident is a simplification of Blair's political position to make his point more comprehensible to his audience. In other words, the position he holds as the leader of the party is a powerful one; he uses an anecdote (1) to illustrate more complicated ideas and thus to simplify them. It is a shorthand explanation of the elements of change that must come into play for the Labour Party to win back voters like the man in the story.

In terms of linguistic resources, the story itself is told much as one would tell a neighbor or friend about an incident such as this. Establishing a casual and intimate relationship with the audience through narrative devices makes the message quite palatable. But the fact that his points are conveyed through conversational means does not indicate that Blair intends to equalize the relationship between himself and his audience. Instead, he creates a synthetic relation of intimacy to convince his listeners. The features of private conversation simulate the closeness of the private setting in the public domain; the purpose is, however, to persuade.

Discussion

1. Having read the anecdote, do you think that Blair accomplished his goal of persuading his audience of the need to change policies?
2. Would you employ such means in trying to convince listeners? When you hear speakers use these conversational techniques, are you positively or negatively affected? Why?
3. In what other situations might the storytelling technique be useful?

8.4.2 Conversationalization: Text 5

We now move on to the next text, in which President Bush participates in a 'conversation' about class action lawsuit reform. In the excerpts that follow, President Bush provides rationales for the reform of class action lawsuits. We will focus on the conversational resources he uses.

It is revealing to note that 'Conversations' are what the White House calls relatively informal meetings between the President and various civic groups.

> I do want to put it in the larger context, though, about why we even ought to take on this issue. As Carlos said, lawsuits are – a litigious society is one that makes it difficult for capital to flow freely. And a capitalist society depends on the capacity for people willing to take

risk and to say there's a better future, and I want to take a risk toward that future. And I'm deeply concerned that too many lawsuits make it too difficult for people to do that.

…We're here to talk about class-action lawsuit abuse. And we've got some experts here to help us understand what class-action lawsuits are all about, and how best to effect good public policy.

http://www.whitehouse.gov/news/releases/2005/02/20050209-15.html
(Accessed March 2005)

1. Which of the conversationalization features below are exemplified in the short excerpt above? List the instances of each feature. For example, 'I do want' indicates the subjective marking of modality, clearly expressing the president's position towards the issue of class action lawsuits.
    a) Frequent use of singular and plural first person pronouns
    b) Informal chatty manner of speaking (repetitions, colloquial speech, mood variation, short sentences…)
    c) Subjective marking of modality ('I think', 'I would like'…)
    d) Inclusion of personal observations and reactions
2. Discuss in writing the purpose that each serves.
3. Do you find President Bush's conversational techniques convincing? Why? Why not?
4. Compare your responses with others in the class.

Application

A second example of conversationalization is evident in this text by Greg Palast, a British journalist, on the same topic, entitled 'Bush Tort reform executive clemency for executive killers'.

Here is Greg Palast's story:

Closing the doors of justice to the ruined and wrecked families of boardroom bad guys is nothing less than executive clemency for executive executioners.

You think my accusation is over the top? Well, please talk with Elaine Levenson.

Levenson, a Cincinnati housewife, has been waiting for her heart to explode. In 1981, surgeons implanted a mechanical valve in her heart, the Bjork-Shiley, 'the Rolls-Royce of valves,' her doctor told her. What neither she nor her doctor knew was that several Bjork-Shiley valves had fractured during testing, years before her implant. The company that made the valve, a unit of the New York-based pharmaceutical giant Pfizer, never told the government.

When the valve's struts break and the heart contracts, it explodes. Two-thirds of the victims die, usually in minutes. In 1980, Dr. Viking Bjork, whose respected name helped sell the products, wrote to Pfizer demanding corrective action. He threatened to publish cases of valve strut failures.

A panicked Pfizer executive telexed, 'ATTN PROF BJORK, WE WOULD PREFER THAT YOU DID NOT PUBLISH THE DATA RELATIVE TO STRUT FRACTURE.' The company man gave this reason for holding off public exposure of the deadly valve failures: 'WE EXPECT A FEW MORE.' His expectations were realized. The count has reached eight hundred fractures, five hundred dead-so far.

Eight months after the 'don't publish' letter, a valve was implanted in Mrs. Levenson. In 1994, the U.S. Justice Department nabbed Pfizer. To avoid criminal charges, the company paid civil penalties-and about $200 million in restitution to victims. Without the damning evidence prized from Pfizer by a squadron of lawyers, the Justice Department would never have brought its case.

http://www.GregPalast.com (Accessed March 2005)

Practice

1. Use the conversationalization features list at the beginning of this section to identify and list all the conversational features evident in this story.
2. Compare Palast's conversationalization strategies with those used by Blair in the anecdote in Section 8.4.1.

Summing up the main points in his article, Palast has the following to say:

> The Tort reformer's line is that fee-hungry lawyers are hawking bogus fears, poisoning American's faith in the basic decency of the business community, turning us into a nation of a people who no longer trust each other. But whose fault is that? The lawyers? Elaine Levenson (the woman with the implant) put her trust in Pfizer Pharmaceutical. Then they broke her heart.

1. Here Palast uses many conversational features that are designed to engage his audience. Go through this excerpt to identify all of these features.
2. Discuss the specific ways in which each of these features engages his readers.

To examine yet other features of conversationalization, we turn back to President George W. Bush, whose conversational style marks his discursive interactions with the public. It is a style that crosses the boundaries between the private and public domains, and by so doing it intrudes on the private domains. This is particularly evident in another of Bush's speeches.

8.4.3 Conversationalization: Text 6

Let's look at the conversational features of Bush's speech to parents, teachers and students at a Virginia high school on 12 January 2005. He is speaking about an education act he signed, entitled 'No child left behind'. In the speech we will be examining, he focuses on the need for accountability. We first quote a longer extract of the speech to show the background to the points he is making and the conversational tools he is employing to make them.

> To keep this country prosperous and to keep this country hopeful, we've got to make sure these public schools of ours stay strong, and we started on that road to strengthening every public school three years ago, when I signed the No Child Left Behind Act. The theory of this law is straightforward, it's pretty easy to understand: that in return for federal dollars, we are asking for results. That makes sense if you're a taxpayer. It makes sense, frankly, if you're an innovative teacher and a

strong principal. We're leaving behind the old attitude that it's okay for some students just to be shuffled through the system. That's not okay.

If you believe every child can learn, then it makes sense to measure to determine whether every child is learning. That's called account-ability, accountability for results. Accountability is so crucial to achieve our goal for every child learning to read, write, add and subtract. Accountability helps to correct problems early, before it is too late. Accountability enables a good teacher to test a curriculum as to whether or not that curriculum is working. Accountability allows prin-cipals and teachers to determine whether methodology is working. Accountability also is a way to make sure parents stay involved in the educational systems across our country.

You know, for a while, in certain districts, a parent – you'd ask a parent, how is your school doing? And the parent's natural reaction is, it's the best there is. In some cases, like the parents here at Stuart High, they're right.

…Accountability system allows a parent or a local official or con-cerned citizen to compare results from one school to another within a district, and from one district to another within a state. And that's important.

http://www.whitehouse.gov/ (Accessed February 2005)

Now let's look at Excerpt A – the first paragraph – in more detail. We have numbered the sentences and bolded some conversational features to facilitate discussion.

Excerpt A

1) To keep this country prosperous and to keep this country hopeful, **we**'ve got to make sure these public schools of **ours** stay strong, and **we** started on that road to strengthening every public school three years ago, when I signed the No Child Left Behind Act. 2) The theory of this **law is straightforward, it's pretty easy** to understand: that in return for federal dollars, we are asking for results. 3) **That makes sense** if you're a taxpayer. 4) It **makes sense**, frankly, if you're an inno-vative teacher and a strong principal. 5) **We**'re leaving behind the old attitude that it's okay for some students just to be shuffled through the system. 6) That**'s not okay**.

The point of this entire excerpt is to convince the audience, if they need convincing, about accountability; in this law, accountability means testing. In the excerpt he is providing a rationale for it.

In this excerpt, we can see two discursive features that are explicit examples of conversationalization. One is the use of first-person plural pronouns. Throughout this segment Bush uses 'we' – not the exclusive 'we', but the inclusive 'we' – with which he both appeals to parents and includes them in the decisions reflected in the law. He describes the law as a joint effort and as reflecting shared goals. The inclusive form seems to suggest that the audience shares with him the goals and the means towards these goals. He talks to the audience as friends, as colleagues whose interests he has at heart. By suggesting that 'we' must ensure that schools stay strong, he expects parents to agree with him and includes them in the decision to strengthen schools. He does so through the repetition of 'we', suggesting that he and they work together to accomplish this.

The inclusive 'we' has a further function here: it excludes others who may argue against what he is doing, setting up a 'we' versus 'them' distinction. 'If you are not with us you are against us' is a refrain evident in many of Bush's speeches. This linguistic choice may stem from an anticipated negative reaction to the law from those who feel differently about 'accountability' – that is, about testing. The use of the inclusive 'we' is an attempt to show a unified front.

A second conversational feature is one we have not discussed in detail, namely the use of personal observations, such as **law is straightforward**; **it's pretty easy**; **That makes sense** (x2); **not okay**.

Evident here are '…claims about what ought to be the case … overtly based on the speaker's own judgements' (Fairclough and Mauranen, 1997: 114).

Evaluating the theory of the law in terms of his own judgments, Bush seems to suggest that he speaks for all. If he finds it was easy for him, the suggestion is that it will, of course, be easy for everyone. When he claims that '…asking for results 'makes sense', he is revealing his own position on the issue. He maintains that it 'makes sense' to demand results for the financial support provided in the new law for educational reforms; this acts as a preamble to his insistence on accountability being built into the law.

Bush's own evaluation of elements of the law is, of course, not just a personal evaluation; it is also a public pronouncement by virtue of his position. Bush's opinion here constitutes an evaluation in the public domain which validates the statement more than it would in the private sphere. The statement, among others, is a good example of the blurring and transgressing of the boundaries between private and public domains. This instance of conversationalization suggests not a softening of power, but an increase in control (Blommaert, 2001: 5). The intrusion of the public into the private, and vice versa, makes it difficult for readers and listeners to decide whether evaluations such as those of Bush above are simply taken from the private domain and applied to the public one, however inappropriate that may be. Fairclough and Mauranen suggest that 'The shift of public discourse towards the lifeworld (the private one) involves a widespread appropriation of the discourse practices of ordinary life in public domains … a simulation of conversational interaction' (1997: 91).

Excerpt B exemplifies two other discourse features: repetition and parallel structure.

Excerpt B

7) If you believe every child can learn, then it makes sense to measure to determine whether every child is learning. 8) That's called **accountability, accountability for results.** 9) **Accountability** is so crucial to achieve our goal for every child learning to read, write, add and subtract. 10) **Accountability** helps to correct problems early, before it is too late. 11) **Accountability** enables a good teacher to test a curriculum as to whether or not that curriculum is working. 12) **Accountability** allows principals and teachers to determine whether methodology is working. 13) **Accountability** also is a way to make sure parents stay involved in the educational systems across our country.

Repetition is often found in oral narratives, where it helps listeners keep track of the main threads of the story. It is also used for emphasis, and to ensure that listeners not only remember the topic, but know its importance. That the word 'accountability' appears 7 times in 6 sentences is a clear indication of how highly Bush values it. The fact that the word is really a substitute for 'testing' does not become entirely clear until later in his speech, but when it does come, the groundwork has been laid and the listeners are ready for it.

This is particularly so because of the reinforcement the idea receives in the parallel structure of sentences 9–13. Each of these sentences has the same grammatical form, again to emphasize the point – in each case, 'accountability' is textually the theme and ideationally the main participant. The claims made for accountability are drummed into the listeners' ears through this parallel construction. This is quite apparent when we isolate the verbal groups associated with accountability:

Accountability:
9.   is crucial
10.   helps correct problems
11.   enables a good teacher
12.   allows principals and teachers
13.   is a way

In each, there is a positive assessment of the concept, emphasizing its necessity, its value in learning and therefore the justification for including it in the new law.

Application

In Excerpt C, which continues from Excerpt B above, you will notice several other conversational features. If you didn't know that this was a public setting and that the president was speaking, you might think you were overhearing a spontaneous conversation between friends or colleagues, because it is so reminiscent of the private domain in which casualness such as this is typically found.

Excerpt C

14) You know, for a while, in certain districts, a parent – you'd ask a parent, how is your school doing? 15) And the parent's natural reaction is, it's the best there is. 16) In some cases, like the parents here at Stuart High (where he is speaking) they're right. … 17) Accountability system allows a parent or a local official or concerned citizen to com-

pare results from one school to another within a district, and from one district to another within a state. 18) And that's important.

1. Go through Excerpt C above and underline or circle all of the conversational features that you can find.
2. Explain in writing the purpose that each conversational feature serves. Compare your responses with those of others in the class.
3. Pick out those elements that seem to you inappropriate in a public domain and that more appropriately belong in the private setting. Defend your choice in writing.

8.4.4   Conversationalization: Text 7

The next text is a speech given by James Wolfensohn, the former president of the World Bank, to a conference at Cambridge University in June 2000. In it, Wolfensohn talks about the uses and contributions of information and communication technology in less developed countries.

We will start with some of the conversational segments of his speech to discuss the specific purpose they serve in the context of convincing the audience of the value of information and communication technology for development. We will focus on instances of conversationalization similar to ones we have been examining in this section. The speech describes the achievements of the World Bank in increasing technology in third world countries and in improving knowledge about this technology. Throughout, Wolfensohn interjects personal anecdotes, and interacts with the audience in a very personal way.

Discussion

Let's look at a few short statements from the beginning of his speech.

1. Consider the quote below and try to identify any features of conversationalization and the possible reasons for these choices.

Excerpt A

And so I am grateful to Keynes for his guidance and his participation
in those negotiations because it has created a job that I am now
involved in and so I want to thank you and my children want to thank
you because of the very large salary I receive.

We at the bank as you know, and let me talk from that vantage point,
are concerned with the issues of poverty in the world.

(King's College, Cambridge, U.K. 24 June 2000)

2. Compare your findings with those of Mark Thompson from the
    University of Cambridge's Judge Institute of Management, who
    used CDA to analyze this excerpt.

Read the following extract from Thompson's critical discourse analysis
of a speech by Wolfensohn.

**Example of a CDA
analysis: a speech**

Interestingly, … (this quote above) is probably the point at which the
speaker is most exposed, since he is unabashedly asserting a claim to be
paid highly in comparison to the development's subjects-some of whom,
we later learn, exist on 'under a dollar a day.

Critical discourse analysis offers an explanation for the way in which
this uncomfortable power relation offers an explanation for the reasser-
tion of an unpalatable (and fundamental) aspect of development mixed
with speech genres of confidence, in which he appears to be confiding
in, and inviting a personal, co-conspiratorial link with his audience;
and humour in which the assertion is made in deliberately unacceptable
terms, thus undermining objection. (2003: 357)

We might add here that this example reinforces the point made by
Blommaert that conversationalization such as this is not a 'softening of
power' at all, not an equalizing element as it appears to be but a trans-
posing of the private 'lifeworld' as Fairclough and Mauranen call it into
the public domain however inappropriately.

By the beginning of (the next paragraph), the Bank appears to be precariously poised as a group of highly-paid experts with no object for their expertise, so the poor are quickly introduced… and normalized within the Bank's development paradigm, in which we first hear that ICTs are to play a major part. (ibid: 357)

Moving on to other excerpts from the speech, we again see many elements of conversationalization. In Excerpt B below, the President of the World Bank personalizes his speech through the use of the first person singular pronoun 'I'. He couples this with another feature we have seen in Bush's speeches, the synthetic 'you'. This further personalizes his speech and creates the impression that he is involved in a dialogue with the audience. It is reinforced by the statement which draws a parallel between his own experiences and those of his listeners: 'I was someone like many of you…' Associating himself with them further draws the listeners into the group Wolfensohn represents, seeming to make them one of 'us'. It is therefore strange that the 'we' he uses throughout the excerpt is an exclusive one. This could suggest that no matter how much the audience shares his experiences, he is still part of an exclusive club to which they do not belong. Wolfensohn takes on an authority that is exclusive to the club of which he is not only a member but a leader. And leaders do things like 'coin a phrase' such as the one he refers to in the last sentence of this part of his speech. He has not only learned a lot about technology, overcoming his past ignorance, but has become a leader in the field. And he does not hesitate to congratulate himself publicly.

Excerpt B

I thought **I** might just tell **you**, not as a matter of theory, but as a matter of practice, what **we** have done in the last five years since **I** have had the privilege of running the Bank. Coming as **I** did, **I** was someone, like many of **you I** suppose, who grew up without any facility for using internet, or using a computer, but very conscious of the fact that this was an extraordinary tool. Just let **me** give **you** a cameo of the last five years in our own institution. The first thing **I** recognized is that it was not just money that was important in development, and so **I** coined the phrase that **we** should not just be a money bank but a knowledge bank. (24 June 2000)

In Excerpt C, he later makes it clear again to this audience how he has been responsible for spreading technology and the knowledge of how to use it.

Excerpt C

> The second thing which happened was that I went to Uganda on a trip and then came back to the United States to Wyoming where I have a small place. The local chamber of commerce had been after me to make a speech for a long time. Finally I got up in front of the Chamber of Commerce and someone asked whether there was something we could do in development. With some sort of instinct, I said 'why don't we link the Jackson Hole High School with the Uganda High School that I just saw, and we can do it by internet and wouldn't it be fun for the kids of Jackson Hole to know something about Uganda…' (24 June 2000)

1. Identify Wolfensohn's use of conversationalization features to appeal to his audience.
2. How does he personalize information?
3. In your opinion, in what ways does Wolfensohn cross the boundaries between the private and public domains?

To summarize, we have been looking at typical features of the conversationalization trend: how speakers and writers use anecdotes, first- and second-person pronouns, questions and other linguistic resources that simulate an informal and chatty relationship for persuasive purposes. We have looked at how these resources do not contribute to an equalizing of power, but rather to a transgression of private domains by the public one. We have seen significant evidence of these strategies throughout the material we examined.

Nevertheless, Thompson cautions against making assumptions about the intentionality of discursive choices such as these, a caution that critical discourse analysts do not make often enough.

Views from the theorists:
Thompson

The task of CDA

To claim that the speech (Wolfensohn's) analyzed here was a set of conscious cumulative constructions on the part of the speaker would be to impute almost impossibly Machiavellian aims... to a person who, it is likely, undertakes his job in good faith, unaware for the most part, of the assumptions and positionality with which speeches such as this appear, upon closer analysis, to be drenched. (ibid: 370)

Thompson acknowledges that analysts can never be sure of intentionality but this does not take away from the task of CDA, which he discusses in this way:

Indeed, it is this very task-uncovering, problematizing, and raising our consciousness about contestable assumptions which have, through sheer use, become woven into the fabric of discursive interaction – at which CDA arguably excels. The submerged nature of many such assumptions merely makes such a task the more pressing. That it is an important task is evidenced by the analysis itself... the links posited between discursive forms... and the discursive power relations. These links are able to show how local-level utterances are in fact saturated with prior assumptions about role, legitimacy, and the nature of the world-in short, about power – and how the inequalities attendant upon assumptions can be reproduced, wittingly or unwittingly, in discursive practice. (370)

8.5   Marketization

Fairclough outlines many interrelated aspects of this trend in his article (1993) from which the features described below are adapted. Our focus, like Fairclough's, will be on how the discourse of advertisement has colonized much of public discourse in general, and the discourse of education in particular. We will examine discourse from the tertiary level of education, considering it a reflection of the more general trend towards consumerism in our early twenty-first century society. Our analyses will cover the discursive ways in which universities describe themselves as institutions and advertise employment opportunities. These discursive choices show clear evidence of the growth and spread of marketization.

To augment Fairclough's data base, we extended our examination to include North American tertiary level institutions in addition to British ones. A further extension is the brief analysis of the interrelationship between the verbal and the visual modes of communication in marketization, calling on our expertise from Chapter 6.

Throughout our discussion in this section, the focus will be on the visual and verbal indications that education has come to be reconstructed on a market basis (Fairclough, 1993: 141).

The following list, adapted from Fairclough (1993), outlines the main features of marketization:

3) Personalization of the reader or listener through the use of the second-person pronoun 'you' often used in the singular; personalization of the institution through the use of the inclusive 'we'. The result is the setting up of a personal relationship between interactants.

4) Incorporation of advertising elements, including self-promotional claims, into university discourse. Related to this is a shift from traditional institutional identities to entrepreneurial identities; in the new professional identities personal qualities and personal features of identity are highlighted.

5) Focus in employment advertisements on the applicant's activities and productivity.

6) Mixing of commodity advertising – as if education was itself a commodity – and prestige or corporate advertising, e.g., the use of trademarks, logos and slogans, as well as in the design and layout of information.

7) Characterizing of the institution and the consumer in particular ways.

8) Interpersonal marking of discourses through modality of probability, obligation and necessity, as well as mood variation with commands evident. This is, of course, another feature of marketing discourse, which we saw in Chapter 4, where advertisers command readers to act in certain ways.

These discursive features represent some of the more prominent shifts of higher-level institutions towards the market mode, where there is evidence of a '…fracturing of the boundary between (the discourse of) higher education and business as regards advertising, and a colonization of the former by the latter' (Fairclough, 1993: 149).

We will begin by looking at some of the linguistic features of this trend in advertisements for two Canadian universities, and in job postings from British, American and Canadian tertiary level institutions.

8.5.1   Marketization: Text 8

Image 8.1: Lakehead University

In terms of verbal choices, one of the most prominent is the personalized 'you' in the heading at the top right, where new information is usually presented. The 'you' is in contrast to the numbers in the previous sentence; the message is that at Lakehead, the individual counts (and is counted).

Visually the message is reinforced by the blurred numerical and figurative representations – where people are depicted in blurred fashion because they are only numbers at other institutions. They are not treated as unique, unlike the two individuals in the foreground. The visual reinforcement of the verbal message drives home the difference between Lakehead as an institution and other places; at Lakehead individuals are valued, unlike the people who get lost elsewhere.

The focus on the main participants in the foreground as opposed to the blurred figures in the background strongly reinforces the message of the verbal text. Here are two participants whose gaze is directed at us, the readers – and potential consumers. The two young people are interpersonally engaging with us through their prominence as well as their gaze. Compositionally, the two are framed in opposition to the blurred figures in the background – the idea clearly being that at Lakehead, students are individuals and not just numbered parts of a multitude.

We can also see prestige elements borrowed from corporate advertising: trademarks and slogans. The university has a wordmark (a verbal trademark) consisting of the words 'Lakehead University' in a specified typeface, size and colour. (The specifications are provided on the university website.) Every public communication from the university must carry this wordmark in the specified format. The design elements of the logo are understated and dignified. The typeface is traditional, the colour dark blue (a colour long associated with a prestigious British institution: Oxford University). Lakehead also has a slogan: 'Realize Your Potential'. This slogan is also trademarked – meaning that no other university is free to use these words as its slogan. The two elements combine to characterize Lakehead as an institution worthy of respect.

From a verbal perspective, the size and different font as well as the bolding of the word 'you' on the top right further reinforces the verbal message of uniqueness. It is a feature you may remember from Chapter 4 as a marker of the language of advertising. It is an attempt to connect with the readers, to create a sense of personalization (however synthetic it is) because the advertisers do not in fact know who they are addressing. They only know that it will be mainly students, and perhaps parents, but not who they are; yet through the synthetic personalization prominent in advertisements, they are trying to create a relationship.

Now look at the discourse on the bottom left reproduced below:

At Lakehead, you will never be 'just a number.' We see you as a person with unique goals and abilities, and distinct potential. With smaller classes and professors who care, we will help you succeed. Come see us in Thunder Bay, Ontario. Call or visit us online to find out more.

The verbal message further reinforces the characterization technique using synthetic personalization to achieve its purpose. Once again, in the first sentence of the discourse, 'you' is prominent as it in the rest of the discourse. The personalization being created here extends to the first-person plural 'we' evident in both the prominent discourse at the top right and on the bottom left. This is an attempt to create a dialogue with unseen readers. Another feature familiar in the world of the market is the use of the imperative form. Here it is repeated twice at the end of the discourse: 'Come see us in Thunder Bay' and 'Call or visit us online to find out more.' Both of these utterances are typical in advertisements for different products. Here the product is education. This is strategic language, designed to get the audience to act, to visit and in the long run, to enroll at this university – to consume education, in short, as they would consume any other product.

The final strategic language element is evident in the wording of the slogan: 'Realize your potential'. This is also in the imperative form, urging students to come to Lakehead to benefit from what it has to offer.

The features of marketization evident here are the characterization of the institution and the reader through the use of first- and second-person pronouns, together with prestige elements from corporate advertising. As well, there is Mood variation as readers are encouraged to come and see and to stay at Lakehead to realize their potential. The university is marketing itself, its services and its facilities in the same way as any other commodity.

8.5.2   Marketization: Text 9

Another example of this trend is an advertisement for Thompson Rivers, a new university in British Columbia. We will see many of the same features, although there are also new ones. Evident are the mood choices of the last example, namely the two examples of imperatives: the first in large letters: 'Apply Now for September 2005', the second: 'Request Your Complete Information/Application Package'. Both are instances of strategic discourse designed to get people to act. But other than this, there is less personalizing since there is no pronoun use at all. Instead, in its place, we see another feature of marketization, namely a shift from traditional identities to entrepreneurial institutional identities.

Image 8.2 Thompson Rivers University

Like the advertisement for Lakehead University, the Thompson Rivers advertisement includes prestige visual elements, such as the crest (which symbolizes the mountains, the river and the railroad that characterize the location in Kamloops). The ad also exploits the exceptional beauty of the surroundings through the large photograph at the top left.

Verbally, the focus is on the new, presented in comparative terms in relation to other unmentioned universities. What is important is the newness of the offerings of this university. The institutional identity of Thompson Rivers University is presented in terms of highly saleable and desirable features, such as one would find in corporate and prestige advertisements. Verbal information is presented in bullet form, as you might find in the business world: 'smaller class size', 'personal attention', 'unique programs', 'new and modern facilities', 'lower tuition fees' and 'involvement in research'. Each of these is a desirable aspect that makes this institution more saleable – so it has adopted elements of commodity advertising, presenting education itself as a commodity rather than in terms of traditional educational values. This is further reinforced by the URL – in large print, prominently placed in the centre of the ad. Thompson Rivers, the ad tells us, is definitely a modern, connected institution.

Reinforcing these elements are the three phrases prominently placed a little off-centre, just beneath the photo of an idyllic scene of a lake and mountains in the background. They are: 'Quality Education', 'Flexible Options' and 'Lifestyle & Recreation'. Of these three, it might be suggested that only the first is a traditional value, a traditional element of the identity of university life. The other features, along with those presented in the bullets on the bottom right of the page, strongly indicate the new institutional identity being created. Without the first feature, the ad could just as well be selling upscale vacation properties.

Discussion

1. As you study the advertisement for Thompson Rivers University, focus on the visual elements. Make a list of the more prominent ones and discuss each in terms of the Representational, Modal and Compositional functions from Chapter 6.
2. Next, describe in writing the ways in which the visual reinforces the values being promoted verbally.
3. Evaluate your own reactions to this advertisement. Which of the elements of this ad appeal to you and which do not? Which of the features being promoted would make you seek more information about this university? Why?

8.5.3 Marketization: Texts 10–13

We now turn to employment opportunity advertisements from four educational institutions: two British, one American and one Canadian. The focus is on how the institutions present themselves, how they describe the candidates they want, and what they require of these candidates. As you will see, there are real differences among the discursive choices in terms of marketization.

The first set of texts is excerpted from job postings from Oxford, a traditional, very well-known and highly-regarded university in England; the second text is from the Open University, also in England, founded in the 1970s with a non-traditional structure; the third set is from Barnard College, a very prestigious women's school, part of Columbia University in New York; the fourth text is from Humber College Institute of Technology in Canada.

Text 10: Job postings, Oxford University

Regius Professorship of Civil Law

The appointee will be a scholar of distinction who will exercise leadership in research and develop graduate studies in his or her area of specialisation. He or she will also be expected to take a leading part in developing the work of the faculty generally.

Coulson Professorship of Theoretical Chemistry

The University seeks to appoint a person with an international reputation in research in theoretical chemistry, broadly interpreted. The new professor will need to ensure the continuing pursuit of excellence in teaching and research in theoretical and/or computational chemistry at Oxford and its wide recognition outside.

http://www.ox.ac.uk/jobs/ (Accessed April 2006)

Text 11: Job postings, The Open University

Professor in The Institute of Educational Technology, Centre for Research in Education and Educational Technology (CREET)

You will make a crucial contribution to its mission of pursuing research which is distinctive and of the highest quality. In so doing, along with many researchers of international repute, you will enhance the effectiveness and reputation of the Open University as a world-class institution.

You will make a strong contribution to one or more of three broad areas of work in IET: The Centre for the Study of Educational Technologies, The Centre for Institutional Research and The Centre for Educational Development. You will be encouraged to develop your own research and scholarship to support the research and development missions of IET. We offer excellent support for research and professional development, including funding for conference attendance and other activities.

http://www.3.open.ac.uk/employment/ (Accessed April 2005)

Text 12: Job postings, Barnard College

Chemistry: General Chemistry Lab Director

Barnard College, an independent undergraduate college for women affiliated with Columbia University, seeks a Ph.D chemist … Requirements: excellent teaching and administrative skills with a strong command of written and spoken English.

Economics: Macroeconomics

…Barnard is an independent liberal arts college for women affiliated with Columbia University. We seek a highly qualified macroeconomist who can thrive in our unique academic environment where both teaching and scholarship are important … Candidates must also contribute to the department's mission of …

Political Science: Comparative Politics

Barnard College is a highly selective liberal arts college for women, affiliated with Columbia University … We are interested in candidates who… Applicants must already have a Ph.D. and several years of demonstrated excellence in teaching …

http://www.barnard.edu/hr/employment (Accessed April 2005)

Text 13: Job postings, Humber College Institute of Technology

Part-Time Professor, Creative Advertising

The School of Media Studies at Humber College is looking for people who work in and are passionate about the creative side of advertising. If you know art direction, concept development, layout, copy, or related areas of communications, we want you to be a key contributor to our new Bachelor's Degree program in Creative Advertising. These are part-time positions so you can experience the joys of teaching with minimal time away from your agency. The first class of this exciting new program enters in September 2005.

http://www.humber.ca/careers.php (Accessed April 2005)

1. Examine Texts 10–13 above, and list all occurrences of each of the following features of marketization. Not all texts exhibit all the features.

   • Personalization of the reader or listener through the use of second-person pronoun 'you' often used in the singular;
   • Personalization of the institution through the use of the inclusive 'we'.
   • Shift from traditional identities to entrepreneurial institutional and professional identities.
   • New interpersonal features including marked modality of probability and obligation.

2. Write a paragraph describing the differences and similarities among the postings. Include information about the features that distinguish the postings from one another. Suggest a rationale for the differences you observe.

Norman Fairclough suggested in 1993 that there was a definite trend towards the commercialization of modern society, evident in and instantiated by the samples of university discourses he analyzed. He suggested that the marketization of universities is one aspect of the marketization of education in general.

1. You have now examined ads for universities themselves, and for positions at these universities. On the basis of this brief examination would you agree with Fairclough's conclusion? If so, what features have you seen that are evidence of this trend?
2. Have you found exceptions to this trend in the discourses above and if so how would you account for this?
3. In what ways does this trend relate to the connection between language and power? In other words, does the marketization of discourse contribute to increases in power? Of whom? How?

8.6   Globalization

To begin discussion of this last trend, we will look at one of the clearest definitions of globalization as a process. It comes from Marcussen in his abstract. Later in his paper, he also examines the discourse of globalization.

Views from the theorists:
Martin Marcussen

Globalization

Globalization is overall considered to be an irreversible process to which national politicians will have to adapt in order to avoid future crises. Thus, we can talk about a structural-determinist discourse, or a discourse which is traditionally applied in neo-liberal circles stating that 'there is no alternative. … The dynamics of the globalization idea can be better understood by focusing on the Ideational entrepreneurs who formulated the idea in the first place, the power-base of the politicians who started to talk the globalization discourse, the role of international economic organizations in diffusing the idea, and the national politicians and civil servants who in the end implemented the globalization discourse in concrete national settings. In other words, the life-cycle of the structural-determinist discourse seems very much to be actor-driven. (Marcussen, 2000)

This last trend refers to the particular area of economic life, but we include it here because globalization as a process pervades much of our lives and it does so through language. To fully understand the connection between language and power it is necessary to understand the role of discourse in what is called our 'knowledge-based economy', where much of what is bought and sold across great distances is done so discursively.

Many people, including Fairclough, Giddens and Graham, have written about the role of language in this new economic trend. In fact, there is a website devoted to the study of globalization, not only in economic terms but in areas that affect much of our social lives in the twenty-first century (www.cddc.vt.edu/host/lnc). We introduce this trend by examining the role of discourse in the process of globalization, in order to make transparent what are often opaque features of this new social phenomenon.

Fairclough suggests that:

Globalization entails 'action at a distance' it means that social processes and social relations are stretched out across huge distances both in terms of mileage and in terms of social and cultural differences. Representations of these processes and relations in discourse therefore become increasingly important in maintaining some sort of order within this complexity – part of what binds people together … is shared representations of what they do. (2001: 205)

Globalization itself is an economic process that benefits some and hurts others. Fairclough, citing Bourdieu and others, claims that 'Those who benefit from it seek to extend it, and one of the resources which they use is discourse of globalization…' (Fairclough, 2001: 207).

The discourse of globalization incorporates discursive features that promote the trend of globalization itself. We will look at globalization as an economic and political process, particularly in Britain. We will briefly examine the discourse of what is called the 'Third Way', associated with the New Labour Party of Britain. Discursive features evident in economic and political processes are also evident in the discourse of the World Bank and other world organizations, such as the International Monetary Fund. These features are pervasive, and lead, according to Fairclough, to a codification 'of aspects of social life'. In other words, there is a '…narrowing down of the range of ways of using language and of the range of discourses for representing the world' (ibid: 207). And this affects our social life, including our daily interactions.

For this reason, we end our book with an economic, social and political trend which is to a great extent defined by, and carried out through, discursive practices.

Once again, we will look at specific discursive features within several different contexts: politics, world trade and development.

Our list of the discursive features prevalent in globalization is adapted from Fairclough's description in the last chapter of his revised *Language and Power* (2001) and from an article entitled 'Critical discourse analysis in researching language in the new capitalism: overdeterminism, transdisciplinarity, and textual analysis' in a collection of essays on the interface between SFL and CDA (Young and Harrison, 2004).

Discursive features of globalization

Globalization is presented as an inevitable reality that cannot be argued against; it is represented, in other words, as a *fait accompli*. This is accomplished through several linguistic resources:

1) Processes are realized in the simple present tense, that is, the timeless present.
2) A cascade of change is presented as a list of examples to produce a cumulative effect that overwhelms the reader with its weight. The examples thrown together are not necessarily related. Presenting them in a list contributes to a sense of cascading inventory in paratactic arrangement.
3) A cumulative list of evidence is presented, described but not analyzed as to cause and effects.
4) Processes are often presented without agency.
5) Actors in material processes are sometimes non-human and inanimate.
6) Processes are often nominalized.

Let's begin by looking at the first aspect, which presents globalization as more complete than it actually is, and further, as a simple fact of life that cannot be changed and thus cannot be argued against. The implication is that globalization has to be accepted, that nations and states have to accommodate to this new trend. The discourse of globalization is thus a discourse of power (Fairclough, 2001: 207). This becomes particularly evident in representations by diverse speakers such as Vice President of the European Commission Sir Leon Brittan, British Prime Minister Tony Blair, World Bank President James Wolfensohn, and former Vice President of the United States, Al Gore.

In the text below by Lord Brittan, we see the language of a *fait accompli*.

8.6.1 Globalization: Text 14

> Globalisation **is** a fact of life, and **will continue** irrespective and independent of the activities of government. It **is** vital that national and international organizations **acknowledge** the impact of globalisation and **respond** accordingly.

(Rt. Hon Sir Leon Brittan QC, 1999)

One of the main features of this example of the discourse of globalization, namely the present tense, is also referred to as the timeless present. This choice is not used to represent future possibilities, but to describe events that exist now and that are part of our lives. One of the strongest aspects is the presentation of an event as completed and as a current reality. The one example of the future tense here only adds to this by predicting with an air of confidence the inevitability of this process. Neither governments nor national and international organizations can stand against it.

8.6.2   Globalization: Text 15

> Globalisation has transformed our economies and our working prac-
> tices […] Any Government that thinks it can go it alone is wrong. If the
> markets don't like your policies they will punish you…

(Remarks by Tony Blair at the Economic Club, Chicago, Illinois, 22 April 1999)

Practice

1. Look at Text 15 above. Identify the aspects of completeness. List these.
2. Compare your list with others in the class.

8.6.3   Globalization: Text 16

Other examples of a preponderance of timeless present realizations of processes are taken from two of Lord Brittan's speeches on globalization. The first excerpt is from his paper, 'Globalization: responding to new political and moral challenges', delivered in 1997 at the World Economic Forum; the second excerpt is from his paper 'The contribution of the WTO (World Trade Organization) Millennium Round to globalisation: an EU view', delivered at a Globalization Symposium in Vienna in 1999.

Text 16a

> Globalisation is widely viewed as one of the most powerful forces shaping the modern world. … What is abundantly true … is that globalisation does require a greater willingness to accept change. Change is not new, of course.
>
> In short there is no genuine alternative to globalisation. Anything else would be a blind alley. (Brittan, 1997)

Text 16b

> Globalisation is a fact of life, and will continue irrespective and independent of the activities of government. The issue is not whether we can accept or reject it, but how to ensure it is channelled in positive directions. It is vital that national and international organisations acknowledge the impact of globalisation and respond accordingly. (Brittan, 1999)

Application

1. Read the two excerpts above to find examples of the timeless present. Explain in writing the purposes that are served by Lord Brittan's choices.
2. Explain in a paragraph or two how the linguistic resources he selects underline the idea of the completeness and inevitability of globalization.

Now let's look at other elements of the discourse of globalization. As we have outlined above, there are several other features to examine. Here we will focus on the paratactic resources in which speakers provide lists of items or events, so that everything that is included in the list appears to be related. This is accomplished not only by the list but by the fact that in paratactic relations each of the items or actions occurs in the same grammatical form.

8.6.4   Globalization: Text 17

Parataxis surfaces in many discourses of globalization, beginning with Marcussen himself, who while analyzing the language resources used, provides examples of this grammatical structure in the process of his analysis.

> Other examples of coupling can be given. In the citations listed at the beginning of this paper, some of the social democratic spokes-persons couple globalization to a certain way of thinking about the economy. A **sustainable**, **healthy**, **sound** and **responsible economic policy** strategy is one which is rigorous on **inflation, budgetary deficits**, **foreign debt** and **currency stability**. Everything is explained in the light of globalization. (2000: 5)

Essentially, this is a list composed of nominal groups beginning with 'inflation' and ending with 'stability'. Each part of the list is in the same grammatical form – in this case nouns. Coupling together the items in this way is intended to be convincing about the strategy involved in globalization. The list of items is joined together by commas or by 'and'. Each item is equal in structure to the other, and joined through what is called paratactic relation: a connection between like items. Listed items can be realized by nouns, as in the case above. They can also be events, realized by verbs, as in the next example.

8.6.5   Globalization: Text 18

> …Let me summarise the new political agenda we stand for: (1) Financial prudence as the foundation of economic success. In Britain, **we have eliminated the massive Budget deficit** we inherited; **put in new fiscal rules; granted Bank of England independence** – and we're proud of it. (2) On top of that foundation, there is a new economic role for Government. We don't believe in laissez-faire. But the role is not *picking winners*, *heavy handed intervention*, *old-style corporatism*, but: education, skills, technology, small business entre-preneurship.

(Remarks by Tony Blair at the Economic Club, Chicago, Illinois, 22 April 1999)

In each of the bolded clauses, there is a list of material processes realized by verbal groups, linked by semi colons. This list of actions is selected to show how active Blair has been in setting out priorities and in carrying out a particular political plan. The list in paratactic form is designed to reinforce his message to the public. This paratactic list supports another list in this short segment; this one is composed of nominalizations followed by yet another paratactic list of different nominal groups. We have italicized the nominalizations and underlined the last list of items in nominal groups.

The point here is that Blair uses paratactic listing to drum his points home. Within five sentences, three paratactic sets result in a cascading of items and events designed to impress an audience with the Blair government's purposeful activity, determination and self assurance.

This linguistic resource of parataxis marks many of Blair's speeches, as we see in the next example from a speech in 1999, entitled 'Doctrine of the International Community'.

8.6.6   Globalization: Text 19

> The lesson of the Asian crisis is above all that it is better to invest in countries where you have openness, independent central banks, properly functioning financial systems and independent courts, where you do not have to bribe or rely on favours from those in power.

(Remarks by Tony Blair at the Economic Club, Chicago, Illinois, 22 April 1999)

Application

1. Go through the excerpt above and identify the paratactic structures.
2. How do the modifications in the groups reinforce the overall effect of parataxis?

8.6.7   Globalization: Text 20

In Text 20, from the same speech, other elements popular in the discourse of globalization are evident, namely material processes without human agency in two out of the three cases. The excerpt opens with a short comment about globalization. Then the speaker talks about the widespread effect of globalization. In the last two sentences there are no human actors.

> Globalisation is most obvious in the economic sphere. We live in a completely new world. Every day about one trillion dollars moves across the foreign exchanges, most of it in London. Here in Chicago the Mercantile Exchange and the Chicago Board of Trade contracts worth more than $1.2 billion per day.

(Remarks by Tony Blair at the Economic Club, Chicago, Illinois, 22 April 1999.)

It is interesting that no-one is named as the mover of the dollars – they just move on their own. In the second case, while it is true that people are employed at the Mercantile Exchange and the Chicago Board of Trade, they are not mentioned, only the organizations themselves.

Once again, one result of the lack of actors – of the inclusion of mainly abstract nouns – is that there is no-one to question or to argue with about any of the points made. This choice seems to express the inevitability of the process of globalization – here are the results without any explanation of the processes. The actions resulting from globalization just seem to occur; the fact that they are presented as agentless once again reinforces the sense of the inevitability of globalization. No-one is in a position to argue against or question it, another sign that the discourse of globalization is a discourse of power. This is also evident in another discourse choice that we will examine in the last excerpt below.

8.6.8   Globalization: Text 21

What is interesting in Text 21 is that while some processes are congruently realized by verbal groups, they are not the processes that actually express the actions with which the excerpt is concerned. Rather, these actions are almost all presented by nominal groups.

We also need improved financial supervision both in individual countries through stronger and more effective peer group reviews, and internationally through the foundation of a new Financial Stability Forum. And we need more effective ways of resolving crises, like that in Brazil. The new contingent credit line at the IMF will assist countries pursuing sensible economic reforms and prevent damaging contagion. We should also think creatively about how the private sector can help to resolve short-term financial crises.

(Remarks by Tony Blair at the Economic Club, Chicago, Illinois, 22 April 1999. Crown copyright material is reproduced with the permission of the Controller of HMSO and the Queen's Printer for Scotland.)

Application

1. As you read through Text 21, list the processes realized by verbal groups; identify the type of process and the participants involved in each.
2. Next, go through Text 21 again and make a second list of the processes that have been nominalized. Are identifiable participants explicitly indicated in relation to these nominalized processes?
3. Explain in writing the implication of these choices.
4. Rephrase the text with fewer nominalizations and more concrete processes.
5. In which version is agency more easily identifiable? Does this make it easier to challenge the conclusions and the actions being described? If so, how? If not, why not? Explain in writing.

Example of a CDA analysis: the discourse of globalization

Read the following example of a critical discourse analysis of the discource of globalization. Fairclough analyzed the following segment of a speech by Blair in 1997, a Speech to European Socialists' Congress.

The critical challenge is to connect our goals to a world that has undergone a veritable revolution of change. Technology, trade and

travel are transforming our lives. Our young people will work in different industries … Many will work in or own small businesses. Jobs for
life are gone. Nine to five working is no longer universal. … Money is
traded across international boundaries in vast amounts twenty-four
hours a day.

Fairclough has this to say about Blair's speech on change:

> …Change is presented as a series, an unstructured list, of effects. The
> processes that produce these effects and the agents involved in the
> processes, are absent. … For instance, 'Jobs for life' represents insecurity
> in employment as a simple matter of fact (using what is probably best
> seen as an attribution process – although 'gone' is a verb, it functions
> more like an attributive adjective), rather than as a result of decisions
> taken by companies to serve their own interests in a particular set of
> circumstances. Where the effects of change are themselves processes,
> e.g. … 'Money is traded across boundaries in vast amounts…' the agents
> of the processes are not specified. Both the main operators in the global
> economy and those responsible for international agreements which have
> helped produce the 'new, new, new world', i.e. large business corpora-
> tions and governments, are absent. The basic design of these stories
> is very simple: this is the way the world is, so this is what we must do.
> (2001: 212–213)

---

1. Review the main features of each trend in the summary chart
   below. Note the features that recur in different trends. Do they
   serve the same purpose in each trend?

CDA questions

Technicalization	Conversationalization	Marketization	Globalization
Condensation through nominalization	Anecdotes and stories	Use of second-person pronouns	Timeless present tense
Lack of concrete actions	Use of first-person pronouns	Synthetic personalization	Cascade of change
Lack of animate actors	Repetition	Characterizing of individuals and institutions	Use of parataxis
Predominance of third-person forms	Colloquialisms	Use of corporate and prestige elements in advertising	Description without analysis
Agentless passives	Short sentences	Modality of probability and obligation	Absence of agency
Value labelling	Questions	Commands	Non-human or inanimate actors
	Subjective marking of modality		Nominalization of processes
	Personal observations		

2. Discuss the influence of these trends in society. Be specific in your examples.
3. To get a more concrete idea of the impact of these trends on your own lives, search the Web, magazines or any other form of discourse where you think these trends can be found, and bring in examples of at least two trends. Exchange these examples with another student and carry out an SFL and CDA analysis of each sample to discover which trend is being exemplified and which features are indicative of the trend.
4. Discuss how the examples illustrate the power of language that we have been examining, in this last chapter in particular, and throughout the book.

We have looked at many different types of discursive events throughout this book, examining language and power in terms of a wide variety of current issues, beginning with an introductory look at politics in relation to war speeches.

Chapters 1 to 4 presented SFL methodological tools and CDA analytical perspectives. With these, we examined the language resources employed to produce or maintain particular ideological stances behind positions of power in relation to the following issues: politics (Chapter 1), gender (Chapter 2), racism (Chapter 3) and advertising (Chapter 4). Each chapter examined the particular connection between discursive issues and ideology. Chapter 5 reviewed the techniques presented in Chapters 1 to 4, examining the language of organizations.

Chapter 6 introduced a new, important development in modes of communication: the use of multimodality. We examined the bi-directional influence of visual and verbal modes of expression. We extended the analytical tools to include visual communication, while continuing the analysis of verbal information. We also compared the influence of one mode on the other, and the contributions of each mode to the overall message being conveyed. Chapter 7 focused on the issue of power in unscripted spontaneous spoken discourse, examining through SFL and CDA how power is exerted in daily discursive interactions.

In Chapter 8 we studied four modern discourse trends and examined the ways they reflect and construct changing social practices.

After working through *The Power of Language: how discourse influences society*, you now have the ability to use SFL and CDA to discern how power and ideology are discursively realized.

Chapter 8 Glossary

Condensation: the use of a great many nominalizations in a discourse, resulting in the elimination of time, place and agency, making the discourse more difficult to understand.

Conversationalization: the use in public discourse of features of the private domain, such as telling anecdotes and stories, in public settings. Used in politics, media and advertising.

Globalization: the process of increasing interdependence and integration of social, cultural, political, and economic processes across local, national, regional, and global levels. The discourse of globalization incorporates discursive features that promote the trend of globalization itself, such as the use of the simple present tense, and listing of things and events through parataxis.

Intertextuality: The connections between texts; texts are connected to others that have preceded it and incorporate parts of previous texts in current ones. Everyone brings texts from their own social and cultural backgrounds to help understand discourse that they encounter.

Marketization: the colonization of public discourse in general, and the discourse of education in particular, by the discourse of advertising; the commodification of education and other public goods.

Parataxis: the joining together of elements of equal value, e.g., lists of nominal groups such as: apples, pears, oranges and bananas; listing of equal elements including verbal groups, adjectival groups etc.

Technicalization: the introduction of technical language and the language of experts into the social policy domain. Political strategists use technical knowledge to underwrite social changes in areas such as education, welfare and social security. In the social policy context, policies presented in technical language are directed primarily at those with a certain expertise but are often used by those without it.

Chapter 8
Further readings

The following readings combine SFL and CDA, since the overlap is so significant that a separation between the two would be artificial. We discuss the authors in the order of appearance in this chapter.

Fairclough, N. and Mauranen, A. (1997) 'The conversationalization of political discourse: a comparative view'. In this article they outline some features of conversationalization in more detail than we have done; they also discuss different aspects of marketization that we have not dealt with but that you could add to and compare with the discussion in this chapter.

Fairclough, N. (1993) 'Critical discourse analysis and the marketization of public discourse: the universities.' Here Fairclough discusses the ways in which universities have been affected by the marketization of discourse. We relied on this article primarily for our discussion.

It would be useful for you to look at this and the previous article to extend your knowledge of this discursive influence on the language of education.

Fairclough, N. (2001) *Language and Power*. In Chapter 10 in the second edition of Fairclough's book as well as in his article (Young and Harrison, 2004), he outlines in some detail the discourse of globalization and also talks about the difference between the discourse of globalization and the globalization of discourse, two different but related trends.

Lemke, J. (1995) *Textual Politics Discourse and Social Dynamics*. In this book, Lemke outlines in some detail in Chapter 4 the relationship between technical discourse and technological ideology. He explains the features of this discourse and the effects on readers of the features used.

References

Barthes, R. (1977) The Photographic Message. In S. Heath (ed.) *Image, Music, Text* 15–31. (Trans. by S. Heath) New York: Hill.

Butt, D., Fahey, R., Feez, R., Spinks, S. and Yallop, C. (2000) *Using Functional Grammar, An Explorer's Guide*. Second edition. Sydney, Australia: Macquarie University, National Centre for English Language Teaching and Research.

Clark, K. (1992) The linguistics of blame, representations of women in *The Sun*'s reporting of crimes of sexual violence. In M. Toolan (ed.) *Language, Text and Context, Essays in Stylistics* 208–224. New York: Longman.

Cotterill, J. (2004) Collocation, connotation and courtroom semantics: lawyers' control of witness testimony through lexical negotiation. *Applied Linguistics* 25 (4): 513–537.

Dobell, K. (2002) Message to employees: workforce adjustment from B. C. Public Service Agency. British Columbia, Canada, January.

Eckert, P. and McConnell-Ginet, S. (1992) New generalizations and explanations in gender research. *Language in Society* 28: 185–201.

Eggins, S. (1994) *Introduction to Systemic Functional Linguistics*. London: Pinter Publishers.

Eggins, S. (2004) *Introduction to Systemic Functional Linguistics*. Second edition. New York: Continuum Publishers.

Eggins, E. and Slade, D. (1997) *Analysing Casual Conversation*. London: Continuum.

Fairclough, N. (1989) *Language and Power*. London: Longman.

Fairclough, N. (2001) *Language and Power*. Second edition. London: Longman.

Fairclough, N. (1993) Critical discourse analysis and the marketization of public discourse: the universities. *Discourse and Society* 4(2): 133–168.

Fairclough, N. (2004) Critical discourse analysis in researching language in the new capitalism: overdetermination, transdisciplinarity and textual analysis. In L. Young and C. Harrison (eds) *Systemic Functional Linguistics and Critical Discourse Analysis: studies in social change* 103–122. New York and London: Continuum.

Fairclough, N. and Mauranen, A. (1998) The conversationalization of political discourse: a comparative view. In J. Blommaert and C. Bulcaen (eds) *Political Linguistics* 89–119. Amsterdam: John Benjamins and Son.

Fowler, R. (1996) On critical linguistics. In C. Rosa Caldas-Coulthard and M. Coulthard (eds) *Texts and Practice* 3–15. London: Routledge.

Giddens, A. (1991) Modernity and Self-identity: self and society in the late modern age. Stanford, California: Stanford University Press.

Gombrich, E. [1972] (1982) *The Image and Eye: further studies in the psychology of pictorial representation* 137–161. London: Phaidon Press Ltd. (The visual image: its place in communication. Originally published in *Scientific American*. Special issue on Communication, 272: 82–96.)

Goodman, S. (1996) Visual English. In S. Goodman and D. Graddol (eds) *Redesigning English: new texts, new identities*. London: Open University Press.

Grant, D. and Hardy, C. (2004) Introduction: struggles with organizational discourse. *Organization Studies* 25(1).

Halliday, M. A. K. (1978) *Language as Social Semiotic: the social interpretation of language and meaning*. London: Edward Arnold.

Halliday, M. A. K. (1994) *Introduction to Functional Grammar*. Second Edition. London: Edward Arnold.

Harrison, C. and Young, L. (2005) Leadership discourse in action: a textual study of organizational change in a government of Canada department. *Journal of Business and Communication Technology* 19(1): 42–77.

Holmes, J. and Meyerhoff, M. (1999) The community of practice: theories and methodologies in language and gender research. *Language in Society* 28: 173–183.

Kress, G. (1985) *Linguistic Processes in Sociocultural Practice*. Victoria, Australia: Deakin University Press.

Kress, G., Leite-Garcia, R., van Leeuwen, T. (1997) Discourse semantics. In T. A. van Dijk (ed.) *Discourse as Structure and Process* 257–291. London: Sage.

Kress, G. and van Leeuwen, T. (1996) *Reading Images: the grammar of visual design*. London: Routledge Publishers.

Krugman, P. (2005) Little black lies. *New York Times* 'Op-ed' page, 28 January.

Krugman, P. (2005) Many unhappy returns. *New York Times* 'Op-ed' page, 1 February.

Lemke, J. (1995) *Textual Politics: discourse and social dynamics*. London: Taylor and Francis.

Lemke, J. (1998) Multiplying meaning: visual and verbal semiotics in scientific text. In J. R. Martin and R. Veel (eds) *Reading Science: critical and functional perspectives on discourses of science*. London: Routledge Publishers.

Locher, M. (2004) *Power and Politeness in Action*. Berlin: Mouton de Gruyter.

Malinowski, B. [1923] (1946) The problem of meaning in primitive languages. Supplement I, by C. K. Ogden and I. A. Richards. In C. K. Ogden and I. A. Richards (eds) *The Meaning of Meaning* 296–336. Eighth edition. New York: Harcourt Brace and World.

Marcussen, M. (2000) Globalization: a third way that gospel travels worldwide. Paper presented at the International Studies Association 41st Annual Convention, Los Angelos, United States, March.

Martin, J. R. (2000) Close reading: functional linguistics as a tool for critical discourse analysis. In L. Unsworth (ed.) *Researching Language in Schools and Communities: functional linguistic perspectives* 275–304. London: Cassell.

Mitchell, D. J. (1997) Creating a better social security system for America. Backgrounder #1109. The Heritage Foundation.

Moir, A. and Jessel, D. (1989) *Brain Sex: the real difference between men and women*. New York: Dell Publishing.

Munby, D. K. and Clair, R. P. (1997) Organizational discourse. In T. A. van Dijk (ed.) *Discourse as Social Interaction Discourse Studies: a multidisciplinary introduction Volume 2* 181–205. London: Sage Publications.

O'Toole, M. (1994) The *Language of Displayed Art*. Leicester: Leicester University Press.

Shapiro, M. (1988) *The Politics of Representation: writing practices in biography, photography and policy analysis*. Wisconsin: University of Wisconsin Press.

Starke-Meyerring, D. (2005) Abstract of talk. (Making connections: intercultural inquiry through virtual teamwork in professional communication.) Lecture given at Carleton University, Ottawa, Canada, 11 March.

Talbot, M. (1997) Randy fish boss branded a stinker: coherence and the construction of masculinities in a British tabloid newspaper. In S. Johnson, H. Meinhof and H. Ulrike (eds) *Language and Masculinity* 173–187. Oxford, UK: Blackwell Publishers Inc.

Teo, P. (2000) Racism in the news: critical discourse analysis of news reporting in two Australian newspapers. *Discourse and Society* 11(1): 7–49.

Teo, P. (2004) Ideological dissonances in Singapore's national campaign posters: semiotic deconstruction. *Visual Communication* 3(2): 189–212.

Thompson, G. (1996) *Introducing Functional Grammar*. London: Edward Arnold.

Thompson, M. (2003) ICT, power and developmental discourse: a critical analysis. In E. H. Wynn, E. A. Whitley, M. D. Myers and J. T. DeGross (eds) *Global and Organizational Discourse About Information Technology: IFIP TC8 WG8.2* 347–373. Working conference, Barcelona, Spain, 12 December 2002. Boston, Massachusetts: Kluwer Academic.

van Dijk, T. (1993) *Elite Discourse and Racism*. London: Sage Publications.

Wodak, R. (1996) *Disorders of Discourse*. London: Longman.

Wolfensohn, J. (2000) Speech: new possibilities in information technology and knowledge for development in a global economy. Lecture delivered at King's College, Cambridge, U.K., 24 June.

Internet sources

BBC Radio 4 *The Westminster Hour with Andrew Rawnsley*. Broadcast 6 February 2005. Retrieved 25 May 2005. http://news.bbc.co.uk/go/pr/fr/-/1/hi/programmes/the_westminster_hour/4241787.stm

Cato Institute (2000) *Cato Handbook for Congress, Policy Recommendations for 107th Congress*. Retrieved March 2005. www.cab.org/pubs/handbook/handbook107.htm

Fairclough, N. *Home Page*. Retrieved May 2004. http://www.ling.lancs.ac.uk/staff/norman/norman.htm

IMF Various material. Retrieved January 2005.
http://www.imf.org/external/np/exr/facts/glance.htm
http://www.imf.org/external/np/exr/facts/globstab.htm
http://www.imf.org/external/np/exr/facts/poor.htm
http://www.imf.org/external/np/exr/facts/prgf.htm
http://www.50years.org/factsheets/SAPs-FactSheet_3.9.04.pdf
http://www.globalexchange.org/campaigns/wbimf/

Lemke, J. Multimedia website. Retrieved 000 000.
http://www-personal.umich.edu/~jaylemke/mxm.htm.
http://www-personal.umich.edu/~jaylemke/guides/multimedia_semiotic_analysis_questions.htm

MVE Project. Transcript of dinner conversations, graduate class. Conversation 6 Nov 2000. http://www.ndsu.nodak.edu/ndsu/kbrooks/MVE/transcripts/americana.html.

The San Francisco News Their best way to show loyalty. (Pearl Harbor editorial) 6 March 1942. Retrieved December 2002. http://ctah.binghamton.edu/student/george/georgeprint.html

The United States of America vs. Fritz Arlo Looking Cloud. Court transcript. Retrieved April 2005. http://web.telia.com/%7Eu71502499/arlo/#feb2004

The United States of America vs. Kaczynski. Court transcript. Retrieved April 2005. http://www_unabombertrial_com – court transcripts. htm.

Names Index

General Index

Lightning Source UK Ltd.
Milton Keynes UK
UKOW06f0056190115

244703UK00001B/6/P